REWRITE YOUR RULES

MORGAN DeBAUN

Ballantine Books / New York

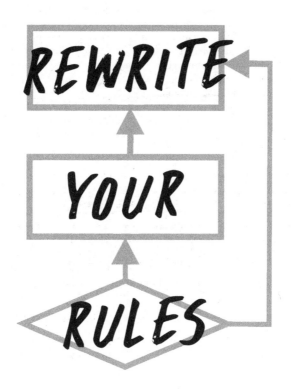

THE JOURNEY TO SUCCESS IN LESS TIME

WITH MORE FREEDOM

Published in the United States by Ballantine Books, an imprint of Random House, a division of Penguin Random House LLC, New York.

BALLANTINE BOOKS & colophon are registered trademarks of Penguin Random House LLC.

Graphics: concepts by Morgan DeBaun, design by Tatiana Temple

Hardback ISBN 978-0-593-72505-4
Ebook ISBN 978-0-593-72506-1

Printed in the United States of America on acid-free paper

randomhousebooks.com

2 4 6 8 9 7 5 3 1

First Edition

Book design by Fritz Metsch

The authorized representative in the EU for product safety and compliance is Penguin Random House Ireland, Morrison Chambers, 32 Nassau Street, Dublin D02 YH68, Ireland, https://eu-contact.penguin.ie.

To my grandmothers, mother,
and the remarkable women in my family,

This book is dedicated to you.
Your dreams, courage, and love have made
my success possible. Thank you for your strength
and wisdom.

Contents

Introduction

Ever feel like you're slogging through life, trying to meet everyone else's expectations, only to end up exhausted and unfulfilled? It's as if society, our jobs, and even our families have set up this elaborate maze of "shoulds" and "musts," pushing us down a path that's not only convoluted but downright tiring. Instead of carving out a life that genuinely resonates with us, we get caught in a cycle of pursuing success as it's traditionally defined—climbing the corporate ladder, chasing after more, and somehow ending up feeling unfulfilled. Perhaps you're at a point where you're questioning if the grind is worth it, or maybe you love your job but crave deeper meaning outside of your work hours. You could be juggling the demands of parenthood while aiming for that next big career move or even standing where I once stood: an ambitious entrepreneur with a vision but no clear road map.

What if, instead of constantly trying to meet external benchmarks, we took a step back and reevaluated? Imagine simplifying the process, focusing on what truly matters, and building our lives around those pillars. That's the headspace I was in and have tried to live in since the fall of 2016 when I called my father while I was on the side of the road, declaring it was time for something new.

"I'm quitting," I said as I walked down 6th Street in San Francisco. I'd called home feeling drained, uninspired, and completely dissatisfied with my job at a Silicon Valley tech company.

"Morgan, that's not a responsible decision."

My dad's voice was firm. He wasn't totally wrong. I'd be lying if I said I hadn't had the same thought. However, it was quickly overshadowed by the unshakable belief that I was here to do more than work my way up the corporate ladder at a large tech company. And while the free food, laid-back office environment (this was prime-time Silicon Valley, there were literal puppies running around), clear upward mobility, and a fast track to a brag-worthy job title sounded good on paper, I knew I would never be satisfied on that path.

To be clear, it wasn't like I was quitting without a plan. I already had an out. I'd been working on a side project for a few months and, while it was far from a safety net, I was fueled by blind passion.

I was twenty-three and had spent months watching tech bros launch start-up after start-up and raise millions in funding for projects that did almost nothing to impact culture in any real way. Yet they were racking up all measures of what we all consider to be "the good life": a flexible work schedule, creative freedom to build, friends as colleagues, and respect. And, I thought, why not me?

It wasn't their superficial signals of success I set my sights on, but rather the ability to see a real dream come to life and make an impact on millions. Not worrying about performance reviews and corporate politics seemed pretty appealing too.

Staring at a computer in a sea of cubicles, I longed for meaningful work. So I left behind the bureaucratic rules that were suffocating my spirit. The rigid structures and chain-of-command mentality stifled my creativity.

The time had come to press forward with the vision simmering inside that I just knew could drive lasting social impact. A vision that would allow me to truly care about the work I was doing. Was it a guaranteed success? Absolutely not. But continuing on an unfulfilling path felt even more risky. I took a leap guided by self-awareness—understanding my core values and strengths. I leapt with resilient purpose, determined to build my skills on my own terms. My entrepreneurial mind would either soar or fail to take flight. A risk I was willing to take.

My journey has taught me that it's entirely possible to design a fulfilling life and career without succumbing to the relentless hustle culture and the success metrics of others. In *Rewrite Your Rules,* we're going to debunk the myth that success is a one-size-fits-all formula requiring endless sacrifice. By questioning the status quo and shedding the unnecessary burdens society has placed on you, you can uncover a more straightforward, more satisfying path to personal and professional fulfillment. This book isn't about throwing all rules out the window but discerning which ones actually serve you, which ones you're better off without, and rewriting a few to fit the grandest vision for your life. Let's explore how to build a life that's not only successful on the outside but deeply rewarding on the inside, using principles that cut through the noise.

I've been the corporate soldier, scrappy founder, confused

romantic, and more. I disrupted the status quo with my companies while still holding true to guidelines tailored to me and only me. Most important, I've made plenty of mistakes and have the bumps and bruises to show for them! Now I spend my time equipping high achievers with the customized blueprints to redefine success and make the changes in their life to get them there. Ultimately, your dreams require rules reflecting your distinct desires for *your* life, not everyone else's.

Since I quit my corporate job, I've gone on to build one of the most progressive and profitable corporations in the media and tech space. I currently lead a team of more than one hundred brilliant co-conspirators as co-founder and CEO of Blavity Inc. What started as a whiteboard vision in my San Francisco apartment living room has exploded into an empire reaching more than a hundred million people each month.

Blavity Inc. operates trailblazing brands in media and beyond, accelerating equity and diverse talent while spotlighting Black culture and identity. Our digital media brands like Blavity, Travel Noire, and 21Ninety amplify and activate a new majority of consumers, influencing how traditional diverse advertising happens through our daily content, newsletters, and immersive in-person experiences. Our community, Afro-Tech, is the premier tech, equity, and wealth-building platform for Black culture and has become an essential destination for diverse global innovators and professionals, with more than fifty thousand people participating in events annually.

In less than ten relentless years, Blavity Inc. hasn't just moved the needle, we've redrawn the scale for access and business equity for multiple industries. We've scooped up accolades from heavyweights like *The Wall Street Journal,* CNBC, *Forbes,* and *Fast Company,* and we've even received recognition from the White House. I've been honored as one of the *Forbes* 30 Under 30 in media, one of *Inc.'s* Top 100 Female Founders, and in the Advertising Hall of Fame, all before turning thirty-five. Blavity Inc. is not just a corporation. It's a movement, a force of change, an engine of empowerment.

But after an exhilarating seven years scaling Blavity into a media force out of Silicon Valley—raising over $12 million from venture capitalists while increasing our team from zero to hundreds of employees—I found myself depleted. The relentless hustle took its toll despite our glittering success. My health needed recovering. Relationships required mending. And simmering under the surface lay aspirations beyond business-building: I felt called to explore holistic living.

This realization became clear not in the buzzing California chaos that fueled Blavity Inc.'s growth, but in the rainforest jungles of Costa Rica during a monthlong sabbatical with friends. Surrounded by nature's rhythms and roaring waterfalls, the clarity one can find only in stillness washed over me. I knew that a radical change was required—one making my overall quality of life my new focus so I could realign my body and my time for sustainable impact. It is very easy for our careers to become our identities, and while I loved the work I was doing, my life begged for a reset in terms of *how* I executed my dreams. The time had come for me to renegotiate my own rules.

I had spent all of my twenties being the responsible one.

The ambitious, hardworking student with many leadership titles. The serious career-driven founder. But I was maxed out.

Are you maxed out too? Have you been looking around wondering how you got here? I know exactly how you feel. I consider myself a high achiever and many who have come to follow me see themselves similarly. We are those who constantly strive for more, even at the expense of ourselves, and, at times, without enough clarity on what we want the result to actually be. As a high achiever, I pushed myself to the top, chasing after what I thought I was supposed to want. But then, something shifted. I started questioning my own mindset about what I could or couldn't do to make my life better.

I caught myself thinking, "Why am I waiting to be married before I buy my first house? Why am I holding off on taking that amazing vacation overseas until I hit a certain income level? And why am I stressing about getting recognition or awards if they don't contribute to my own personal goals and values?" I needed to accelerate the ease I was welcoming into my life, to make smarter choices about how I was spending my time and what I was willing to put on autopilot through delegation and smart systems. I needed to design an environment for myself where I could continue to be an intense high achiever (let's face it, that is who I am!) and *also* live a life full of joy. And I want that for you too. Why? The truth is, we really do want success both in the tangible and intangible, and there's nothing wrong with that. But *how* we get there is often flawed.

With *Rewrite Your Rules* we're going to take control of how you're navigating the ups and downs of life to position yourself to achieve success on your own terms. In part one, Master Yourself, you'll gain clarity on your core values, beliefs, and priorities. By getting brutally honest about what you value and what you stand for, you'll build the mental toughness to handle whatever life throws your way. In part two, Master Your Methods, I'll reveal the key to setting goals that actually matter, prioritizing like a CEO, and taking action even when you don't feel like it. Whether it's through ruthless efficiency, strategic delegation, or simply caring less about everyone else, you'll develop a no-nonsense approach to living your life. Last, in part three, Master Your Growth, we'll explore how to keep pushing yourself to new heights, even when you feel like you've plateaued.

REWRITING THE RULES

Close your eyes for a moment and picture a life where the impact of how you spend your time resonates deeply, success is a constant companion, and personal freedom is not just a wish but your everyday reality. It may seem like a fantasy, especially when facing an endless labyrinth of decisions and unpredictable challenges. You long for quality time with your family, but the climb up the professional ladder demands so much. You dream of immersing yourself in creative pursuits, yet weekend responsibilities drain your energy before you even begin. But here's the exciting part: As you journey through this book, you're not merely flipping through pages, you're walking a path with me, unraveling a decade of entrepreneurial discoveries and lessons that you will be able to apply to every area of your life, be it work, passion projects, or daily living. I'm kind of known as the straight shooter, no-filter type of friend. I tell it like it is, even if it ruffles some feathers. I believe that life's too short to beat around the bush or sugarcoat things. If there's an elephant in the room, I'm the one who's going to point it out and say, "Hey, let's deal with this." I have an uncanny ability to see the holes in someone's playbook and help them reroute. Often getting them to their destination a bit faster, having enjoyed the process a lot more. I've had the privilege of advising some seriously impressive people—we're talking CEOs of *Fortune* 100 companies, top fundraisers for presidential campaigns, founders with companies worth over $300 million, the real deal. And you know what I've realized? So many of us are living from someone else's playbook, even as we're out there playing at the top of our own game. And it's just not sustainable. This book is more than words. In it, I offer invaluable frameworks and mindset transformations, each designed to empower you. Together, we'll navigate through these insights, helping you firmly grasp your life's vision and turn it from a mere dream into a vibrant, tangible reality. This moment is a celebration, a turning point where you start taking control of your destiny, one page at a time.

I've been a cubicle warrior, struggling entrepreneur, and scared-shitless risk-taker, and I have found myself in every uncomfortable situation that you can imagine a Black female leader in corporate America might find herself in. (There. Are. Many.) For years, emails from curious professionals, both seasoned and green, have accumulated in my inbox wanting to know how I did it. In the digital era, everyone seems to be peddling a new hack, trick, or system, yet few offer the battle-tested mental armor and strategies that allow us to drive our ambitions forward. People have asked me: "Morgan, how do I smash through fear to ascend the corporate ladder?" "How do I turn my side hustle into a thriving empire?" "How do I maximize my potential, impact, *and* wealth simultaneously?" "How do I avoid burnout in pursuit of an extraordinary life?" That's why I created my signature coaching program, WorkSmart, to provide an arsenal of field-tested strategies for those seeking transformative change in business and life.

Over the last decade, I've advised more than ten thousand small business owners and professionals stepping into the next stage of business and personal expansion. But here's the thing: Our journey of growth never truly ends. I want to give my community a resource they can continually reference as new challenges emerge and their goals evolve.

If you've picked up this book, chances are you see yourself in parts of my story. You are a high achiever chasing bold dreams and determined to actualize your potential. Yet somewhere along the way, your relentless drive has left you feeling frustrated or maybe even working backward, like key pieces of the puzzle are missing. The realization creeps in that keeping up the ambitious path you've laid out requires harmony between pursuing your goals and enjoying the journey.

I'm a total nerd when it comes to devouring start-up, self-help, and entrepreneurship books, so I can tell you with complete confidence that there is a major connection between the science of personal growth and the strategies of high-performing CEOs across the world. As I consumed book after book written by the most revered business leaders and self-help gurus, I noticed a glaring gap. The vast majority of these bestselling staples were written by white men, yet they're marketed as containing universal advice. Try as I might, I struggled to find practical frameworks that took into consideration the everyday realities and unique challenges faced by ambitious women and people of color—the new majority in this country.

What some celebrated male leaders failed to acknowledge were the extra hurdles and demands so many of us juggle day-to-day. The never-ending balancing act of managing a household, the pressure of being the first in our families to reach new heights of success, caring for elderly parents, limited affordable childcare options, impossible mortgage rates, and battling bias and discrimination at work—all while trying to get ahead professionally and financially. The emotional and mental labor often falls disproportionately on our shoulders.

I knew I couldn't be the only one desperately seeking life and career strategies that spoke directly to my experience. Through my work, I began to hear stories from people of color and women expressing how they were burning out and barely keeping their heads above water. The narrative thread was clear: They were putting tremendous pressure on themselves to have it all—raise healthy families, have successful careers, pursue personal passions—because society told them they could, and should, do it all flawlessly and effortlessly. Aren't those rules a bit antiquated?

Whether seeking balance between career goals and quality family time or polishing up passion projects on weekends, you'll find customizable frameworks that will accelerate your growth while leaving the burnout behind. Let's get to thriving on our own terms—not default rules rigged for someone else's definitions of "making it." Call me a little sentimental here, but I think it's time we start living for those moments that make us genuinely smile, not just for the next accolade or promotion. And yes, you can have both—just make sure it's what you actually want. In *Rewrite Your Rules,* I promise to walk beside you with care, patience, and a little positive pushing while offering real tools (not those internet "hack your life" bits) I wish I had years ago!

Maybe you're where I was a decade ago, burning the midnight oil on a passion project, or maybe the midnight oil is burning you with infinite responsibilities. I want to show you there's another way, a smarter way that leads to the deliciousness, richness, and fullness that you've been craving. From career to love and everything in between, my life has been a series of big, beautiful breakthroughs, and I want you to experience the same.

Let's be real: The relentless pursuit of success often fails to deliver the balance and fulfillment we crave. In our quest for achievement, we become like heat-seeking missiles, locked on to targets while our personal well-being, relationships, and downtime fade into the background. Our minds fixate on the next milestone, promotion, or launch, while our bodies grow weary and our loved ones feel neglected. The very drive that propels us forward also narrows our field of view.

Even when we know we should come up for air, FOMO sets in—the fear that stepping off the treadmill means missing out on opportunities our peers will seize. But make no mistake, they too are likely running on fumes, secretly longing for relief, yet wondering if taking a break will irreparably set back their ambitions.

It doesn't help that many of us have tied our identities and self-worth to the realization of our goals. They've become so intertwined that slowing down, even briefly, leaves us grappling with feelings of failure and loss of purpose. We ask ourselves, "Who am I, if not the person chasing the next goal, actualizing my potential?" Even if we're worn out and depleted, at least we can avoid the frightening prospect of "wasted talent" by staying the course.

But eventually, the truth demands a reckoning: No one can operate at full throttle indefinitely without consequences. Health wanes, relationships suffer, creativity dulls, and motivation frays as this cycle intensifies. As goals are checked off, exhaustion creeps in alongside the next round of ambitions.

Eventually we must confront the glaring absence of boundaries in our drive for achievements. Any separation between professional demands and personal needs has gradually eroded. We've allowed our drive to dominate nearly all aspects of life, leaving little room for fuller dimensions like self-care, community, family, and pursuits unrelated to climbing ladders. Trying to perfect this delicate balance between ambition and harmony feels impossible when they operate as competing forces under old rules. But with understanding and intention, perhaps we can rewrite the rules.

This was the urgency I discovered from over ten years of pushing full throttle. I created this book to provide high-achieving people the essential elements they were missing: practical wisdom and strategies to achieve their dreams without succumbing to exhaustion. This book provides the blueprint to unite your ambition with fulfillment at every stage and harmonize your choices to result in living your best life. It answers the soul-searching question of how to sustainably achieve greatness on your own terms.

Consider this book your trusted companion—a road map, journal, and sounding board—as you navigate rewriting the rules to live life on your own terms, steeped in daily joy and purposeful living. Whenever you need fresh ideas, perspective, or encouragement, I've got your back.

WHY NOW?

Can I just go ahead and say it? The world feels like it's on fire. We find ourselves in a time of both pivotal global change and accelerated growth fueled by innovation.

During such periods of volatility, it is not always easy to chart a clear path forward that feels good, looks right, and lands you at your definition of success. An always-on sensationalist news cycle, 24/7 rage-inducing social media feeds, and an escalating cost of living can make even the most ambitious person want to bury their head in the sand until conditions improve. And, more often than not, we are burned out by the day-to-day. When we look up, months have passed without our having made real progress on our personal and professional goals or sticking to that new routine. No matter how hard you try, your goals, dreams, and measures of success don't feel any more within reach.

I'm going to give it to you straight: It doesn't matter how many external fires need to be put out, achieving success is largely a matter of accepting that the only obstacle standing between you and your dreams is yourself. There is no better day than today to start your journey toward a big leap, to tear up everyone else's rules that have come to define your life and create your own. I know you've heard that before, and yet you still find yourself in the same place, holding this book. But I guarantee that will not be the case if you put these chapters into action. It's time to recognize and own your inherent power to shape both your present-day reality and your future.

And let's be honest—it's also about recognizing when it's time to hunker down and work hard, temporarily surrendering to increased focus and relentless discipline in order to unlock the door to your next level of potential. That's when you step into the greatness that's always been waiting for you.

You want it all, don't you? That skyrocketing career, the passionate relationship, the intellectual hobbies, the social life of a Kardashian, all while getting a solid eight hours of sleep every night. It's a lovely picture to paint, but let's just cut the crap for a moment. That's not a dream, it's an illusion. The sooner you stop chasing it, the better. Time doesn't give a damn about our dreams. It doesn't care how many things we want to cram into our day. It's finite, unyielding, and completely indifferent to our complaints. We have twenty-four hours, just like everyone else. Not a minute more, not a second less. But there's a way to serve your purpose in the world without depleting yourself to get there, wherever "there" is for you.

In order to get the most out of this book you need to have

not only the desire to prioritize your growth, but the commitment to do so as well, regardless of your starting point. The things that I will be asking you to do will stretch you and are designed to transform your mindset and how you move in the world. My goal for you is to have less friction between where you are now and where you want to be. My goal isn't to change the ambitions you have for your life but to make sure that they actually happen again, and again, and again. I had a vision. I built it, grew it, and guess what? I find myself cycling through that same process. Whether it be in business, love, friendships, painting, or even gardening, I use these frameworks and approaches to meet every new phase and stage in my life. I will provide the tools but it's your responsibility to use them.

An extraordinary life requires you to be *extra*. You want a lot? You have to do a lot. But not in the way conventional hustle culture has taught us. By incorporating the methods in this book you'll reduce your risk, mitigate the likelihood of failure, and maximize your happiness and freedom so that you *fully* enjoy the journey. And, if you feel you've read several self-help books and still find yourself in a similar position, know that I'm going to challenge you to *act* on what is in this book. It's not always going to be fun. Oh, man, at times it's going to be straight-up uncomfortable!

I have witnessed firsthand how small, consistent actions compound over time into transformation. If you implement the strategies in this book relentlessly, growth is inevitable. In six months, you may be astonished when reviewing your expansion. I encourage you to email me your wins and lessons as you advance. You can reach me at MorganDeBaun.com. Your stories will help me refine this work to further empower the next generation of leaders.

WHY NOT YOU?

In this very moment, pause and take in the world around you. You're at a unique point in your journey, surrounded by a history of experiences and opportunities only you can see. To truly flourish, immerse yourself in a rich understanding of who you are, savoring your values like a fine wine. Our world often tries to script our lives, but I urge you to gently push that script aside. Instead, wrap yourself in the embrace of your strengths, acknowledge your weaknesses with a soft touch, and look at yourself with the same warmth and compassion you'd offer a dear friend. Now, let's come to accept something: You can have it all, but not all at once.

Your vision of "all" is deeply personal and it's important to recognize that it will change over time. Your "all" could be a nightmare for someone else! As you grow and experience different aspects of life, your priorities will naturally shift. This is a normal and healthy part of personal development. Having it all isn't about achieving everything simultaneously, it's about understanding and accepting that life unfolds in stages, each with its own set of opportunities and challenges.

The key I want you to remember as you're reading through this book is that your priorities, your dreams, and your definition of happiness are uniquely yours. This means acknowledging what you're equipped to manage at this moment. Attaining your goals is a process that occurs over time, not immediately.

I encourage you to embark on this journey with a journal, capturing your thoughts and responses to the strategies and exercises presented in each chapter. And don't stop there. For further insights, tools, and resources that can assist you in this transformative process, I invite you to visit MorganDeBaun .com. Here, you'll find additional support and community to help you continue your journey of growth and self-discovery beyond the pages of this book.

With this book, you'll swiftly navigate from challenges to solutions, gaining an irresistible blueprint that transforms your approach to success. It's a must-read for anyone serious about turning their goals into reality. Here's a sneak peek at the powerful transformations awaiting you:

- Feeling stuck between professional growth and happiness? Blend personal satisfaction with professional achievements for a balanced life.
- Amassing money without direction? Start employing your finances to simplify your daily life and recover valuable time.
- Struggling to lead and scale effectively? Develop systems that enhance both your business and personal life, boosting your overall leadership capabilities.
- Scared to make the wrong next step? Transform your fear into a powerful asset for resilience and strategic foresight, turning obstacles into opportunities for success.
- Confused about risk-taking? Revolutionize decision-making for impactful, calculated risks.
- Want to be more successful in less time? Learn to work smarter, not harder, for quicker success.

- Finding it hard to build a supportive network? Learn to create a purpose-driven team in all areas of life, ensuring you have the support needed for success.
- Struggling with work-life balance? Master the art of pacing work and personal life, knowing when to accelerate in your career and when to focus on personal growth.

Your dreams may not include becoming the CEO of a large company. But no matter what your purpose and passion in life may be, I'm going to teach you how to adopt and own the CEO mindset so you can become a titan in your own world and create your own rules by which you choose to lead your life.

PART 1

MASTER

YOURSELF

You've heard it all before—the rules to achieve the so-called good life: Go to school. Get a good job. Buy a house. Have a family. Work until you retire. And somewhere in the middle of all that, find happiness. But if you're reading this, chances are those rules feel a little too one-size-fits-all for your taste. They might even feel like a straitjacket, constricting and uncomfortable, designed for somebody else's life, not the vibrant one you were meant to lead.

In twenty-first-century American society, there's a strong current that pushes us toward conformity and compliance. From a young age, we're taught to value harmony, avoid rocking the boat, and follow a prescribed path laid out by societal norms. This conditioning seeps into every aspect of our lives—from our career choices to how we interact in our personal relationships. There's an unspoken rule that we should take the path of least resistance—avoid conflict and align with what's expected of us.

But here's the thing: This isn't a mandate. It's not the only way to live, nor is it necessarily the path to success or fulfillment. In fact, it's often those who dare to stand firm in their beliefs, who refuse to bend their vision to fit into someone else's box, who end up leaving the most significant mark on the world.

Take a look at history, at the people who've made real, lasting change. They weren't the ones who followed the crowd. They were the rule-breakers, the visionaries who saw a different way and had the courage to pursue it, even in the face of opposition and misunderstanding. They understood that to make a real difference, to create something truly unique and valuable, sometimes you have to go against the grain.

And it's not just about making a mark on the world, it's about living a life that's true to you. Remember, you are the CEO of your life. I use the term "CEO" a lot in this book, and I want you to embody the idea that you are the chief executive officer of your life. You're the boss. You're the decision-maker. You're the person in control. Like any effective leader, you need to recognize that everyone around you—your colleagues, friends, even family—has their own set of interests, perspectives, and limitations. They're seeing things from their vantage point, which might be vastly different from yours. They don't have a full understanding of your dreams, your challenges, or your potential.

As the CEO, it's your responsibility, then, to guide your life in the direction you believe is best. That might mean making tough decisions, decisions that might not be popular or understood by everyone. But these decisions are crucial because they stem from a deep understanding of your own values and vision.

Breaking free from societal conditioning requires a conscious effort. It's about continually questioning the status quo and asking yourself whether the paths laid out before you truly align with who you are and where you want to go. It's about being okay with the idea that your journey might look different from others'.

Being a visionary of your own life isn't just about seeing the future. It's about the ability to envision the future in a unique and imaginative way and work from a core purpose that drives you. With a clear and inspired view of what *could* be, visionaries have the drive and determination to turn their ideas into reality. Visionaries see what others can't, and they're not afraid to buck the naysayers. They're the ones who take risks and chase their dreams, no matter how unconventional they may seem. And, let's be real, they're the ones who make life a little more interesting. The term "visionary" is often reserved for titans of industry, but there's no reason your ambitious self can't assume that title in your own life. From setting your sights on innovating an empire to switching careers, and even locking down that house and 2.5 kids, deciding you're the visionary of your life is the first step to making anything happen.

In the first section of this book, we're not just going to dream, we're going to redefine what success and contentment look like for you. We'll uncover the values that give you the most energy. We'll learn how to set goals that make you jump out of bed in the morning, excited to start the day. This isn't about rejecting everything you've ever been told, it's about questioning whether those things are truly what you want for your life. Let's strive for success, but do it in a way that reflects what is most important to you and, hopefully, makes the world a better place along the way.

By the end of part one, you will have identified what you actually expect from yourself, your work, and the order in which you need to prioritize these things. We'll create space to deeply focus on who you are today and who you want to be tomorrow. In this time, we'll get real about your strengths and weaknesses, and then brutally honest about your current situation.

It's all up to you: Take charge or stay stagnant. As you navigate the complexities of life, remember that you have the power to write your own rules. You have the strength to stand firm in your convictions and the wisdom to know when to pivot and adapt. This section will help you create a vision that is dynamic, fulfilling, juicy, and beautiful to the eye of the beholder—*you*. Your vision and purpose do not need to appeal to anyone other than yourself. They are for you and you alone. But, you will need a vision that is so vivid you can close your eyes and see it, feel it, smell it. Embrace the role of a visionary in your life, and watch as the path unfolds in ways you might never have imagined. Throughout this section, I will guide you toward a tangible vision by walking you through:

- Understanding yourself, where you've been conditioned and what you value;
- Defining and prioritizing your own personal Six Pillars of a good life;
- Creating a personal Wealth Code to transition to utilizing your finances as a tool for enhancing life quality and gaining back precious time.

1

THE PURPOSEFUL LIFE: SIMPLE, NOT EASY

August 11, 2014. That miserable Monday morning stretched on under harsh fluorescent lights. I strained against the glare of my computer screen, fingers flickering furiously to meet the data cleanup deadline for the leads we were uploading. The shine of start-up land felt dull as I kept toggling to Twitter, hungry for updates.

It had already been two agonizing days since the news shattered my world. Back home, Michael Brown, an unarmed eighteen-year-old, had been killed by police. It made me sick not knowing what was unfolding on those suburban St. Louis streets. Friends posted grainy videos from protests growing restless. Reporters seemed slow, absent. Fear and fury twisted inside me as the office bustle blurred into oblivion.

Black America was on fire, but somehow, no one in the room I was sitting in felt the same emotional gut punch as me. For a moment, visualize the typical sexy start-up office environment in downtown San Francisco: A high-energy scene dominated by Ivy League white boys. T-shirts and jeans. Some zone in on their computer screens, while others pace the floor wearing headsets and tossing stress balls. A few are found in the middle of a beer pong game, and some are caught stuffing their faces with free food while also tending to the dogs they brought to work that day. It's exactly what you'd expect to see in a start-up-culture movie. Now, close-up on me, sitting smack in the middle of it all. A twenty-four-year-old Black girl from St. Louis, with big natural curly hair and fair skin. On any given day, the one emotion that overwhelms me is loneliness. Don't they know worlds are burning minutes away from where we stand? I need clarity. Understanding. The closure of truth. But all I find are disjointed fragments of information.

At the time, I worked for Intuit, a financial software company that makes technology for small businesses and consumers. I was one of the few Intuit employees assigned to the sales floor of the business development team at Demandforce, a start-up tech company that they had purchased a few years prior. Professionally, it was at the tail end of my two-year program with Intuit, during which I rotated through different parts of the company, and the time had come for me to make a decision about which division I wanted to join. I had to honestly ask myself three questions: (1) Do I want to stay at Demandforce and build my career here? I would join the fast track and climb the corporate ladder. (2) Do I want to return (and commute every day) to Intuit's main campus in the southern Bay Area and work on a different product within the Intuit product ecosystem? (3) Am I done with working here and at pretty much any big tech company like it?

To be frank, I had an inkling that I was done with corporate life overall! Working at Intuit's Demandforce office was my first exposure to a scaled start-up and my first *up-close* interaction with the stereotypical tech start-up environment you hear about in the media. The successful entrepreneurs had raised millions of dollars in funding, employed a bunch of their friends to build a distinctive product, and then sold the start-up for more than $400 million. I worked at their company for five months and picked up some pointers: The product was based on community, they had an amazing sales team, and ultimately the staff there were just ordinary people.

Blavity, at the time, was a side hustle. Something I was tinkering with during my nights, early mornings, and weekends. It was growing, but its growth was constrained by the amount of time I spent working a day job. Just months before, I had wrangled my friends from college Jonathan Jackson, Jeff Nelson, and Aaron Samuels to fly into Nashville and have a co-working weekend in my parents' basement with a goal to launch the first version of Blavity's product, an online newsletter. My vision, if nothing else, was clear: I wanted to create a platform for the Black community to see themselves and their stories reflected in the media and to feel empowered to effect change. I was serious about what we were building and knew Blavity was something special.

Prior to that weekend, Jeff and I spent roughly seven months brainstorming and building the first version of the site, hiring engineers from Upwork (a site that connects businesses with freelancers), and I had been sending out weekly emails filled with Black-created content. We huddled down and narrowed in on what each of our roles would be to get to the next milestone: Jonathan focused on building our brand, Aaron made our initial business model, and Jeff built the product. We were just getting started on the formation of the company. It lacked our full-time commitment and was still moving slowly. I had no idea that intense, all-encompassing energy would rush through my heart on August 9, only two months after sending out our first Blavity newsletter, and push me into the throes of full-time entrepreneurship.

The death of Mike Brown happened on a Saturday, and there were no tweets, no articles; it seemed there was absolutely *nothing* from Black media until Monday. Along with the surge of other emotions that surrounded his death, I felt both confused and disappointed that Black media failed to cover these events in real time. There were white reporters dropping down in my hometown of St. Louis with a *white lens* on Black pain. Venture-backed millennial media brands like Mic, VICE, and others were covering the emerging Black Lives Matter movement but I couldn't find this same coverage in Black media. I couldn't take it. I was angry! I felt disappointed to see that Black media of the time put most of their focus on following entertainers and celebrities rather than current issues and social justice.

In my cubicle at Demandforce, I felt small in a sea of whiteness, but every evening, when I switched to my personal laptop to work on my passion, I became an energized giant suiting up for war. The stark black-and-white of my emotions during those weeks between August and October 2014 provided the clarity that I needed to quit my job and put all of my eggs in one basket: Blavity.

I'm often asked how I knew it was time to make that shift.

I would ask myself, "Where am I uniquely positioned to make the most difference in the world?" I knew that being one of six thousand employees wasn't the best position for me to make the greatest impact. Similarly, the year 2014 fell amid a period when the media industry was completing the transition to digital, hastened by changes in consumer consumption and the advancement of technology. Magazines were reducing their print schedules and moving online. Local newsrooms filled with reporters who took weeks to write a single piece of content were running out of advertising dollars, which were now being diverted to social platforms like Facebook and Google. Thanks to mobile phones, the entire market for receiving information had changed. And here I was, in the middle of the shift, working in Silicon Valley. I had insight and access to the latest developments.

That, however, was not enough to justify quitting my job. The X factor was this: I was one of a few thousand Black people working in the Bay Area, while Atlanta and New York were the epicenters of Black media. Who else in the universe, at that exact time, could intelligently formulate a space that unapologetically combined Black media and technology with digital content and social impact focused on Black millennials? The odds were slim. We're talking about fewer than three thousand Black people working in product at a technology company in the Bay Area at the time, only some of whom were part of my generation. And when you narrow down who had the time, the desire, the ability to build a team, the personal resilience to get through it—we're down to about ten people in that area, at *that* moment, who could have created Blavity. So when the idea came to me, I saw my identity all over it. I was uniquely positioned to bring it to fruition, and the possibilities of its success were in plain view.

That Saturday afternoon of August 9, from my desk, I went down a serious rabbit hole while attempting to follow Michael's story, which proved extremely difficult. This was at a time when Twitter's algorithm was changing, making it nearly impossible to see everything that was trending. It was tough to come across accurate information. Plus, because I was from St. Louis, I could see the difference between the bit of static information being reported and the real-time experience of people on the ground, many of whom were using Periscope or Vine because Instagram and Facebook didn't yet have live streaming.

What I could find was that Michael Brown Jr., only a few days before his first day of classes at a technical school, had been shot by a police officer around 12 P.M. He was walking with a friend from his apartment to his grandmother's house in the middle of a two-lane street. When a police officer drove by, they told him to use the sidewalk. The sequence of events that came next: an exchange of words, a heated confrontation, and Mike, who was unarmed, was shot multiple times and killed at the hands of the officer. Mike's body remained in the middle of Canfield Drive that day for four hours in the summer heat. The people in the neighborhood were enraged. Protests erupted. People were being arrested left and right, and the community was attempting to bail out as many of them as possible.

Although Blavity was barely a seed in the ground, I found ways to do my part. I started to curate as much information as I could and instructed our subscribers and social media following to keep up with certain people's Twitter accounts, like DeRay Mckesson, Johnetta "Netta" Elzie, and Brittany Packnett, who were all reporting real-time, on-the-ground updates. I reached out to my Washington University alumni and asked how Blavity (read: me) could be helpful. I didn't have much to give, but I had time, an email list, a few developers, and a strong desire to get as much information out as possible. Soon after that weekend, Jeff and I spun up a blog, and I started to pay bloggers out of my pocket to cover Black issues, Black creators, and social justice.

By September, Blavity had ramped up traction. And I was more focused on my company than I was on my day job at Intuit. Being the best employee was no longer my priority because I had made a heartfelt commitment to growing Blavity from a passion into a career, being of service, and being a part of this moment.

In October, I officially left the damn cubicle. I told Jonathan, Jeff, and Aaron I was quitting my job and was prepared to put all of my time, life savings, and energy toward building Blavity. I'd identified my unique positioning in the tech space by recognizing how underrepresented and underserved the Black community was in terms of content and access to resources. I knew that this venture had to happen.

THE PURPOSE PRINCIPLE

What's your purpose? I know—intense question, but, as I mentioned, intensity is in my blood. Your true answer goes beyond superficial motivations like money, praise, or status. You need to have a reason that you connect with so deeply that you're willing to put in the hardest work. I know you've asked yourself in weary moments: Why am I pursuing this dream despite everyday obstacles feeling incredibly difficult? Why do I persist when easier paths exist? Why not switch careers or spend time helping the people I care about most? What magnetic purpose keeps pulling me forward, empowering me to refuse to let tough days claim victory no matter how appealing giving up may feel at times?

My real question is this: What do you care about?

From shaping the next generation of young minds from within the confines of your own home to building resources for your local community, making your ideas a reality isn't always easy. It's a shitstorm of sleepless nights, thankless work, and a merry-go-round of disappointment. But you're not here because you thought it was easy, are you? No, you're here because you see the bigger picture and you want to carve out a piece of it. You're ready to roll up your sleeves and dive into the mud.

Enter the Purpose Principle.

When I talk about the Purpose Principle, I'm really talking about *meaning* and how we extract it from our lives. Do we see our place and purpose in this crazy world? Is there value in what we do day-to-day?

Why does it matter, you ask? Every successful, impactful CEO has a why, a purpose, and for a good reason. Meaning is hugely connected to our happiness and ability to thrive, even in darkness. Viktor Frankl, a psychiatrist who survived Nazi concentration camps, knew this firsthand. His book *Man's Search for Meaning* shares how having a "why" to live for helped him and others survive and even grow during such hardship. Frankl emphasized that even in the most limiting of circumstances, we have the freedom to find purpose. He exemplified the power of this inner freedom and control over our attitude. Frankl believed finding meaning is the primary motivational force in humans. Even when everything is taken away, we can endure suffering if we have a "why" to live for. He called this drive the "will to meaning." The more meaning we uncover, the more motivated, joyful, and alive we feel.

Purpose fuels resilience and helps you uncover a vision for your life you can be committed to at your core. I've witnessed this truth again and again in my own life and work. Those with a clear sense of meaning have a fire in their bellies that gets them through challenges that would exhaust others.

In my coaching practice, I've observed that those without a driving purpose often struggle with feeling lost, drifting, or frequently jumping from one thing to the next seeking fulfillment. The difference is night and day compared to those who wake up knowing their why. Psychology research backs this up too. Studies show purpose provides inherent motivation that is sustaining rather than draining. When we act in alignment with our purpose, we experience boosted moods and self-control. Our precious reserves of energy and attention aren't depleted as easily. Having a purpose is not difficult to act upon. Researchers have also found that having meaning in one's work predicted perseverance on challenging tasks months later, even better than factors like work satisfaction.

The impact that clear meaning can have on one's success not only applies to outcomes for individuals. I've seen this ring true in mission-driven enterprises with a clear, strong purpose. Their missions guide policies that have a positive impact on their people. Take FreeFrom, a grassroots non-profit organization in the United States dedicated to helping domestic violence survivors achieve economic justice and long-term financial stability. Their why informs a positive workplace culture in alignment with their values, which include a minimum $80K annual salary, a bring-your-children-to-work policy, complete health coverage, and unlimited menstrual leave. They are committed to hiring and supporting QTBIPOC folks and survivors. In fact, several members of their team are first-generation college attendees with no generational wealth to their name.

Trader Joe's, a name synonymous with vibrant aisles and quirky products, stands out in the crowded grocery sector not just for its Hawaiian-shirt-clad staff, but for its mission-driven approach that deeply resonates with its customers. At its heart, the Trader Joe's mission is about delivering exceptional value to its shoppers. They've nailed this by offering an array of unique, quality products at prices that don't break the bank. It's like walking into a treasure trove where you're bound to find something new and exciting, but without the fear of an extravagant price tag. This mission-driven focus has cultivated a fiercely loyal customer base who don't just shop, they advocate. Getting groceries at Trader Joe's is an experience, a community, a lifestyle. Their mission statement is: "Providing our customers outstanding value in the form of the best quality products at the best everyday prices. Through our rewarding products and knowledgeable, friendly Crew Members, we have been transforming grocery shopping into a welcoming journey full of discovery and fun since 1967." This approach has also translated into remarkable business success. In 2020, Trader Joe's reported an impressive average revenue of approximately $2,130 per square foot, nearly double that of its competitors. Trader Joe's has grown into a powerhouse with over 500 stores across 43 states and territories, boasting annual revenues of over $13 billion.

Ultimately, your purpose only needs to feel big and important to *you*. It should help you make order out of chaos; it should give your goals and tasks direction. Your Purpose Principle doesn't have to be some grandiose, world-changing thing. It just needs to be something that you're passionate about, something that you can commit to and aspire to be better at every day.

Maybe your Purpose Principle is about bringing people together through the power of food, creating delicious meals that break down barriers and create a sense of community. Or maybe it's about fighting for gender equality, standing up for what's right, and making a difference in the world.

Or maybe your Purpose Principle is more short-term, like building a company that makes recycling more accessible in your school district, or experiencing the raw beauty of nature by visiting every national park in the country.

My Purpose Principle, as I mentioned before, is to create more economic equity for my community through storytelling, wealth-building, and advocacy for small businesses because I'm dedicated to elevating the voices of emerging Black leaders and forging a legacy of financial freedom for both my family and myself.

I use my Purpose Principle as a filter for my decisions and

actions, and I let it be the driving force behind everything I do. Is what I'm doing helping me amplify Black voices, secure my own financial independence, or create more economic equity for my community? Yes, I'm all in. No? Then it requires a deeper look at why I'm spending my energy this way (more on this later!).

I know that getting distracted from your purpose can happen all too easily. I speak from personal experience. When I first started to taste success—raising money and expanding a team—it subtly nudged me off my original path. I found myself increasingly engrossed in the mechanics and the day-to-day operations, and, slowly, I started losing sight of the reason behind all the hard work. I became completely out of balance, with no personal life, no hobbies, and poor health. The point of assembling this network of brands within Blavity, and fostering an active community, wasn't solely for the attainment of start-up accolades or about the frantic pursuit of the next round of funding. It was about driving toward a tangible impact and doing it on our own terms.

The moments in my journey when I found myself straying, I forced myself to readjust my approach. Whether I needed to steer the leadership of the company toward longevity and resilience, build a strong, mission-driven company culture, or create an institution that could live beyond my tenure as CEO, I pivoted in order to keep my gaze firmly fixed on the original purpose my co-founders and I had set. I also needed to ensure that my personal needs didn't get lost in the shuffle. Oh, and I made a heck of a lot of mistakes along the way. I'll spill more on that later.

HOW TO DEFINE YOUR PURPOSE PRINCIPLE

Defining your Purpose Principle is a critical step in building a life of meaning and fulfillment. Just as successful investors have a clear investment philosophy to guide their decisions, your Purpose Principle serves as a compass for navigating the complexities of life. It's not about chasing fleeting trends or short-term gains, it's about aligning your actions with your core values and long-term vision. By taking a thoughtful and intentional approach to crafting your Purpose Principle, you'll create a resilient foundation that can weather the inevitable ups and downs of life. Embrace the power of purpose and watch as it transforms your journey in profound and unexpected ways.

Living with meaning isn't about ticking off items on a to-do list, it is about centering a core foundation from which your actions find strength and belief. We often hear the phrase "I do this because . . ." and sometimes that's the greatest place to start. What's your "because"? It's about making your work, and everything in your off hours, an extension of your being, not just a way to pay the bills. Identifying your "why" might seem like a massive, daunting task. Yet it's crucial to provide a road map for your life and work. When the waters get rough, and they will, knowing your Purpose Principle will keep you steady. It will be the fuel that keeps your engine running even when you feel like you're running on empty. Here are the three steps I want you to take to create your Purpose Principle.

Step 1: Reflect on your passions and values.

Take some time to think about the things that truly matter to you. Consider your interests, hobbies, and the causes you care about deeply. Ask yourself:

- What activities make me lose track of time?
- What issues or topics do I feel strongly about?
- When do I feel most alive and fulfilled?

Step 2: Identify how you want to make a difference.

Imagine a world where resources are not an issue. Think about who you would help and how you would do it. Consider:

- What problems do I want to solve?
- What communities or groups do I feel connected to?
- How can I use my unique skills and experiences to contribute?

Find that special place where you're meant to make a difference and start chipping away. It doesn't have to be some life-changing, world-shattering idea like curing cancer; it can be something as small (yet important) as playing music in nursing homes to bring the elderly joy every week. Your purpose could be creating a supportive community of like-minded people, or filling a hole for an underserved group in a specific market. Your purpose might be to learn how to nurture and grow seeds in order to eat more organic and healthy meals.

Step 3: Craft your "because" statement.

Complete the phrase "I do this because . . ." or "Because I'm . . ." to articulate the driving force behind your actions. Your "because" should be a compelling reason that motivates you to keep going even when faced with challenges. It should be something that:

- Aligns with your core values and beliefs
- Provides a sense of meaning and purpose
- Inspires you to push through when things aren't going your way

Using your reflections and "because" statement, develop a clear and concise Purpose Principle. This should be a statement that:

- Encapsulates your passions, values, and desired impact
- Serves as a guiding light for your decisions and actions
- Can be easily communicated and understood by others

If needed, refine your Purpose Principle based on your experiences and insights. Remember that your purpose may evolve over time as you grow and change. Here are four examples of Purpose Principle statements, each reflecting a unique set of values and goals.

Environmental advocate: My Purpose Principle is to champion environmental sustainability through innovative conservation strategies and education, because

I'm all about fostering a harmonious relationship between humanity and nature for future generations.

Community connector: My Purpose Principle is to strengthen community bonds by creating inclusive and supportive spaces for cultural and artistic expression, because I am committed to celebrating diversity and fostering understanding and unity among different communities.

Health and wellness coach: My Purpose Principle is to promote holistic wellness and healthy living by guiding individuals on personalized health journeys and advocating for accessible health resources, because I believe that true well-being is the foundation of a vibrant and fulfilling life.

Empowered caregiver: My Purpose Principle is to foster a nurturing and creative home environment, while also pursuing my personal passions and engagement at church, because I care deeply about balancing caregiving with self-growth and spiritual fulfillment.

This is such an important foundational exercise and I want you to take the time you need to get it right. Back when I was so tired of being stuck in an office at Intuit and Demandforce, my Purpose Principle kept me afloat. When that period of my life finally passed, my Purpose Principle got me through a grueling hunt for Blavity's venture capitalists and hours upon hours of good old-fashioned hard work. For me, my Purpose Principle was defined by a deep, relentless desire to connect myself with Black audiences, and them to one another, using technology. I was confident this would bring us to the forefront of mainstream media. This desire is what drove me through all the ups and downs of early entrepreneurship. It's the reason I stopped projecting what I was "gonna do" and actually took off! My Purpose Principle dragged me up and out of the worst holes, and when you define it for yourself, it will for you too.

PEOPLE ARE NOT YOUR PURPOSE

While exploring the concept of a Purpose Principle, it's crucial to recognize that it's not merely about fulfilling roles, whether as a partner, parent, daughter, son, or in any other capacity. It's easy to fall into the trap of defining our purpose through the lens of our relationships or the expectations of others, but true fulfillment comes from honoring our own authentic desires and values.

I know it's easy to get caught up in the idea that our purpose should be tied to the people we love, like being the best mom or husband we can be. And while those roles are certainly important and can bring so much joy and meaning to our lives, they shouldn't be the sole defining factor of our purpose. You are a multifaceted individual with your own dreams, passions, and aspirations. Your Purpose Principle should reflect that inner spark that makes you come alive, regardless of your relationship status or family situation.

Think about it this way: If you define your purpose entirely around being a good spouse or parent, what happens when your children grow up and leave the nest, or your relationship dynamics change? Your sense of meaning and fulfillment shouldn't crumble just because your external circumstances shift. When you make your purpose all about another person, you're essentially handing over the reins of your life. You're putting your happiness and fulfillment in someone else's control.

Instead, your Purpose Principle should be a constant thread that weaves through all aspects of your life. It should be something that you can pursue and find joy in, whether you're single or married, a parent or not. It's important to clarify the distinction between having a Purpose Principle that *involves* others and one that is *dependent* on others. While it's okay and even wonderful to have a Purpose Principle that involves others and seeks to make a positive impact on the world around you, it's crucial that it comes from a place of internal motivation and personal values, rather than external validation or dependence.

Embracing your Purpose Principle allows you to take ownership of your life's narrative. It's a statement that says, "I am the captain of my journey, steering toward what truly matters to me." This approach might initially feel selfish, but it's a profound truth: Living in alignment with your authentic purpose allows you to show up as the best version of yourself. This not only enriches your life but also positively impacts those around you. Sacrificing your own fulfillment doesn't do anyone any favors.

Give yourself permission to prioritize your personal growth and gratification. Delve into your passions and values, those elements that form the core of your being. Remember, your purpose is uniquely yours; prioritizing it isn't selfish, it's essential. It's time to shift from living for others to truly living for yourself.

YOUR JOB IS NOT YOUR PURPOSE

Your work is a means to an end—a way to engage in day-to-day tasks, find satisfaction in progress, and derive meaning from your endeavors. My personal "because" has always been to generate uplifting experiences, forge connections, and promote wealth advancement for young Black individuals in this country, all while amassing wealth and freedom for myself, my loved ones, and my friends. From the moment I founded Blavity in my modest San Francisco apartment to now, I've remained steadfast in that vision and never gotten too hung up on the specifics of how I was going to get there.

In the grand scheme of things, it's vital to remember that your job is but a tool, a vehicle that propels you toward your ultimate purpose. Defining your purpose isn't a one-time task, it's constant. Your purpose will inevitably change as you grow and evolve, and that's okay. You're not locked into a single purpose for the rest of your life, just like you're not locked into a job forever, but for a season. Attaching your purpose too closely to your job can lead to a fragile sense of self. When your job is your sole source of identity and fulfillment, any change in your professional status—whether it's job loss, retirement, or dissatisfaction at work—can cause an existential crisis. What matters is that at any given moment, you have a purpose that provides you with sustained energy and motivation to bring your big, juicy vision—which we're about to create in the next chapter—to life.

I once coached an Atlanta-based lifestyle blogger named Rosalynn who felt her flame for writing was dimming. Though she loved connecting with readers on food and family, years of grinding to keep content flowing left her longing for freedom. Rosalynn confided to me that her why was the joy she felt creating everyday memories with her family, traveling the world with her partner, Harvey, and watching her three kids bloom, rather than continually trading magical memories for blog income. While her family was certainly a significant part of her life, Rosalynn's Purpose Principle was rooted in her internal sense of fulfillment and the activities that energized her, such as traveling, nurturing her children's growth, and being present in the moment. These experiences and values were integral to her personal identity and purpose, separate from external validation or dependence on others. By restructuring her business and creating space for more meaningful experiences, Rosalynn was honoring her authentic self and the things that truly mattered to her. After a deep advising session, we got to work on rewriting her rules. If pouring boundless energy into posts and videos now drained rather than energized her, it was time to reorient. Rosalynn restructured her business to profit without daily demands, hiring a team and freeing space for annual adventures without income loss. By amplifying smarter income streams and maximizing platforms built over time, she carved out fresh opportunities for a reset in her life.

Now every year Rosalynn embarks with her crew to quietly disconnected locales abroad, even taking a thirty-day sabbatical. She pauses her email and shifts her content toward posts capturing delicious local food and travel hacks rediscovered away from unrelenting deadlines. While content frequency temporarily slows, her niche audience delights in the sporadic dispatches from foreign destinations.

By bravely stepping back to rediscover her inner yes, her resounding why, Rosalynn wrote her own rules and found work she once loved waiting patiently for her again *and* more balance for time with her growing family. The key was quieting that inner voice that says, "You can't do that!" and breaking through to a new level of permission.

DON'T GET TALKED OUT OF YOUR PURPOSE

Most successful companies started out as crazy ideas. You don't change the world with something that's been done before. Everyone—and I mean everyone—will have the experience of someone trying to talk you out of your wildly awesome purpose at some point.

"That's not a good use of time."

"It'll never work."

"People don't have a need for that."

Don't listen! The world's biggest brands all started with ideas other people called straight-up crazy. Take Airbnb. Can you imagine how many folks thought the concept of staying in a complete stranger's home while traveling was absolutely nuts? But Brian Chesky, Nathan Blecharczyk, and Joe Gebbia felt the why behind it—helping people belong through shared spaces that were cheaper than a hotel—and stuck to their guns.

I bet Shan-Lyn Ma and Nobu Nakaguchi, the founders of Zola, were laughed at more than once when they suggested that the wedding registry industry needed an overhaul. And what about Calendly? I'm sure many people told founder Tope Awotona that no one needed another calendar app. It turns out we did!

As we explored with FreeFrom and Trader Joe's, businesses have mission statements. But it's the founders who have a purpose. Founders don't have to justify their why, and neither should you.

As the founder of yourself, what do you care about? When we consider the concept of personal purpose—it matters not whether our driving motivator is to change the world or simply bring meaning to our own small corner of it. The human heart doesn't know the distinction. What matters is that we identify and connect with that inner fire, unique to each of us, that infuses our lives with a sense of mission and personal accountability. Your purpose may be to rescue abandoned animals until each one in your community finds a home. Your friend's may be to mentor young adults in the juvenile detention system seeking direction. Another's may lie in artistic creation or fostering entrepreneurial innovation. The choice is not right or wrong, world-changing or insignificant. It is simply a calling that resonates in our gut.

When challenges arise, lean on your Purpose Principle for strength and clarity. Remember:

- Your purpose is unique to you and your journey.
- Living with purpose takes courage and commitment.

- Your purpose has the power to positively impact yourself and others.

By following these steps and staying true to your Purpose Principle, you can navigate the ups and downs of life with greater resilience, clarity, and fulfillment.

2

BE A VISIONARY

The persistent clicking of my keyboard ricocheted off the bare walls of my Los Angeles apartment. It was past midnight. Another long day of advising passionate entrepreneurs that mirrored the endless hours I poured into my own start-up. I took a long sip of lukewarm green tea, hoping to ride one last wave of alertness as I wrapped up my final session.

After ending the call, I stared blankly at the clutter surrounding me. The strewn papers and haphazardly stacked books told the story of three chaotic years relentlessly chasing my vision. And yet . . . despite the accolades and rapid company growth, an unease was bubbling within me.

I flashed back to the fatigue clouding the eyes of the entrepreneurs I had advised that evening. They were dealing with the same churning internal conflict—trying to reconcile their sky-high ambitions with the fractured personal lives crumbling around them.

I knew the truth. My perfectly curated social media presence shouted ambitious and fearless founder. But behind closed doors, I was barely keeping it together on take-out meals and four hours of sleep a night. When was the last time I'd made a dinner date with friends? Attended a yoga class? Read a novel? My dreams of success were slowly mutating into stress-fueled nights and an isolated existence bereft of joy.

How could I guide others to fulfillment when my own life was veering off course? There had to be a way to harmonize success with satisfaction beyond the highlight reel I was selling.

Over hundreds of conversations with similarly disillusioned high achievers, the solution crystallized. We all wanted to be the best at our craft and defy the odds through sheer grit and determination. But in the process, we often sacrificed key aspects that make life rewarding. We'd put achievement above balance. I knew I could have it all—just not all at once. By making mindful trade-offs aligned with my core values, it was possible to build an ambitious and balanced life. It was possible to rewrite the rules of hustle culture.

I asked myself: Beyond profits and prestige, what makes me come alive? What would I regret not prioritizing in ten years? In a moment of stark reflection, I faced an undeniable truth: I had become overly consumed by my work, a workaholic detached from my authentic purpose. This realization was both a jolt and an awakening. I realized that chasing influence and business success, even with its admirable cultural impact, would never satisfy me. I needed so much more. I needed to eventually invite more creativity, adventure, connection, and earnest relationships into my life. Over time, through my own personal trial and error, and many advising sessions, six key pillars emerged, encompassing all facets of a balanced life: Money, Stability, Freedom, Relationships, Passions, and Wellness.

To truly transform my life, I realized I had to renegotiate the terms I had unconsciously accepted. I needed to reprioritize what truly mattered and redefine what success meant to me.

DEFINING THE SIX PILLARS

Imagine yourself ten years from now. What does your ideal life look like? What trade-offs did you make to architect the existence you aspire to? I invite you on a journey to clarify your priorities so we can reverse engineer the vision guiding your choices today.

I like to start conversations around vision-building with the Six Pillars framework to keep you accountable to priorities that are authentic to your values, beliefs, and interests. Like columns supporting a home, properly managing these pillars constructs a satisfying vision. Living in concert with a vision that can't be extinguished because it's a natural extension of yourself is what will push you beyond stagnation. Research shows that in business, organizations with a clear vision and mission statement have employees who are more committed and motivated to stay. The same is true for our own lives. If you give yourself a clear vision that you feel connected to, you're more likely to stick with it.

I believe that we are always performing a balancing act within these six life pillars. With dedication and determination, properly managing these pillars will bring you closer to the day-to-day life you desire.

Foundational Pillars

Resources such as time, energy, and attention are limited, and so it is essential to consider the pillars that create a strong foundation for a balanced life: Money and Stability. Without financial security or a stable environment, it becomes challenging to focus on personal growth and fulfillment in other areas. I recommend you pick one of these pillars to prioritize. You could, of course, pick both depending on the season of life that you're in, but that will leave very little room for personal growth. But in some scenarios, like the start of a new family or after a particularly unstable time in your life, prioritizing both makes total sense!

Money: This pillar relates to your monetary situation, materialistic desires, and financial freedom. It's about earning enough money to adequately save, invest, and budget to live the way you want to live, while still affording to do the things you love.

Stability: This pillar refers to feeling safe and secure in your professional and personal life. It's about feeling confident and grounded, and having peace of mind.

Growth Pillars

Freedom: This pillar is focused on creating a life that feels unbound. It's about breaking free from whatever shackles feel apparent in your life. It's about having the ability to choose your own adventures, pursue your creativity, and be who you intrinsically are. It's about independence. It wrestles with the question: Do you feel in charge of your life? And if not, who or what is?

Relationships: This pillar is about the people who make life worth living. It centers building and maintaining meaningful relationships with family, friends, and romantic partners.

Passions: This pillar centers your pursuit of interests, hobbies, and activities that bring joy and fulfillment to your life but do not make you money. Its focus is on making time for the things that make your heart sing.

Wellness: This pillar focuses on taking care of your physical and mental well-being. It includes eating a balanced diet, exercising regularly, getting enough sleep, and finding ways to manage stress and anxiety.

These universal pillars manifest uniquely for each person reading this. For instance, a freelancer's definition of stability will differ from a government worker's. A child-free woman's definition of relationships may differ greatly from that of a dad of four. Freedom will look different for a *Fortune* 500 employee who is balancing his desire for a raise with wanting more time at home compared to a person who is employed and wants to work four days a week. The framework stays constant; your definitions shift. It's important to define what each pillar means to you and clarify what you value in each one. It creates an opportunity to get crystal clear on what matters most so you can make choices aligned with your authentic self.

When your goals, mindset, methodology, and desired results flow from your core values, you have a solid foundation for a fulfilling vision. Let's dig deeper.

THE SIX PILLARS

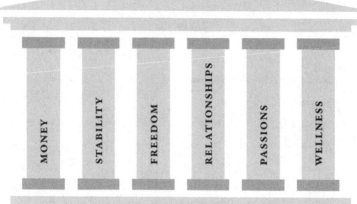

QUESTIONS TO ASK YOURSELF
TO DEFINE YOUR PILLARS

MONEY

- How much income do you require to thrive at the highest level?
- What specific material items or experiences are most important for you to attain?
- How do you define financial freedom for your life vision?

STABILITY

- What stress or worries reduce your resilience and bandwidth?
- What makes you feel most grounded and supported?

- What are the essential conditions for you to feel peace in your daily life?

FREEDOM

- What currently restricts your autonomy?
- What would make you feel liberated in your work and personal life?
- What adventures, creative pursuits, or modes of self-expression are you craving?

RELATIONSHIPS

- Which of your relationships are reciprocally energizing and nurturing?
- What interactions feel most rewarding and in sync with your ideal life?
- What intimacy or support do you feel is lacking?

PASSIONS

- If you had unlimited free time, what activities would you pursue?
- When do you feel happiest and most energized?
- What interests or hobbies would you love to cultivate if you had the resources?

WELLNESS

- What regular self-care practices help you feel balanced and centered?
- Where do you struggle most with maintaining your physical and mental health?

> • What adjustments might increase your energy, resilience, and inner calm?

Spending time answering these questions will likely be very revealing. Maybe you'll realize new things about yourself, or receive confirmation and validation of what you already knew to be true. Use this increased self-awareness to articulate what each pillar represents for you. For example, if leaving a meaningful mark on the world emerges as a part of the legacy you want to leave behind, your Passions pillar may include activities that make a difference in your community, like getting involved in local politics. If being financially comfortable is important, then your Money pillar will be focused on maximizing earning potential, making smart investment decisions, and understanding the sacrifices that need to happen in order to achieve those things.

Take time to write out your own meanings for each pillar. Be honest with yourself about what matters most right now. Dig deep to understand your motivations and what influences your quality of life. Free-write or brainstorm activities, habits, relationships, and feelings associated with each pillar. The more clarity you have, the easier it will be to prioritize in alignment with your truest values and needs.

BUILD YOUR VISION

Imagine this: a vision as your personal road map to the future. It's not just any picture, but a vivid, detailed image of where you're headed, the heights you aspire to reach, and the life you dream of living. Anyone can create a vision, but a *visionary* will never play it safe. You need to be honest and not modest about what you want success to look like in your life.

In addition to an overarching vision, it's helpful to get specific by creating pillar-specific visions for *one to three* pillars you want to prioritize at the moment. (Not all six! More on why shortly.) These vision statements will help you dive deeper into your ideal future specifically related to your three-priority pillar. For example, this was my overall vision in 2018:

> As an entrepreneur growing my media company, Blavity, I envision creating an empowered life in which my work fuels positive social change while building my income, establishing industry relationships, and growing as a leader.

My priority pillars at the time were Money, Freedom, and Passions. My longer pillar-specific visions were:

> **Money vision:** I see myself earning income from Blavity as a CEO that provides basic comfort for myself, and building my social media following to create new streams of income to offset my salary as a founder. I envision feeling financially free to pursue creative passions outside my company when needed for fulfillment.

> **Freedom vision:** I aim to build an inclusive team culture that allows me to work with diverse voices while creating an office

environment that is full of life, productivity, and smiles. I see myself delegating responsibility as we grow so I can focus on higher-level strategic vision and external representation for our brand.

Passions vision: I envision finding time to improve my health and finding a spiritual community in Los Angeles. Keeping my physical, mental, and emotional health balanced will enable me to show up fully as a leader, friend, and community builder beyond my CEO role. I envision establishing a legacy as an advocate for diverse founders and an example of unconventional business success.

> Ultimately, I see my work through Blavity creating positive ripples that affirm people while still allowing simplicity and centeredness in my personal life. My pillars work harmoniously, not in conflict. I can drive impact while living my truth—this is the extraordinary future I know I can build.

Now it's your turn.

Let's walk through this process of creating overall and pillar-specific visions for your current season in life. Read this next section in a private place where you can focus. I want you to turn off your notifications and sit quietly with me.

Having a clear plan can make all the difference between living a happy, fulfilled life of abundance and freedom, and living reactively to the outside world. Visualizing your future isn't about setting in stone a ten-year plan, but rather sketching a flexible road map that guides your decisions and actions. A visionary not only holds their vision within sight, but is also able to see around the corner into the future, and come up with innovative strategies to take themselves to the next level.

To transform your life, you need to recognize where you are now and vividly envision where you want to be. What does your dream life *really* look like? Uncertain? That's a starting point for change.

We need to shake you out of the fog and get *clear* on the vision that will pull you forward and catapult your growth. Imagine your ideal future self. Dream big, then make it bigger—think epic *impact*! Ambition pushes us to expand our vision beyond our current circumstances or assumed limitations. Write it in vivid detail. Are you a mogul? Philanthropist? Humanitarian? Unleashed creative? Loving matriarch of your family? Don't limit yourself!

An ambitious vision propels you to a higher realm of success! Olympic athletes don't envision coming in third place, they practice visualizing that gold medal around their necks, their winning strides, the crowd roaring their names. Multibillion-dollar entrepreneurs don't daydream about helping a few hundred users, they visualize global monopolies and disrupting other industries into extinction! See, a mediocre vision equals mediocre results. An ordinary vision of your life will result in an ordinary life lived. To hit big goals, you have to turn up the heat on those visions and make them bigger, better, bolder! No more keeping one foot timidly in today. Fully occupy the shoes of your audacious future self.

When your vision feels crazy, you're on the right track. Limiting your dreams to what appears easily achievable is, in essence, a subtle form of self-defeat. Life bestows upon us what we have the courage to envision. It's crucial, therefore, to liberate your ambitions and push the boundaries of your imagination. Become addicted to the power of declaring your bold vision daily. Let it infiltrate your subconscious, influencing each decision.

FAST-FORWARD!

What year is it right now? Okay, fast-track your imagination a few years ahead. You're sitting across from me at a café, and I ask you, "How is life?"
You respond, "Life is good!"

- What exactly is a good life?
- What are you saying in that conversation with me?
- Where are you living at the time?
- What does your friend circle look like?
- How much time do you spend with your family?
- How much money do you make?

Put yourself in that moment and answer these questions *today* for where you see yourself in the near future.

PILLAR BY PILLAR: A TIME FOR EVERYTHING

We ambitious people think we can excel at everything simultaneously—the thriving career, adventurous vacations, quality family time, passion projects on the side. Before we know it, we've overcommitted to so many things that exhaustion sets in from trying to be on top. Let's get empowered by evaluating our pillars to understand our authentic priorities, then match our mindset and methods accordingly. This builds self-awareness to connect our vision to our values, not someone else's expectations.

Here's the catch many high achievers resist at first. It's not sustainably possible to maximize more than three pillars at once without compromising quality and sanity. Similarly, you can't put too much stress on just one pillar. Just like a house, if you don't balance the weight of one pillar and add excessive weight to another, the house will eventually become unstable.

I know we think we can master it all simultaneously. We pride ourselves on being the Jane-of-all-trades who can smoothly manage twenty things at once. But that magical juggling act is an illusion for most of us.

Attempting to maximize every single aspect of life all at once spreads our mental bandwidth dangerously thin. I know, we ambitious folks set sky-high expectations for ourselves—careers laden with promotions, passion projects that take the world by storm, loving and adventurous relationships, hobbies mastered in our spare time, all while maintaining inner calm and wellness. We pride ourselves on excelling across the board. More important, we *expect* to excel across the board. So stepping back feels equal parts unnatural and terrifying. By doing all of the things and trying to keep all those plates spinning, we fail to give our true focus and determination to any one priority pillar. Things slip through the cracks. Frustration builds as our drive feels fragmented across mediocre results. We start exhausting ourselves trying to "do it all," which ironically means accomplishing very little anywhere.

Admitting you can't healthily manage it all can sometimes conjure up your deepest fears—wasted potential, falling behind, not living up to immense pressure from within. But we have to give ourselves some permission here. Dialing back focus does *not* mean defeat, it means getting strategic with your mental bandwidth so you can actually show up powerfully for your chosen priorities right now.

There's a theory called limited cognitive resources that presumes our minds budget and allocate our attention, much in the same way we do with our finances. If you blow your whole paycheck on concert tickets, you won't have much to spend on groceries. Attention distribution works similarly. When your resources are depleted, you can't perform very well. The truth is we need to mindfully budget our cognitive resources across only one to three compatible pillars in a given season. Attempting the whole portfolio at 100 percent intensity will drain you faster than an overdrawn bank account.

Trying to be the best in every aspect of our lives is a perfect recipe for frustration and disappointment. Instead, let's try something different. Let's prioritize the three pillars that are most important to you at the moment, based on your vision and goals, and give your all in those three areas first. You don't have to be a one-dimensional person, but you *do* have to be a well-rounded individual who knows when and *where* to put in the work, in addition to making sacrifices to hit the target. Think about it as if you're putting your other pillars in maintenance mode. You're going to continue to operate on a day-to-day basis and not actively put more energy into trying to improve or optimize these areas of your life. So, can we agree, moving forward, to cut ourselves some slack if we need to reel our focus back a bit? Scaling back to your top one to three pillars for a season is not admitting defeat whatsoever. If anything, it's responsible and strategic so you can truly show up for those priorities. Pillars can be revisited and revised at any time—one month, ninety days, a year, or whenever you're ready to make a shift. Different seasons require different levels of focus and dedication.

In fact, as I write this book, I am actively prioritizing my Stability, Freedom, and Relationships. I want to make a difference in helping more people live fuller, happier lives, but I'm not willing to sacrifice my personal freedom. So, I chose to write a book to hopefully answer many of my email inquiries for advice on life and business.

I'll be honest, I want to make a lot of money. Yet, now that I'm older, I'm not willing to do so at the expense of my relationships with my family and romantic partner. So, after six years of building my career in California, I left Los Angeles to buy a new home in Nashville, Tennessee, with the intention of being grounded near my family while pursuing my next phase of ambitions outside of my career. Yes, I still want my company to reach new financial heights, but now I aim for my company to continue strong financial growth without jeopardizing stability or solvency along the way. We've intentionally slowed revenue expansion to fuel manageable, sustained progress. I restructured my life to align with the pillars most important to me right now.

In my twenties, my pillars looked a lot different. It was all about Money, Freedom, and Passions. I prioritized money by creating value in my start-up instead of a nine-to-five income with no equity. I valued freedom of expression and work on my own terms as an entrepreneur. I lived my passion to build something to serve people who I felt were overlooked by mainstream media. In retrospect, I dedicated my twenties to relentlessly turning my passions into a career at the expense of my overall wellness or any meaningful personal relationships.

Take a moment to prioritize your Six Pillars. What stands out as nonnegotiable in this phase of your journey? Which three pillars are driving your current desires? Where will you strive for mastery in your current season of life? Let's shape your vision around the answers. In this exercise, I invite you to grab a notebook and find a quiet space to prioritize and order the Six Pillars—Money, Stability, Freedom, Relationships, Passions, and Wellness—according to their importance to you in this moment. Consider what you need right now to help you design a fulfilling and balanced life. Consider the trade-offs: Are there any pillars that you may need to deprioritize or sacrifice in order to achieve your goals in your top three areas? Reflect on how you feel about making these trade-offs and whether or not they align with the overall vision for your life.

WATER THE GARDEN

I understand it's tough to let go. But consider the concept of gardening, specifically a garden that contains a variety of plants—vegetables, flowers, and trees. Each type of plant represents different aspects or pillars of our life, such as career, relationships, personal growth, etc.

In the vast garden of our lives, we might feel compelled to tend to every plant with equal vigor, ensuring that each one grows strong and healthy. However, this approach can lead to exhaustion and, ironically, might not yield the best harvest. Instead, let's embrace a more strategic approach to gardening our lives.

First, identify the three pillars that are most crucial to your current season of life. Perhaps you decide that your money, a relationship, and wellness by way of physical training are where you want to focus your efforts. These areas will receive the bulk of your attention: the best spots in the garden for sunlight, the most water, and the highest-quality fertilizer. You're not neglecting the rest of the garden; rather, you're optimizing your resources and efforts to ensure that these priority pillars thrive.

The other plants in the garden are still cared for but in a more maintenance-focused manner. You water them enough to keep them alive and tend to their basic needs, but you're not actively trying to maximize their growth at this moment. This doesn't mean these plants are less important, it simply acknowledges that you have limited resources (time, energy, attention) and must allocate them where they can have the greatest impact according to your current priorities.

As seasons change, so too might your focus within the garden. The vegetables that were once a priority might give way to nurturing a fruit tree that's come into season. This flexibility allows your garden to be dynamic and responsive to the changing conditions and your evolving goals.

Consider your relationships. Yes, you might not be the social butterfly you usually are, but a simple text or a brief coffee meetup still keeps the connection alive. It's the quality, not quantity, of time that maintains these bonds. Your hobbies too can find a smaller, yet still significant, slot in your schedule. Maybe it's half an hour of reading instead of a full afternoon or a weekend morning of photography rather than a whole day out.

The essence here is to keep your eyes on the garden and grand vision of your life. This selective focus isn't forever; it's a phase of growth, a period where certain pillars stand stronger so you can make transformative shifts in your journey. This period of intensity can be as long or as short as you want. Trust in the process, knowing that in time, equilibrium returns, and the temporarily quiet pillars will once again share the spotlight. Remember, life's balance is not static, it's dynamic, constantly adjusting and realigning based on where you are and where you're heading.

If you miss a call on an important date or skip a class, don't dwell in guilt. Life is about navigating priorities, and sometimes balls will be dropped. It's not a failure, it's a natural part of balancing a complex life. Each dropped ball is an opportunity to pick it back up later, perhaps with a new perspective or renewed energy.

Your life circumstances often set the tempo for priorities, and each milestone comes with its own set of challenges and opportunities. Revisit this values-clarification exercise whenever you face major transitions, feel unbalanced, or need direction. As your pillars shift, realigning your mindset, goals, and daily rituals will help you follow through on what matters most in each season of life.

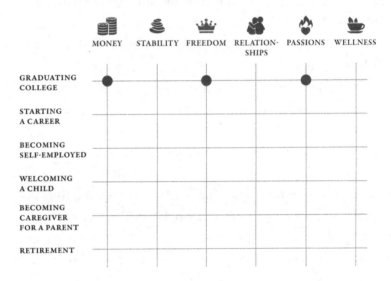

MAPPING LIFE MILESTONES TO PRIORITY PILLARS

For instance, if you're fresh out of college, your priority might be to build a solid foundation for your career (Money), innovation (Freedom), and self-exploration (Passions).

On the other hand, if you've recently welcomed a child into your family, your focus could shift away from your own personal growth and toward health (Wellness), providing (Money), and making the world a better place for a new life (Passions).

MAPPING LIFE MILESTONES TO PRIORITY PILLARS

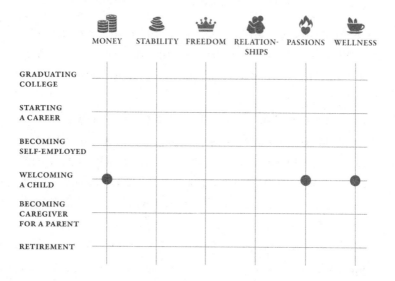

An entrepreneur in a high-risk, high-reward venture might prioritize Money, Freedom, and Passions, accepting the lack of stability in the short-term to achieve their long-term goals.

These chapters in our lives are often written by significant events and transitions that naturally steer us toward specific paths. Embracing these shifts, instead of resisting them, can help shape our actions to meet the demands of the present, enhancing our overall life experience long-term. It should be noted that even if your priority pillars change with life seasons, the overall vision that encompasses all pillars usually remains the same.

LET'S PRESSURE-TEST YOUR TOP PILLARS

Now that you've defined each pillar and begun to craft your overall vision, it's time to pick the one to three pillars where you'd like to focus your limited energy and resources. But how?

Sometimes it's helpful to start with a simple binary question: How much control do you want? Pillars like Freedom, Passions, and Wellness are all about *you,* and they are totally in your control. The other half—Money, Stability, Relationships—well, they're a bit more dependent on the will of outside forces. Not that you don't have a major influence on the trajectory of your path, but you cannot deny how much the economy, your environment, and the people around you will impact the journey to your goals.

Intuitively, we know that certain pillars will go together. Being able to afford vacations and getting a promotion at work are compatible goals. Or, if you're too focused on building your Money *and* Stability pillars, you might not have much time for your Passions. It's all about balancing and prioritizing. They're all important, but which ones are the most important for your vision right *now*? And which ones naturally fit together? These questions can help you arrive at a good starting point.

By acknowledging these natural value tensions, we can intentionally focus our energy on up to three priority pillars that align with our current aspirations. This focused channeling of effort allows us to make meaningful progress. Although we may need to let other pillars simmer at a lower intensity for a period, it doesn't mean we deem them unimportant. I want you to own your priority pillars proudly. When the season shifts, we can return to the pillars we haven't been focused on. As we move through this book, I'll show you how I've done this a few times. Over the arc of your life, this fluid rebalancing act enables you to thrive across multiple dimensions, creating overall alignment and fulfillment.

Think about your Purpose Principle. Now cross-check your purpose with your Six Pillars. Can you find alignment? Does it match up with at least one of your priority pillars? Ideally, you could see how all six of them factor into the Purpose Principle you've created. This is how you know that both your vision and your why have the fuel you need to reach all your goals.

Keep these priority pillars top of mind while you read this book. Maybe write them on a piece of paper and use it as a bookmark. If you're reading digitally, tape it to the back of your phone or tablet. Set a timeline for reassessing your priorities and progress—I like to do this at the start of each month. Recognize that your priorities may change over time and that you will need to regularly evaluate whether your current focus still makes sense with your overall vision and values. Schedule a time in the future to revisit your priorities and adjust your goals as needed. No, really. Put it on your calendar! Your future self will thank you.

3

DESIGN YOUR WEALTH CODE

Thirty years old and six years into the business, I was feeling pretty good about myself as I walked into the first meeting with my wealth manager, Adam. I breezed in a bit cocky, sure he'd be impressed with my financial track record. After all, I had worked my butt off day and night for years to build a successful business and had continued to make responsible fiscal decisions along the way. Blavity was now a humming machine, and my name started to appear on so many of those coveted industry lists. I was making a decent salary and maintaining a solid savings account, and I had secured a few angel investments. I was definitely living a quintessential "wealthy" life, or so I thought.

As soon as I sat down across from my wealth manager, I quickly realized I had a lot to learn. Despite a diversified portfolio of income that included my W-2 pay stubs, consulting fees, angel investment valuations, speaking engagements, and brand deals, Adam still dropped a major truth bomb on me. "You're rich and making a good income, but you're not wealthy." Had I been drinking water, I would have surely done a spit take. Excuse me?

In chasing the capitalist dream of wealth and status, I had bought into the grind—work hard, stay humble, and happiness awaits on the other side of the finish line. I had followed the path laid out for me around career, money, and success.

As Adam and I went through my portfolio, something unusual happened. We didn't just talk about how well my investments were doing. Instead, he shifted gears and started questioning my relationship with money itself. "Are you utilizing your wealth to genuinely enhance your life?" he asked. "Instead of focusing on growing your income, we should think about how you can leverage your assets to live the lifestyle you want."

The lifestyle I wanted. Not the balance I wanted to see on my bank statements. Not the impact my work was making. Not the increase in my consulting gigs or brand deals. I had to do a double take to check whether I was in the right place. I was meeting with my wealth manager, right?

There I was, after years of sixty-hour weeks, building what I thought was my empire. But Adam's questions made me pause. Was I chasing more money just for the sake of it? I had to face it—despite my achievements, I was still caught up in a race that I hadn't even questioned.

I realized that I had, without knowing it, become a bit of a wealth collector. Stacking savings and diversifying investments had become a sport for me. But what was it all for? I was quickly becoming financially secure, yet I felt the weight of my commitments. It dawned on me that maybe, just maybe, there was more to life than this relentless pursuit.

That's when I decided to flip the script. I began writing my own Wealth Code, one where money wasn't only a future promise but also a tool to enhance my everyday life. I wanted to fund the things that truly mattered—travel, passions, adventures. These weren't distant dreams anymore; I wanted to live my life with fullness *daily*. Not eventually.

My new ethos was simple: value ease and time over money. No matter how much money you have, it can't buy more time. Time is the real currency of life.

A few weeks later, I shared this newfound perspective with Adam. I shared my vision of spending a few months out of the year in Costa Rica, buying a house, hiring a seasoned executive team so I had more time for my personal life, and saving for a family. Saying these dreams out loud made me realize that something had to change. "Don't get me wrong— financial stability is critical, especially coming from humble beginnings," Adam said. "But the time has come to get intentional—put your money to work improving daily lived experiences aligned with your values."

That was my turning point. I decided to recalibrate my reward system. It was clear that my pillars were out of balance. I had the vision; I just needed the right road map to steer myself away from the endless pursuit of "more."

I said no to speaking engagements and brand partnerships that fell below a certain monetary threshold. If an opportunity came to make an extra set of money above my threshold, I mentally would allocate 50 percent toward a bucket list experience, small treat, or something that brought ease to my life. I started saying yes only to opportunities that aligned with my new philosophy.

The realization was stark: I wouldn't progress in my vision of wealth if I kept grinding away with ten-hour days, giving little time to personal pursuits or passion projects. For too long, I'd been laser-focused on reaching a certain income level, not realizing that the next phase of my life was about how that wealth allowed me to live.

Now, this wasn't merely a theoretical shift, it was about making tangible changes to how I lived my day-to-day life. The problem was that I had spent too much time thinking about my definition of success as a linear set of milestones tied to outcomes instead of how I was actually experiencing each day along the way. The rules of financial success meant: debt-free, self-employed, diverse stock portfolio, homeowner. Why did I view these milestones as the end points?

I had to understand what true wealth meant to me, beyond conventions, and shape my reward system accordingly. I planned to front-load my career in my twenties to enable more balance in my thirties. Now it was time to clarify my next-level vision and truly reap those dividends. With more financial freedom, I could start living by design rather than default.

As I matured, I started realizing it wasn't just about having a fat bank account or a big house. It was about using whatever resources I had (large or small) at the time to work for me, to create the kind of freedom that let me do the things that mattered most. Instead of thinking about money, debt, and cash as something to acquire or conquer, I needed to shift my thinking about money to be a tool that fuels the life I dreamed of. I know you might be thinking, "Morgan . . . wealth? I'm currently just trying to keep up with my bills." But stay with me for a bit, we're going to get there.

True wealth has little to do with money in a traditional sense. It comes from living your deepest values, fulfilling your greatest potential, and making a difference with your time here on earth. I know this sounds a little woo-woo coming from me, but know this is a practical experience I've had and I urge you to open your mind to. Money is simply a resource—one that allows us to invest in things of true worth, like relationships, personal growth, and service.

This journey wasn't just a financial awakening for me, it was a holistic evolution. True affluence comes not from abundant cash flow but from abundant life flow. It emerges when our purpose, talents, and energy are unleashed to their highest ends.

As I embraced this new mindset, I began to live a life of true wealth—a life where each day was fulfilling, aligned with my core values, and rich with experiences that mattered. And that, my friend, is the real measure of success.

DO YOU HAVE A RICH MINDSET OR A WEALTHY MINDSET?

In today's society, the terms "rich" and "wealthy" are often used interchangeably, but they represent two vastly different mindsets. Being rich is commonly associated with the accumulation of material possessions and the attainment of a certain income or revenue status. Many people are stuck in a cycle where being rich is the ultimate goal. They think they should be busting their butts to make more money, buy more stuff, keep getting promoted. They're driven by a need to feel relevant and have a higher status than other people around them: their family, their friends, their followers on social media. When you're in school, everyone is eager to ask what you want to do when you grow up. But no one asks, "What do you love doing? What's important to you? How much time do you want to spend building relationships and family? What does a healthy life look like for you?"

We're trained to follow a set path: education, job, family. But what happens when we check off these boxes? We end up with good-paying jobs but often we're not happy on a day-to-day basis. It's a trap that many fall into, believing that reaching a specific financial milestone will bring happiness, relevance, and fulfillment. However, this narrow focus on materialistic goals can lead to a life devoid of true joy and purpose.

A rich mindset is one that is constantly seeking more, driven by the desire for status and validation from others. It's a never-ending cycle of consumption, where the acquisition of the latest gadgets, a bigger house, and designer clothing becomes the primary goal. This mindset is perpetuated by societal pressures and the belief that these status symbols are the key to contentment and success.

Maybe right now you are living paycheck to paycheck and ready to get out of debt, or you're a creative entrepreneur trying to scale by balancing financial success alongside brand growth. Or maybe you're comfortable with a corporate nine-to-five job but really want more time and freedom to pursue your passion and turn it into a side hustle. We all start with our own unique baseline of truth, but wherever you fall on the spectrum, you likely need to adjust your mindset around wealth. Instead of asking, "How can I make more money?" reframe the question: "How can I embrace a wealthy mindset?"

I understand the instinct drilled into many to equate net worth with self-advancement. Especially for those working paycheck to paycheck or fighting to build stability from nothing. When you're barely getting by, being told money isn't everything sounds laughable, even insulting. You'll do whatever it takes to increase income because your survival depends on it. Yet, I want to push you to start to think differently about your income, savings, and spending habits. I want you to make decisions that will incrementally move you toward the life you envision for yourself.

Research suggests that the hustle for ever-increasing paychecks often distracts us from cultivating true contentment in life. Consider a 2010 Princeton study that analyzed the correlation between salary and happiness across the globe. Researchers found that while financial resources do enhance life satisfaction to an extent, there is a cutoff point where more money fails to boost reported contentment and fulfillment. This plateau occurred at an inflation-adjusted income level of $75,000 at the time of the study. Once people were making enough money to have their basic needs met, added zeros on paychecks did not correlate strongly with increased day-to-day happiness.

Instead, the study suggested that nurturing social bonds, living with purpose, engaging personal passions, and cultivating gratitude have more impact on feelings of life satisfaction versus added dollars alone. Think of the smartest person you know. While financially comfortable, chances are they invested themselves in personal growth, relationships, or service—using money as fuel for purpose. They know net worth means little if their inner light dims. This truth applies regardless of tax bracket or background.

As you embark on this journey of rewriting the rules for yourself and work through this chapter, you'll probably notice something: Most of the changes you make will seem glaringly obvious. Somewhere along the line, we were conditioned to crave things society told us we should desire. Most of us have been chasing the wrong things for way too long. We're nudged to splurge on status symbols, seeking the validation they bring. Our culture often steers us away from what feels right in our gut, leaving us second-guessing our desires based on others' perceptions and expectations. And that, my friend, is a recipe for a life half lived.

By contrast, the wealthy mindset recognizes that the true value of money lies in its ability to create space for the things that bring genuine joy and fulfillment. It's about utilizing your financial resources to cultivate a life that aligns with your values and passions, rather than simply accumulating more for the sake of status.

With a wealthy mindset you'll begin to think more holistically about what "more" means to you. You will be focused on what matters in your life when the finance factor is removed. What's left? What are the most important elements? When you shift to a wealthy mindset, you open yourself up to a world of possibilities and abundance. Money still matters, but a wealthy mindset is about adapting your relationship with money in a way that can be sustained.

Money is simply a resource—one that allows us to invest in things of true worth, like relationships, personal growth, and service. Money is a tool, not the end goal. Financial wealth presents a choice—we can be shackled by materialism, indulgence, and ego or liberated into more meaningful living.

CHASE JOY, CULTIVATE WEALTH

What if I told you that you can design a wealth-fueled existence whether you're an aspiring entrepreneur, entry-level employee, or still finding financial footing after setbacks? Start creating your new rules by examining what true affluence means to you specifically. You can absolutely design an abundant existence at any income level. I've seen it countless times!

Imagine waking up every morning with a sense of excitement and purpose, knowing that you're living your life in the present, aligned with your deepest values and passions. Picture yourself surrounded by the people, mundane experiences, and activities that bring you the greatest fulfillment. This is the power of a wealthy mindset—a transformative way of thinking that empowers you to create a daily life that truly resonates with your core.

This journey is not about following a one-size-fits-all formula. It's about tapping into your own unique source of joy and using that as a compass to guide your choices. It's about creating a life that is authentically yours, one that allows you to thrive emotionally, mentally, and financially.

Before chasing any dream lifestyle, get crystal clear on your inner truths: What makes you come alive? What does an abundant day-in-the-life entail beyond material possessions?

For me, wealth means total location independence, so that for at least a month each year, I can be immersed in an inspiring culture as I build my business remotely. It means hours in my home studio painting abstracts with vivid colors and sparing no expense on new tools or canvases to express my creativity. Most of all, though, it means free time to fully indulge my entrepreneurial spirit. Yours may involve having the freedom to prioritize family and spend quality time with loved ones. Or perhaps it means creating a passive income stream that provides a sense of security and allows you to pursue your true passions without the constraints of a traditional nine-to-five job.

As you take this leap into a new way of thinking and living, you may feel a mix of excitement and apprehension. Change can be intimidating, especially when it involves challenging your long-held beliefs and patterns. But rest assured, the rewards of embracing a wealthy mindset are immeasurable. By aligning your financial decisions with your true desires and values, you'll experience a profound sense of contentment, purpose, and abundance that permeates every aspect of your life.

So, are you ready to unlock the door to a life filled with joy, meaning, and true wealth? In the following sections, we'll explore practical strategies and exercises to help you cultivate a wealthy mindset and make financial choices that support your vision of a fulfilling life.

THE RICH TO WEALTHY MINDSET MAP

Let's dive deeper into understanding what brings you true joy and satisfaction. I invite you to fully engage in this mapping exercise, to sit with yourself and do the work. This is an opportunity to gain profound insights into your values, your passions, and the life you truly desire to create. By taking the time to thoughtfully complete this exercise, you'll lay the foundation for a life that is rich in purpose, meaning, and authentic happiness. So, grab a pen and paper, and let's embark on this transformative journey together.

1. Brainstorm Your Wealthy Life: Spend fifteen minutes freewriting about what an abundant lifestyle looks and feels like for you. Try to capture daily activities and meaningful priorities beyond superficial wants.

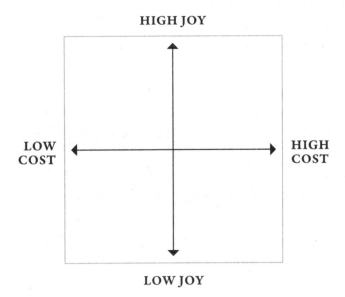

2. Draw a large square on a piece of paper and divide it into four equal quadrants.

Label the top left quadrant as "**High Joy, Low Cost**," the top right quadrant as "**High Joy, High Cost**," the bottom left quadrant as "**Low Joy, Low Cost**," and the bottom right quadrant as "**Low Joy, High Cost**." In each quadrant, list activities, experiences, or purchases that fit the respective categories. Consider the following questions as you fill out the quadrants:

- What activities, tasks, or experiences bring you the most happiness and fulfillment?
- Which tasks, activities, or experiences are relatively inexpensive and which come with a higher cost?
- What are mundane activities that make you smile and that fill your heart?
- What tasks, experiences, or activities save you time or provide a sense of abundance and freedom with your time?
- Are there any volunteer opportunities or ways to give back to your community that align with your values and bring you a sense of purpose and fulfillment?
- Which of your current expenses or purchases bring you little joy, regardless of their cost?

3. Reflect on the items you've listed in each quadrant.

High Joy, Low Cost: These are the activities or experiences that bring you the most happiness without a significant financial burden. Consider how you can incorporate more of these into your daily life.

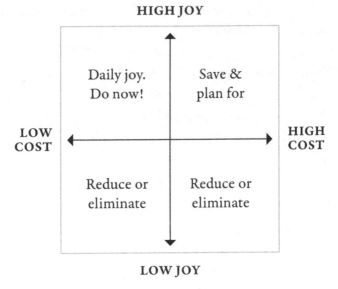

High Joy, High Cost: These are the activities or experiences that bring you great joy but come with a higher price tag. Consider how you can prioritize these experiences and plan for them financially.

Low Joy, Low Cost: These are the activities or expenses that don't bring you much happiness but also don't have a significant financial impact. Consider whether you can eliminate or reduce these expenses to free up more resources for things that bring you joy.

Low Joy, High Cost: These are the expenses or purchases that don't bring you much happiness and come with a high cost. Reflect on whether these expenses align with your values and consider how you can reduce or eliminate them to allocate more resources toward things that bring you joy.

Use the insights gained from this exercise to inform your financial decisions and create a plan for aligning your spending with your values and passions. Consider the following steps:

- Prioritize expenses that fall into the High Joy categories, especially those with low costs.
- Plan and save for the High Joy, High Cost experiences that are most important to you.
- Reduce or eliminate expenses in the Low Joy categories, especially those with high costs.
- Reallocate the resources saved from reducing Low Joy expenses toward High Joy experiences or savings goals.

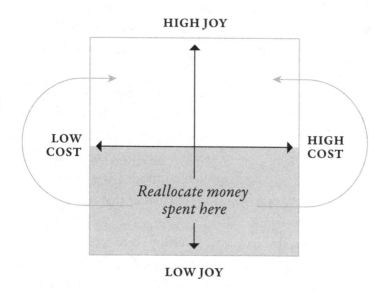

4. Use your reallocation and take action.

This is an exercise in optimizing your life in a powerful way to get change now, not eventually. And remember, this is not necessarily from having more money, but from utilizing what you have more effectively. Take the trends in your quadrants and start to build a new definition of success and wealth for yourself. Write down these findings and build your own Wealth Code.

By completing this quadrant exercise and reflecting on your findings, you'll gain a clearer understanding of how your financial decisions can support a life filled with joy and fulfillment. Prioritizing the mundane and optimizing these aspects of life can significantly enhance your sense of wealth, but it's often overlooked. The power here lies in recognizing that true wealth is not measured only in extraordinary achievements or grandiose possessions, it's also found in the simple, everyday moments that constitute the majority of our lives.

When we shift our focus to refining and appreciating the mundane—the daily routines, the small habits, and the ordinary tasks—we begin to transform our overall experience of life. Use these insights to create a spending plan that aligns with your values and helps you cultivate a wealthy mindset focused on the experiences and activities that bring you the most happiness.

Remember, this exercise is a starting point for aligning your financial decisions with your passions. Regularly revisit and update your quadrants as your priorities and circumstances change, ensuring that your spending consistently reflects your values and supports your journey toward a fulfilling life.

CREATE YOUR PERSONAL WEALTH CODE

Take a moment to identify the recurring elements that define success and wealth for you. These form your Wealth Code, a new guide to help you focus your Money pillar and offer a values-based code for spending. Your Wealth Code will become a set of principles that you can refer to whenever you're faced with financial decisions, big or small, ensuring that your choices are consistently moving you closer to the life you desire. By challenging yourself to be specific about how you are defining success and utilizing money, you'll make choices that are deeply rooted in your authentic definition of wealth, and you'll create a reality that is a better reflection of your most cherished values and aspirations. For example, here are the things that wound up in my priority quadrants broken into themes.

1. I Live for Experiences

   I live for awe-inspiring experiences *now* instead of someday. Jungle landscapes, a remote Airbnb, an eight-course tasting menu with two of my closest friends—my income funds what stirs my spirit most. Before each purchase, ask: Will this purchase create meaningful memories and connections? I prioritize travel, online classes, dining out, and entertainment over material goods.

2. I Respect My Time

   I respect my time above all—I outsource everything not in my zone of genius, such as administrative work. Hours saved go to relationships and fun. My Wealth Code values time as the most precious asset.

3. I Practice Conscious Spending

I consciously spend without guilt on my carefully chosen joys, then I am frugal elsewhere. I will even eliminate things that society tells me I should want or need.

4. I Uplift My Community

I prioritize generous giving, consistently allocating a portion of my income to trustworthy causes and charities. I surprise strangers and loved ones with acts of kindness by donating to people's personal creative funds or leaving a large tip at a local small business.

5. I Fuel My Greatness

I invest in myself without restraint. I pursue education, experiences, coaches, advisers, and personal health that grow my talent, impact, knowledge, and longevity.

The point is to get clear on what wealth means *for you*. Then craft your code and build supports to actualize that specifically (we're getting to that). Claim the power to define wealth on your terms, aligned to inner truth.

I understand some of you might feel a sense of distance or disconnection, thinking, "Morgan, this all sounds great, but my baseline is nowhere near where yours was. I'm not even close to being rich. The cash in my pocket is already promised to a stack of past-due bills." This is a valid concern! After all, it's challenging to think about building wealth when you're focused on making ends meet. But the beauty of the Wealth Code is not about how much money you have, it's about your mindset toward it. From $50 to $500,000, this mindset can help you achieve more holistic abundance. The journey to wealth starts with believing in the possibility of financial freedom, regardless of your current bank balance. Let me reassure you that the concepts of living a wealthy life are absolutely accessible, no matter where you are on your journey.

Use your Wealth Code in practical ways as a guide when making decisions tied to your Money pillar. Whenever you're considering a purchase or investment, refer to your Wealth Code. Ask yourself, "Does this align with my guiding principles? Will it contribute to the experiences, values, and activities that bring me true joy and fulfillment?" If the answer is yes, then you can proceed with confidence, knowing that you're making a choice that is in harmony with your authentic definition of wealth.

As we rewrite the rules of your life, let your Wealth Code inspire your short- and long-term goals that we will work on together in this book. When you're envisioning your future and setting targets for yourself, make sure they are grounded in your personal definition of success and wealth. Ask yourself, "If I achieve this goal, will it bring me closer to the life I truly desire? Will it allow me to more fully express my Wealth Code?" By aligning your goals with your guiding principles, you'll be more motivated and inspired to pursue them.

In making this shift, you'll no longer focus on earning every dollar. Instead, you'll create a life that is meaningful regardless of each money milestone you hit. You recognize that true wealth is about more than just financial success. To shift from a rich mindset to a wealthy mindset, we must first redefine why we're chasing success and how the money we make is utilized. Allow your Wealth Code to be a dynamic, living set of principles. As you grow and evolve, your definition of prosperity may shift as well. Let's continue to make progress creating a life that allows you to spend your time and energy on the things that matter most to you, using a practical method that can help you make this shift.

DITCHING THE SHOULDS

Let's get real about societal ideals of "making it" for a sec. Because the truth? A lot of that is just noise keeping us small. As we design our Wealth Codes, one hiccup I see is people holding back on what they really want. Naming aspects of the "successful" path that we'll ditch because they're misaligned from our vision can be an eye-opening exercise.

For me, I realized early on that car ownership had no place in my wealth story. Though society screamed it was essential, my vision knew better—all that money drained on monthly payments and maintenance held me back from investing in me. So, I decided to ignore pressures and walk on my own path.

In my twenties, I channeled those savings into central apartments near work, using commutes as forced self-care time to listen to podcasts. I leveraged public transportation and budgeted Uber as needed into my plan. My daily steps kept me far healthier in body, mind, and spirit than a sedentary commute ever could.

The point is, designing your Wealth Code means releasing society's "shoulds" in favor of *your* happily ever after. What could you relinquish? Are there material shackles subtly weighing you down each day? Name them. Then align actions consciously to who *you* are, not the invisible script telling you what brings success.

Here comes the fun part: dreaming without boundaries. Now that we've established what abundance means for *you* (and only you!), let's get tangible. Go back to your Wealthy Mindset Map and try to estimate how much your wealthy life would cost. Break it all the way down to a monthly expense. This isn't about trying to make you feel scared or defeated. Quite the opposite, in fact! This is about helping you realize how achievable your dream might actually be, or the trade-offs you can make to get there. Dreams have the power to ignite our imaginations and inspire us to pursue a life of fulfillment and abundance. Yet, as beautiful as dreams may be, they can often feel distant and intangible. That's where attaching a realistic price tag to your dream becomes a game changer. It brings your aspirations down to earth, making them more concrete and within reach.

Research is your best friend in this process. Take the time to delve into the specifics of your dream. Let's say you want to spend winters in Bali doing yoga. Immerse yourself in the logistics of what it takes to live in a foreign country part-time. Explore the housing options, research the cost of living, and calculate the monthly expenses. Look into yoga studios, retreats, or training programs in the area and consider the associated costs. Factor in transportation, utilities, food, and any other necessary expenses. The key is to be thorough and meticulous in your research, leaving no stone unturned.

Estimating the cost also helps you develop a mindset of possibility. How often will you use these things? Consider for a second how often you use the things you currently own. Often, we underestimate what is truly attainable and overestimate the challenges and sacrifices involved. But, when you break down the dream into tangible figures, you may be surprised to find that it is more within your reach than you initially thought.

Refuse to let your current mess prevent you from not just dreaming of the vision, but also writing it down. I realize for many, abundance currently means covering urgent necessities alone. Yet I urge you to know at your core that you deserve prosperity. Regardless of how long that takes. However humble the start. Say it out loud: "I deserve prosperity." When you're ready to turn that fantasy into reality, take bold, imperfect action. If you want to have it all at some point in your life, you'll have to start allowing yourself to embrace the change *now*. You have to completely ignore what other people expect, think, or want you to do. Sometimes, your dream lifestyle won't match what society says you *should* be doing at your current age or stage in life. You have to be honest with yourself about what *you* really want and be willing to ignore the opinions of others. Remember, you are designing your life for yourself, not for anyone else. If you want to get the most out of our time together, I'm telling you to aim big with me. I can handle it!

FROM VISION TO REALITY

As we close out part one of this book, let's take a moment to appreciate the ground we've covered together. You've embarked on a critical process of clarifying your life's vision, prioritizing the most important life pillars in this season, and understanding the role of money in crafting a wealthy, fulfilling existence, while homing in on your unique purpose with your Purpose Principle. You've dared to challenge conventional paths, seeking a more holistic view of success that resonates deeply with your personal values and aspirations.

The journey ahead in part two, Master Your Methods, is all about the "how." You've laid the foundation, now it's time to build upon it. This next section will equip you with practical tools and frameworks designed to accelerate your progress. We'll delve into strategies for working smart, not just hard, leveraging your strengths and resources to move closer to your goals with efficiency and purpose.

Remember, the path to rewriting the rules for a successful, unconventional life is not a one-time effort. It's an ongoing process of growth, learning, and adaptation. I encourage you to use this book as a living resource, returning to it as you evolve and as your circumstances change.

PART 2

MASTER

YOUR METHODS

Creating a vision is just the first step. Now that you know what you want, it's time to focus on learning how to get there. This is where most people mess up. Many can have an idea, but few commit to the work, put the personal infrastructure in place, and have the discipline to execute their plans.

In this section, we'll explore the tools you'll need, including the mental models, habits, and networks that will support you in living out your Purpose Principle and executing your vision. We'll look into how to cultivate relationships that will support you, not just professionally, but in staying true to your vision. You'll learn how to adapt to changing circumstances with agility, making sure your goals remain in sight even as the landscape shifts. How are you going to approach the plan you put into place? Are you going to live, or lead? *Living* is all about going through the motions. You wake up, go to work, come home, maybe watch some TV, and go to bed. Rinse and repeat. There's no intentionality, no direction, and no real sense of the value of your time. It's just existing. *Leading,* on the other hand, is about taking charge of your life. It's about setting goals, making plans, and taking action. It's about being intentional with your time and energy and using them in a way that moves you closer to where you want to be.

BALANCING VISION AND REALITY

I always sensed my career would be a big part of my life. But it took hard work to make my vision a reality. We all have inklings about our purpose. But for me, the early days were more hustle than balance. I thought if I hustled hard enough up front, everything would just fall into place by my late twenties. That's not quite how it works. You have to keep moving the game pieces around the board, redirecting your life when it becomes unbalanced.

When I was twenty-three years old, the call of start-up life beckoned me to leave the comfort of my job and join the legion of founders in San Francisco. Now, let's be real, the odds weren't exactly in my favor. A measly 2 percent of venture-backed founders were women, and the numbers were even more dismal for Black founders. But I, ever the determined soul, was resolute in my quest to defy the statistics and wasn't going to let the data get in the way of building something revolutionary.

To stack the deck in my favor, I started working on my big idea months before I ever considered quitting. I did this by assembling a formidable founding team, each member complementing my skill set and personality. Enter stage left: Jonathan, the charismatic extrovert working at LinkedIn who's never met a stranger. Aaron, the confident negotiator with dreams of business domination, a management consultant at Bain who lived in NYC and was a serial networker. Then there was Jeff, the meticulous technical architect who almost never slept and enjoyed building systems to organize data. Oh, and did I mention they're all men? Now, I certainly didn't pick them just because they were men, but I absolutely was aware that having men by my side building this business would prove helpful. As a 4'11", not technologically savvy Black woman from St. Louis, my chances of raising venture funding solo were about as likely as spotting a unicorn on Market Street in downtown San Francisco. All my cofounders were paid in sweat equity via shares of the company, different levels based on how much availability they had to invest in the project at such an early and risky phase. I knew nothing about media, had zero ideas about starting venture-backable start-ups, and had no experience in accounting, growth hacking, or raising money. In order to bring my vision to life, I knew I needed to start with a well-rounded team and a compelling vision people could get behind.

Once I had a solid support system to brainstorm with, Jeff and I spent our nights and weekends putting in the work on the initial version of our product, tailored specifically for our core audience: Black millennials. Now remember, this was during the era of people tasting weird food in BuzzFeed videos that were racking up a million views in a day, and media start-ups were raising seed rounds north of $10 million. Meanwhile, I was still juggling my day job and searching for

ways to generate some extra income to invest in hiring con-
tractors and fellows for our budding venture.

As fate would have it, my San Fran roommate at the time
decided to up and move to Hawaii with her boyfriend, pre-
senting me with a golden opportunity to increase my
monthly cash flow. I assured her not to worry about finding a
replacement tenant, as I wanted to have control over who my
next roommate would be. I hiked up the rent by $300 and
even managed to convince my next apartment mate to split
the utilities bill 50/50, netting me an extra $50 per month.
Just like that, I had $350 more each month to funnel directly
into Blavity's growth.

Now, bear in mind that I was earning $85,000 a year while
living in downtown San Francisco. Depending on where you
live, that may seem like more than enough, especially with a
roommate. But, if you've ever lived in California—and in the
Bay Area no less—you may feel for me. My disposable in-
come was stretched thin due to California's high taxes, rent,
transportation, and food costs. Luckily, the bustling start-up
office where I worked frequently had free food up for grabs.
So I kept a sharp eye on those emails announcing leftover
meals and unapologetically packed a plate to bring back to
my cubicle where my trusty Tupperware lay in wait. I even
started walking to and from work instead of relying on the
occasional Lyft.

Through these cost-saving measures, I managed to gener-
ate about $450 in additional cash each month. I then directed
all that extra income into the second version of Blavity's
product: a website that would become the foundation for our
thriving media brand.

With a solid team, a public product, and momentum building, I realized there was one crucial element missing: having the time to truly invest in taking Blavity to the next level. I was pushing the limits of my productivity, working three hours in the morning and another two to three hours at night after my day job. But I could feel the constraints of that pesky full-time job weighing me down. My Purpose Principle was rearing its head, and I could clearly see that I was slowing the growth of Blavity's potential, of my own potential, by keeping my nine-to-five.

The time had come to make the most significant decision of my life: quitting my job. Let's revisit the call I made at the opening of the book in more detail. With a racing heart, I contacted my parents to inform them of my decision. My dad's fury was palpable through the phone. From the moment I started Blavity, he never missed an opportunity to express his disapproval. There were even times when I'd avoid going home for the holidays because I couldn't bear to sit at the dinner table when the conversation inevitably turned to my "hobby," as he dismissively referred to it. "Morgan's doing this hobby now," he'd say, his voice dripping with skepticism.

But despite the tension and my dad's strong opposition, I knew I had to take the leap of faith. It was time to give Blavity the undivided attention and energy it deserved, to turn my so-called hobby into a thriving, successful venture that would prove all the naysayers wrong.

My dad, a highly successful doctor (thanks in no small part to my mom's incredible partnership), always had a keen eye for thinking and living outside the box. He viewed my leap into the world of entrepreneurship as a distraction that could derail my "real career." So, with a dose of tough love, he laid down the law: "You're going to negotiate a consulting agreement with Intuit. And that's final."

I knew deep down that his advice was sound. Surviving on a diet of boiled eggs and oatmeal would require more than the few hundred dollars I'd managed to save and the proceeds from my early stock investments. So, swallowing my pride, I followed my dad's advice and approached one of my former bosses about becoming a contracted consultant instead of a full-time employee.

As a consultant, I could regain my time by working remotely, running events to teach low-income taxpayers how to file their taxes for free. The role was meaningful in its own right and, crucially, allowed me the freedom to set my own schedule. During tax season (January to April), I was constantly on the move, traveling to more than thirteen cities across California and managing hundreds of volunteers and multiple site coordinators. It was intense, but I could handle it in my sleep. And the best part? I was earning over $100K for just six months of work each year.

The arrangement wasn't without its sacrifices, but it granted me the freedom to work remotely, replace my income, and continue doing something I loved: helping people. Plus, it left me with both time and money to devote to Blavity. I kept that consulting gig for three years, using the salary to pay myself so I wouldn't need to take money out of the business. I kept the consulting gig even after I raised $500,000 in pre-seed funding and we brought on our full-time employees. With each passing day, I could feel my vision inching closer to reality.

For me, rewriting my rules was about prioritizing progress in the business and not pursuing the emotional validation of "vanity success" we all see in TechCrunch. If I had let indecisiveness rule my perspective of business opportunities, I never would have been willing to put my own money on the line or leave my job to begin with. I would not have been okay with leaving my job and having co-founders who kept theirs until we could afford a salary for them. If I had been stubborn and asked them all to chip in equally in terms of time and money, I wouldn't have necessarily had co-founders! Not because they wouldn't have done it if they could have, but because given their particular life circumstances it wasn't a financial and career risk they were able to take.

One thing you need to know about me is although I have a high tolerance for risk, I'm strategic with every move. The narrative surrounding founders who blindly quit their jobs and lived in their cars on the streets of San Francisco—that wasn't for me. When incorporating lessons from this book, you have to continue to push yourself to evaluate different pathways of success. Those who have kids to feed or loans to pay can't make a decision to jump blindly into whatever risk comes your way without also considering how you will de-risk when you get there! Quite honestly, it's not as simple as always going with your gut. The moral of the story? When you're chasing a different type of life, it pays to be a realist.

And now, my friend, it's time to get really real. I spent months building the vision, assembling a team, and creating a strategy to get this thing off the ground. But, at some point, it was time to execute using the new rules I was writing. Now, it's your turn.

It's time to roll up your sleeves and put in the work. It can feel a little overwhelming to be faced with taking action and defying conventional standards of *how you get to your end goal*. This is where the rubber meets the road and your commitment, big ideas, and support system are all tested. Ideas are fun to dream about, but what happens when they become real? Let's find out, together!

Remember: There is no official "right" way to get to the finish line. In this part of the book, I will introduce frameworks and advice on how to adopt a data-driven mindset and approach, build a network to lean on, and make big strides to keep your momentum. As we transition to the next part, keep an open mind. The best tools for your personal growth are yet to come.

4

DARE TO BE DATA-DRIVEN

Have you ever wondered what sets apart those individuals who seem to effortlessly achieve their dreams from those who are always fantasizing about what they want to accomplish but seem to fall short? The answer lies in a powerful tool that you can start using today: data. The thing is, as noble an endeavor as getting your life in order may be, you can't fix what you don't measure. So, we're going to start counting everything. And I really do mean everything. From all the trivial little minutes scrolling social media to your moods and when you find the best energy for productivity (looking at you, witching hour folks). When you start crunching numbers on yourself, life gets crystal clear, trust me on this one. It's not always easy, but it's a necessary step if you want to make meaningful changes and reach your full potential. By understanding reality through numbers, you gain clarity that enables positive change across relationships, health, finances, and more. It's not about judging yourself harshly, it's about empowering yourself with knowledge so you can make informed decisions and take purposeful action.

People who live extraordinary lives or accomplish things that go against the norm don't reach the peaks of success without a data-driven mindset. All the most successful leaders I know adopt a rigorous view of their time, energy output, restorative input, and everything in between. Embarking on the perpetual journey of self-improvement is an exercise in self-awareness and tenacity. It demands that we objectively recognize where we excel and where we struggle so we can fearlessly address areas for growth.

Tracking my personal data transformed my productivity not just in work but in keeping myself honest with the joyous things too. People around me did not all of a sudden begin treating me like a boss just because I wore a founder hat, they started treating me like a boss because I began to act like one. Until you decide you're the boss of your life, no one else will. And it's impossible to be a boss until you're making decisions based on hard data.

The very existence of resistance within the data presents opportunity for positive shifts. So embrace your inner data geek and start measuring what matters most to you. Through consistent tracking, we transform seemingly random numbers into an empowering road map toward aspirations like healthier relationships, financial freedom, and improved well-being.

It could be argued that human beings have been tracking their personal data for almost as long as they've been in existence. From cave paintings to leather-bound diaries and all the way to Apple Notes, we have a natural tendency to record the goings-on in our lives. It's certainly not a new concept, but few adopt this habit rigorously. Some people don't want to go on a fact-finding mission for fear of what they might discover, and how that might hold them accountable to change. And change is scary! But, again, you're not here because you're afraid to turn your flaws into assets.

Tracking your personal data helps you become more self-aware and informed about your habits, allowing you to make more effective decisions about how to improve and optimize them. By consistently tracking your progress and assessing where you stand in relation to your growth goal, you'll have a clearer idea of what steps you need to take to get there.

One international survey looked at 505 participants who used self-tracking technologies, like apps and wearable devices, to explore their own experiences and found the activity of self-tracking can be very beneficial in increasing motivation, promoting a healthier lifestyle, and driving real behavioral change. In fact, 59 percent of participants reported using their self-tracking tech for extra motivation—the highest proportion of answers, which was followed by monitoring progress (53.55 percent) and data collection (42.39 percent).

The research concluded that tracking your own data can provide a reliable and efficient path toward self-knowledge and improvement. Overall, the feeling of achieving certain goals with consistent progress is intrinsically rewarding and can lead to a snowball effect of engaging in more activities you can track, which leads to positive outcomes.

By taking a realistic and proactive approach to your personal data, you'll not only improve your overall well-being and make it more likely to keep engaging in positive behavior, but also lay the foundation for achieving your vision. When we embrace data-driven decisions, we gain a distinct advantage—a clear, objective perspective. By basing our choices on facts, rather than emotions or biases, we can navigate through the complexities of life with greater clarity and purpose. That's why diligently tracking personal metrics is so essential: It provides an objective reality check when our ambitions blur facts. Don't avoid updating your sleep diary just because it reveals chronic deprivation. Don't stop balancing monthly budgets just because it means your income can't sustain your vision yet. A few days of insights can have a profound effect on what you're actually doing, not just what you *think* you're doing. This objectivity ensures that our decisions are rooted in reality, reducing the chances of misguided choices based on assumptions or incomplete information.

Think about it. Instead of just viewing your data as random unconnected information, what if you saw it as an opportunity for transformational change? This paradigm shift can be super powerful, both in your personal life and in business. By embracing this mindset, you can lay the foundation for growth and progress in all areas of your life. So, don't just let your personal data float around aimlessly. Take control of it and use it to your advantage. Trust me, it'll make a huge difference in achieving your goals in life.

SELF-ASSESS YOUR BEHAVIOR

We simply cannot expect to change anything without radical self-honesty. So now it's time for the fun part. You can evaluate your data and your progress toward personal data mastery at four levels. Each level is defined by a combination of strategic, operational, and habitual data-driven practices. Tracking your data leads to unavoidable truth. And while the truth may sting for a hot second, it hands you the power to transform. Time to make an audit of your data. (Yes, the audit is the fun part—I am a CEO after all!)

Level 1: Data-aware

The first level of your personal data mastery journey is really about exploring the data you have. You understand that you need to collect data to drive the right decisions and actions, but you aren't capitalizing on your data's full potential. You lack standard best practices for how and when to use data, as well as policies for data management. What data should you track? How should you organize it? These are questions you're still figuring out.

In many cases, there is a significant disconnect among different areas of your life, blurring any clear direction on how data should be used to drive success. As a result, each aspect of your life has data and you may be looking at disparate data points across different tools.

At this level, decisions are often being made with little to no data and are typically just a result of gut intuition or momentum. Actions are rarely measured for impact, making it impossible to truly learn from each iteration.

Level 2: Data-informed

The second level of your personal data mastery journey is where we start to see some progress. In this phase, you're beginning to see the value of investing in analytics tools, data organization, and best practices. You're curious about the data that already exists in the tools or gadgets you're using in everyday life and want to explore different meanings and processes. Plus, you're on the hunt for any gaps that need filling.

At this stage, you start prioritizing investments in data and looking daily at what it's telling you. You establish intentions and reflect on how things are going. Adding success metrics to each goal or habit becomes the norm, and so does postmortem analysis when things go awry. You upgrade your life to gain access to self-serve data tools that help answer your day-to-day questions and prioritize improvements in your Pillars or toward your vision in real time.

Level 3: Data-optimized

Now the fun begins! This is when data access has been more democratized across all of your worlds and embedded into your daily life. Data drives your personal strategic and operational practices. Every initiative aims to drive personal growth through data-driven decision-making. You're starting to understand how to drive your key performance indicators by optimizing your daily experiences.

Trusted and complete data is now readily available to you when driving toward your pillars and daily execution. But beyond that, you know how to use data to design effective and valuable personal experiments to enhance your experiences. Investment decisions are driven by past learnings, and goal prioritization is mapped to personal impact.

Level 4: Data-transformed

You've made it to personal data mastery. Data is now part of your DNA. Every aspect of your life and process is totally focused on an awareness of the metrics that matter and there's a culture of sharing it throughout your personal network, work, and family.

That means that everyone in your life is looking at the same numbers and dashboards, and any new habits are quickly learned as they're integrated into your routine. You can predictably invest in the right areas that drive your personal growth levers across your relationships, passions, wellness, and more, and you can commit to personal goals accordingly.

What level are you? Maybe you're just getting started looking at data or you've been using data for your wellness goals but not really in your relationships or in business. The real power comes in knowing your current spot and having the drive to climb higher. Remember, mastering data is not just about numbers and charts, it's also about making smarter decisions in your approach to your life, goals, and decisions. So, take a moment, assess your level, and get ready to embrace the next steps in your data-driven journey.

TOOLS AND SYSTEMS FOR TRACKING

Once you know where you stand, you can fearlessly evolve. So let's figure out what can be tracked. No, I don't mean stalking your ex online. I mean paying attention to your behaviors, actions, and habits. I track everything and I want

DATA MASTERY:
FROM "DATA AWARE" TO "DATA TRANSFORMED"

DATA AWARE	DATA TRANSFORMED
TOOLS You're just dipping your toes into the data pool, perhaps tracking steps on a fitness app or looking at your bank account to see daily expenses.	**TOOLS** Data has become your compass for daily living, shaping everything from budgeting to health, productivity, and personal growth.
DECISIONS You see data as useful but haven't fully integrated it into your life. You know it's there but don't pay attention that much.	**DECISIONS** You make decisions based on patterns and insights from your data, like choosing a healthier lifestyle because you understand how your nutrition impacts your mood.
DAILY BEHAVIOR Your daily decisions are still guided by intuition more often than by the numbers in front of you.	**DAILY BEHAVIOR** You use advanced tools to not just track but also analyze and forecast your progress, setting smarter goals.
GROWTH MINDSET You are sporadically checking in on your progress without a consistent strategy. You don't consider data a part of why you aren't making progress toward your goals.	**GROWTH MINDSET** Data isn't just a tool; it's a lifestyle. You're constantly learning from it and it influences your conversations, your habits, and your pillars.

you to do the same. Track your time. Track your moods. Heck, track your damn avocado consumption if it's relevant. On a daily basis, I monitor the amount of time I'm in meetings, how many ounces of water I'm drinking, how much time I spend on social media apps, and how many hours I sleep per night.

Now, tracking everything may seem unrealistic. For the next two weeks, I would like you to track something every day. In order to form any new habit, getting started is the key to learning what works and what does not. The good news is that it doesn't have to be complicated.

If you want to focus on your Wellness pillar, consider tracking the following categories: emotional well-being, mental wellness, and physical health. For physical health, start monitoring factors such as sleep quality, fruit and vegetable intake, and daily steps. To track your mental wellness, you could keep a record of hours spent in therapy, time spent walking outdoors, and minutes per day dedicated to meditation. Without making any changes to your current lifestyle, assess how you are currently performing in these areas that contribute to your personal growth.

You can apply the same approach to other pillars of your life, such as Relationships. If you're facing challenges in maintaining healthy relationships, begin by identifying the areas you want to improve. For example, track instances where you have positive or negative experiences with communication or expressing boundaries. Keep a record of how often you meet with friends, call your parents, or go on dates. Pay attention to whether you are the one initiating interactions to determine if a relationship is one-sided and possibly no longer beneficial to you.

There are a variety of tools and apps available that make it easy to track your data in a way that's simple and convenient.

Collecting your data and being detail-oriented about it is the only way to know if you're on track.

MONEY

We live in the twenty-first century, which means you can transfer funds, deposit checks, and manage your stock portfolio while lounging poolside on a Friday afternoon. The trick is to get yourself set up. You don't have to be a mathematician to be a financial wizard. There's an app for that. In fact, there are several. Make sure you have all the right apps and accounts in place to track how you're spending and saving. Having all the right tools in place can empower you to visually see where you're spending and offer insight into where you can make adjustments to meet your goals.

FREEDOM

When it comes to tracking your efforts to break free from mediocrity and live life on your terms, your best tool will be a calendar (either a physical planner or digital calendar, or even both). Log everything you're doing! You'll be able to look back and see how you were spending your time. Were you stuck in meetings all day? Did you attend any conferences, sign up for classes to level up your skill set, or hit up any networking events? Consider what your calendar tells you about how you're spending your free time. Keep a log of all the movies and shows you're watching to gauge how much of your time is spent on Netflix and chilling. You'll easily be able to spot opportunities to create more freedom in your life.

RELATIONSHIPS

Granted, tracking the quality of your relationships can be a bit more subjective than tracking other types of goals, but there are a few ways to do it. I recommend keeping a journal. Go buy yourself a nice one you love to look at! This is where you can track your thoughts and feelings about your relationships over time to give you a better understanding of how your relationships are evolving. Also, go back to that calendar. Make sure you record date nights, romantic getaways, family get-togethers, and social events. You can also block off quality time and track how often you're honoring the time you've set up for yourself. For example, if your vision is to have a closer relationship with your partner, you could set a goal of eating dinner together three times a week. Put it in the calendar and invite them, to hold you both accountable. Looking back at it will help you identify patterns or trends.

PASSIONS

If you're working on your hobbies, side hustles, and making space for personal enrichment and growth, it's important to track the time you're dedicating to the things you love doing. This is one area that can be so easy to routinely ignore into oblivion. Keep a record of how much time you've spent on your hobbies each week. Incorporate them into your calendar—make time for them. Try learning how to bullet journal, use a spreadsheet, or tap an app to track your progress. Meeting with an

accountability partner, mentor, or teacher can be an
advantage in this area to help keep you on track and give
you another measurable touch point to use.

WELLNESS

Technology is your friend when it comes to wellness. Use a
wearable device to help track your steps, daily movement,
and sleep. And there are plenty of apps to help track food
intake, as well as how many guided meditations you've
completed. Being able to see how well you're eating,
sleeping, moving, and breathing can be utterly revelatory
when it comes to finding areas (both big and small) for
optimization and improvement in your overall well-being.

LISTENING TO YOUR INTERNAL DATA

After two weeks of tracking your baseline data, it's time to
start analyzing it. As you dig into your numbers, look for
areas where you repeatedly fall short of your goals or areas
where you're consistently overperforming. As you read this
book, imagine yourself as a subject in a research study, or as
your own manager administering a performance review.
When you're tracking your data, dissociate from yourself in
order to be honest and reflective.

Facing less than impressive data points can sting. Our ten-
dency is to downplay or rationalize away information that
conflicts with our lofty self-perceptions. But pragmatic self-
awareness is key to continued growth. I get how easy it is to
only log our wins, then conveniently "forget" to track days
when we didn't hit the goals. Trust me, I've considered hiding

not-so-hot business bank statements straight in the trash instead of sending out my annual investor reports. But the sooner we get real about where we're doing well and where there's room for improvement, the faster we can bounce back even stronger.

You should choose metrics that are the most meaningful, already a part of your daily life, and relevant to your goals. You'll also want to select elements that you can realistically track over time. By keeping records of this information, you can start to triangulate patterns in your behavior, across all your pillars. For example, you might notice that you always feel stressed and overwhelmed on days when you don't get enough sleep. Or you might realize that you tend to let friendships fall to the wayside when you're focused on making money.

This information is incredibly valuable because it allows us to make more informed decisions about how we live our lives and be able to pivot when necessary. If we know that we tend to ignore our personal relationships when we're focused on work, we can take proactive steps to scale back time in the office and put more dinner dates on the schedule.

But keeping track of our data isn't just about identifying negative patterns. It's also about celebrating our successes. By tracking our progress, we can stay focused and build on our own momentum. For example, if your goal is to exercise more regularly, you might keep a log of your workouts. Seeing the strides you've made over time can be incredibly motivating and can help you stay committed to your goals.

I'll never forget the time I spent the night at my parents' house and walked into the living room to find my sixty-four-year-old dad sitting cross-legged on the floor. "Good morning, what are you doing?" I asked. "I'm practicing lowering my heart rate," he replied. I was shocked to see my workaholic dad was meditating! I could tell he was a bit embarrassed, so I sat down next to him in silence. When he was finished, I asked him when he started meditating. A few years prior, my dad had become a grandfather to my nephew, and he explained that when he first became a grandparent, he started reading research papers about the most effective ways to manage his stress and increase his longevity. He started using his Apple Watch to track his heart rate throughout the day and his blood pressure on a weekly basis to get a better understanding of his health habits.

But my dad didn't stop there. He also makes sure to walk or play Wii after every evening meal to reduce any blood sugar–level spikes, doesn't eat after 7 P.M., and takes weekly hot baths to keep his stress levels in check. He's a master at using his own data to increase his longevity and quality of life, and, as a new grandpa, he's leaving nothing to chance.

Taking a few minutes each day to reflect on your thoughts and experiences can be incredibly helpful in improving self-awareness. Don't let the idea of it overwhelm you! Start small and find tools that work for you. You don't need to write a novel; journaling a few sentences about your day can be enough to get started.

You might just be surprised at the positive impact it can have on your life.

MANAGING FRICTION AND ROADBLOCKS

Inevitably there is going to be tension between where you are and where you want to be. I can also guarantee you that there will be roadblocks: a failure, a rejection, an unexpected obstacle. They hurt. They're frustrating. So let's discuss how to look at the data and handle the areas where you constantly fall short of your goals or encounter obstacles that prevent you from reaching your ambitions. This is the point at which you can begin to see where and how improvements can be made. You cannot let these setbacks define you! The boss within knows that roadblocks are there to be overcome, not to become the excuses that hold you back. It's a normal response to avoid evidence that conflicts with how we see ourselves. But resist that urge! You must get obsessed with finding solutions, not complaining about problems. Each roadblock contains clues and data to help you push past your plateau.

For example, if you've been tracking your daily steps and notice that you're consistently falling short of your goal, you might need to adjust your workout routine or find ways to be more active throughout the day. It could be as simple as walking to pick up a coffee in the morning or buying a walking pad so you can take a meeting or two while walking at a slow pace!

Or let's say you've been tracking your daily expenses and notice that you're consistently ordering last-minute delivery after a long day at work, even though you meal prepped earlier in the week. We have all been there. And, occasionally, this can be a nice treat-yourself moment. But leaning on this shortcut too often could be a roadblock preventing you from achieving your financial goals. By acknowledging this obstacle, you can work on planning your meals to last through the end of the week, or walk to get takeout instead of paying a 35 percent premium for a delivery service! It's not about restriction as much as reallocation. Splurge on that delivery! Just don't do it five times a week.

If your focus is adjusting your behavior to meditate daily to support your wellness goal . . . but you've literally only tracked two sessions this week, what micro-adjustments can boost consistency?

If your Freedom pillar aims for location independence but your expenses exceed remote work income, how can you increase earnings or trim costs? If your Relationships pillar is your focus and you're working on prioritizing quality couple time yet your calendar has no dates scheduled, what fun ideas can you book for this upcoming weekend, even if it's just a walk to grab coffee or running errands together? Are you getting my point?

Instead of shortcuts, it's important to tap into grit, which was first defined by psychologist and researcher Angela Duckworth as "perseverance and passion for long-term goals." Grit is all about the hard work that goes into keeping up motivation, effort, and interest in your goal. It doesn't matter what downturns, failures, or stagnation you encounter, those who embody grit see life as a marathon. Every roadblock whispers a secret lesson to us—it's a moment to pause, reflect, and grow. Use it to fuel the stamina you need to get you through the hardest peaks and the valleys.

LEARN TO ANALYZE MACRO DATA

When it comes to looking at the data, it's important to consider things beyond your control. Let's not ignore the big external forces that can have a major impact on your life, like the economy, technology, and culture. These are all factors that can make or break your success. Don't be caught off guard by external roadblocks you could have seen coming from a mile away. Let's get ahead of the game and stay on top of the external data factors that may be having an impact on the pace at which you can grow.

When I was fundraising for Blavity, I found myself up against a big challenge that almost cost us the funding we desperately needed. At the time, there were numerous media companies raising money to address the millennial audience, and we were but one little drop in the bucket. I knew that we had a unique vision and business model that could truly set us apart, but getting the investors to see that was proving to be difficult. My early conversations with venture capitalists left me with polite rejections after only one meeting. They would hear the pitch, review our data, and ask a ton of questions via email, only to dismiss me in the end. It was incredibly frustrating, and I couldn't figure out what I was doing wrong.

After a few hard passes, I decided to dig deeper and find out why I wasn't getting the investment I needed. I requested feedback from a few of the VCs who seemed interested but ultimately passed on us, and what I learned was shocking.

It turned out that they had various media companies in their portfolio and were overextended in that space. They weren't in the market to make more investments in media. It was a big fat waste of time and resources for me and the team. Right idea. Wrong people.

I had failed to do my due diligence in researching the investors and their portfolios. I hadn't taken the time to understand their investment history and the macro trends in the industry. If I had, I could have saved myself hours of time and hundreds of dollars on flights, and avoided showing my cards to people who were only interested in gaining intel on the market. This experience taught me the importance of understanding both the micro and macro factors at play when pursuing a big goal or decision. I realized that I needed to do more research, ask the right questions up front, and analyze both the individual elements and the larger external factors that could impact my success.

The challenge for me was to learn from my mistake and apply this new knowledge to future fundraising efforts. It was a tough lesson, but it ultimately made me a better entrepreneur and leader. Understanding external trends can be a game changer in making informed decisions and achieving your goals, no matter what they are.

For instance, if you're looking to enter the housing market, it's great to get your personal data wish list requirements all lined up. Make sure you know what you want as far as square footage, have a down payment ready that covers closing costs, and have a spreadsheet that helps you feel secure about how you're going to make your monthly mortgage payments. But, before you start your search, you'll need to do your research on external factors you can't control, like interest rates, property taxes, school ratings, and how competitive the market is in your target neighborhoods. You could be primed and ready to go on your end, but if the outside data doesn't line up, it could be a waste of time. Maybe you decide to wait until the buying environment is more in your favor, or you reevaluate your internal data and course-correct your house-buying goal to meet the market.

Likewise, you should also keep an eye on industry trends if you're growing your side hustle. Let's take the example of a full-time, salaried video producer who is looking to leave his job to start his own production company. What trends are happening with companies looking to outsource their video production work? What does the competition look like? Is it a noisy space that requires some major differentiation or is there ample room to consume market share? Is artificial intelligence technology enabling more small businesses to self-serve and reduce their dependence on the exact service you're offering? By understanding the macro trends, you can make better decisions about how to grow your business and what to expect in terms of how the market will receive you.

But how do you stay up to date with these developments? It's simple, really. Take some time each week to research the latest trends and news in your industry. There are plenty of ways to create a steady inbound stream of knowledge. Follow industry experts on LinkedIn, subscribe to newsletters written by trade publications and thought leaders, attend annual conferences, and join the relevant industry associations or memberships for people who are just like you. By staying informed, you'll be better equipped to make decisions and set realistic expectations for yourself.

Remember, the key to success is a combination of realism

and optimism. You need to be realistic about where you currently stand and optimistic about where you can go. With the right mindset and strategies in place, you can achieve anything you set your mind to. Long-term planning becomes an art form when guided by data. By analyzing the patterns and insights gleaned from our information, we can create a road map toward our aspirations. With data as our compass, we craft a future that is both purposeful and strategic.

PUTTING IT ALL TOGETHER: YOUR DATA-TRACKING

Let's take a CEO-level approach to continuously extracting value from your personal data. Don't let the idea of tracking your personal data seem intimidating or overwhelming. Start small with the prompts below to make it manageable and enlightening. The key is turning insights into impact through mindset shifts and focused action.

1. What two to three metrics aligned with your priority Pillars will you track to start? Choose something meaningful and feasible.

2. What simple tools can you leverage? Apps are not required! Calendars, notes, and journals work.

3. Which daily behaviors will you log? Actions and habits provide tangible tracking.

4. How much time can you realistically commit? Even five minutes a day is a great start.

5. How can you make tracking seamless? Put tools somewhere visible to reduce friction.

6. When will you schedule time for tracking? Treat it like an important meeting with yourself.

   Things to consider:

- How can you segment your data for deeper insights? Break it down by time, categories, and behaviors, and see if you can find any trends.
- Are you missing any key metrics that would help tell the full story? What else would be useful to track?
- Who can you enlist to help analyze and interpret the data? Get an outside perspective if you are finding it hard to read. Sometimes someone not as close to your data may see something you don't.
- Be kind! Data can reveal tough truths. Have self-compassion as you learn and be focused on growth, not judgment.

Be patient with yourself as you build this new habit. Tracking is a journey of self-discovery, it's not about judging yourself. Over time, insights will emerge to guide your growth and achievement. Trust the process!

5

BUILD YOUR TEAM LIKE A CEO

Years ago, my calendar was filled with back-to-back investor pitch meetings, while my inbox flooded with employee questions or approvals I lacked time to answer. Blurred days bled into sleepless nights as I darted between cities pitching our vision, then led early-morning all-hands calls fueled on coffee and adrenaline. My co-founder Jeff was entangled in his own chaos, navigating a full-time job at Mailchimp while managing the start of a new family and keeping our website up and running and protected against hackers. Meanwhile, Aaron was starting his business school journey in a city miles away while focusing his attention on launching Blavity's first sales team. As for Jonathan, well, he was settled in the hustle and bustle of NYC, dedicated to building valuable relationships with prospective clients and being the face of Blavity on the East Coast.

As founder and CEO, I felt the burden to single-handedly keep our company alive. More often than not, I felt like I was the glue holding all the pieces together back at our headquarters. This meant I took on a multitude of roles, from setting up our first office in downtown Los Angeles and planning our first EmpowerHer conference in NYC to managing our website's product features and overseeing content and social media managers. I even played recruiter (the most time consuming!), hiring and onboarding staff.

But the chaos didn't stop there. In the midst of it all, I was also chasing our first round of funding. Days blurred into nights as I hopped from one city to another, sleeping on friends' couches while meeting potential investors. My once-structured schedule was now a jumbled mess of back-to-back meetings and flights. Days were spent walking into team huddles, frazzled and unprepared, and nights were dedicated to drafting emails for prospective investors. And despite all this madness, I still had my consulting job with Intuit in the early mornings and on the weekends so that I could keep funneling as much cash as possible into Blavity.

The weight of it all was suffocating. Doubts began to creep in. I started to question: Why did it feel so hard for me? Was I cut out for this? Was this level of struggle normal? Sure, all founders faced challenges, but was it supposed to be *this* hard? I couldn't help but question whether biases were at play that made hurdles higher for me as a young Black woman. I observed my male peers effortlessly raising rounds or jetting between meetings while I felt trapped doing admin work. Were doors just opening wider for them? Did their employees expect less of them as a day-to-day operator?

Four years in, Blavity's business and company culture seemed on the brink of collapse, needing a stronger foundation than just me to hold everything together. There was simply no more time in the day or efficiency left to squeeze out. There was no way to "hard work" myself out of this mess, and it was clear that more output wasn't the solution. Something had to give.

So, I took a step back. I could see the road ahead; if I didn't act, things would spiral further out of control, we might lose traction, or, worse, risk losing a co-founder. The company needed momentum to prove it was worth everyone's effort. It was time to make a radical decision. I knew that I needed more time to focus on my most important responsibilities. I knew that I needed to create more space to think and be intentional with my actions and behaviors. Do you ever feel like you're constantly operating from a step behind? Like if you could only squeeze a few more hours into each day you could finally feel like you're not *always* running out of fuel. That's how I felt.

I needed help, and I needed it bad. So I had this wild idea: What if I hired an assistant? I mean, it seemed crazy at first. Assistants are for those high-flying execs, right? Not for someone like me, trying to prove herself in this cutthroat world. But the more I thought about it, the more it made sense.

I took the plunge, and let me tell you, it was a game changer. I started focusing on the big picture—setting the vision, pitching to investors, bringing in the right people. My assistant took care of the rest. It was like suddenly I had space to breathe, to think. I wasn't just reacting to things anymore, I was leading. I had renewed energy for plotting ambitious growth trajectories that compelled top talent to join despite our early stage. My assistant became my force multiplier.

With my team helping to lighten the load, I was granted a newfound freedom that allowed me to evolve into a CEO who could effectively meet the needs of our company and guide it toward growth.

This whole experience taught me something crucial about leadership and success. This is another moment when I realized I had to rewrite the rules. You've got to look at your situation and say, "What works for them doesn't work for me, and that's okay." It's not just about working harder, it's about working smarter, about building a support system that allows you to thrive.

So if you're feeling overwhelmed, if you're feeling like you're stuck on this never-ending treadmill, maybe it's time to ask yourself: "What can I change? How can I do things differently?" Because trust me, sometimes the most unconventional choice is exactly what you need to move forward.

YOUR DAILY TEAM

If you're anything like I was during my transition from builder to leader, you might find yourself wearing every single proverbial hat in your life. From cooking meals and cleaning the house to handling taxes, reporting to work, and even fixing your flat tire. It's easy to have very little time to focus on what needs to happen to achieve the vision you've set for yourself. Yet, what you have to understand is this: For you to grow and thrive, it's crucial to nurture your relationships with the people you engage with every single day.

The constant juggling made me wish I could clone myself just to get it all done. I'd watch enviously as my friends seemed to effortlessly manage their successful careers while keeping the household running like a well-oiled machine and even finding time for wine nights. Meanwhile, I felt constantly behind, crunched for time and craving more sleep than catnaps.

Yet I wrongly assumed that needing help made me weak or ineffective compared to those who could "do it all." Our society likes to tell us we need to be lone warriors, conquering it all through individual grit. But denying our human limits only leads to burnout and diminishing returns in the long run, making us less capable of achieving those big, hairy visions.

The truth is, to thrive you must nurture an entire network of people to share life's burdens and responsibilities, from your partner to your neighbor. This daily support tribe helps balance strengths, uplift spirits on hard days, and unlock capacity you didn't know you had. With aligned, capable help comes the most precious resource of all: time. The freedom to wholeheartedly focus time and mental bandwidth on your highest, most rewarding priorities—the ones that fuel your purpose and actualize your legacy over time.

I had to shift my mindset to recognize that delegating tasks didn't make me inadequate, it made me a more visionary leader. Building a team enhanced my strengths rather than highlighting my weaknesses. Collaboration would help my gifts flourish, not flounder. With the right team behind me I could play from my front foot instead of always reacting to chaos in the moment.

Does this resonate with your experience? What could you achieve with just a bit more time and space to breathe and focus? Where do you need aligned assistance right now to save your sanity or better capitalize on strengths?

THE TRUTH ABOUT *YOU*

Now that we're on the same page about why you need a team in your corner, let's explore what that looks like and who can help lighten the load. But before we can learn to do that, I need to level set by imparting a few cold, hard facts.

Fact #1: You are not perfect. Let's face it, no one is. Perfection is as elusive as a unicorn is fictional. You might stumble, trip, or fall flat on your face, and guess what? That's okay. Every scrape is a battle scar, each mistake a new lesson learned, and all missteps are dances in disguise.

Fact #2: You are gloriously and wonderfully human. You come with a unique set of strengths, quirks, and, yes, even weaknesses. Continue to embrace that. It's these qualities, the good and the not-so-good, that make you who you are.

Fact #3: You can't do everything by yourself. Trying to be the lone wolf, bearing the weight of the world on your shoulders? Let me tell you, even Atlas had to put the sky down eventually. There's no shame in needing help. In fact, it's a mark of wisdom to recognize when you need it and the strength to ask for it.

So let's face these hard truths straight on. No flinching. No retreating! Once you acknowledge these realities, you will be able to build an A-team to balance your skills and lift your burdens. I can guarantee that increasing your capacity to reach the vision requires expanding your team. Take an honest inventory—where do you consistently fall short no matter how hard you grind solo? What goals or tasks perpetually slide down your list? Where are you feeling overwhelmed and stretched too thin? These shortfalls signal areas for delegation and collaboration.

It's critical to build a team around you with complementary strengths. I want you to keep this in mind when you are feeling the urge to hoard all of the tasks on your list or do everything on your own.

CEO TASKS VS. OPERATING TASKS

When I first started my business, I was the hardest-working employee. So I get it. Hiring felt scary. I worried about whether I would get a return on my investment when bringing on a contractor. Then there's home life, and hiring someone to help me at home also felt weird. I worried about trusting someone else with things that were so intimate, like laundry, cooking, and scheduling appointments. I worried about losing time redoing tasks that were performed incorrectly the first time. I worried about losing the very little discretionary money I had if the person I hired didn't work out.

Ultimately you need to ask yourself, what kind of support will have the most impact on your core pillars. Let's dig deeper into this question by completing an exercise I do with all of my direct reports and small business owner clients. Taking part in this exercise helps my team gain a greater understanding of the sheer scope of all the work, decisions, and responsibilities they take on on any given day. This practice can work for anyone and can be applied to any aspect of your life.

CEO Tasks vs.
Operating Tasks Exercise
List out your CEO Tasks and Operating Tasks.

CEO VS. OPERATING TASKS

CEO	OPERATING

Grab a sheet of paper (or a fancy notebook, if that's your style) and draw a line down the middle. Label the left side

"CEO Tasks" and the right side "Operating Tasks." Now let's define these two categories.

CEO Tasks are tasks that only you, the leader of your life, can do. These tasks require your unique skills, decision-making abilities, or vision to craft your life's purpose and direction. CEO Tasks also bring you energy when completed.

CEO TASKS CAN BE CLASSIFIED INTO FOUR CATEGORIES:

Vision and Life Purpose: Goal-setting, defining values, career aspirations, personal development goals, major life milestones

Innovation and Creativity: Exploring new ideas/ opportunities, creative problem-solving, developing inventions/projects

Leadership and Relationships: Attending events/birthdays, dating, networking, giving praise/feedback, quality time with relationships

Health and Well-being: Fitness, learning new skills, reflection, emotional wellness, self-care, overall health improvements

Operating Tasks are tasks that can be delegated or outsourced, or tasks you simply dread doing. These tasks might require expertise in specific areas or involve day-to-day chores that don't necessarily need your personal touch. These should be tasks that you both aren't all that great at and don't enjoy. You might do them today because there is no one else doing them, but if you had all the money in the world, they would be one of the first things to go!

OPERATING TASKS TYPICALLY FALL INTO FOUR
CATEGORIES:

Administration: Scheduling, researching, driving,
  responding to emails/calls, paperwork
Finance: Paying bills, budgeting, bookkeeping, taxes
Family Care and Household Duties: Childcare, shopping,
  meal preparation, planning holidays, home maintenance,
  dog-walking, school or daycare drop-off and pickup,
  laundry, cleaning, and yard work
Specialized Operating: Marketing, sales, web development,
  styling, social media, legal matters

Anything that is repeatable and could be done on a daily,
weekly, monthly, or quarterly basis is a task that could fall
into the category of an Operating Task. At this point, you
should have compiled your data as I outlined in the last chap-
ter. Take a look at your data and calendar from the last four-
teen days and jot down everything you've done or had to get
done to make your life move forward. Be specific! Now start
making those lists!

DELEGATE TO REDUCE CONTEXT-SWITCHING

Armed with your compiled list of CEO Tasks and Operating
Tasks, you're now in a position to start acting like the em-
powered boss you truly are. Our aim here is simple but
powerful: Carve out a plan that frees up your time and en-
ergy so you can channel them toward focusing on those CEO
Tasks. These tasks are not just any line on your to-do list,

they're game changers that make a substantial impact on your life, and create room for your pillars to shine.

Take a moment and turn your gaze back to your two lists. I'm going to guess it feels like *a lot*. This may be how you're currently spending your time, but is this an accurate reflection of how you *want* to be spending your time in the future? Only you can decide that.

Sure, you could take on these tasks all day, every day. You know you can, because you're already doing it! But here's a reality check. Half of these tasks in the Operating Tasks column are quietly robbing you of the time you could be investing in your CEO Tasks column.

Now, before you have a chance to say, "But Morgan, I can multitask. I can get both the lists done in a day," I want to stop you. You can't. I mean, you can, but not to the very best of your ability. Not to make the gains you need to reach the goals you've set for yourself.

For example, let's imagine you're knee-deep in an important project, pouring your heart and soul into it, when suddenly an email pops up demanding your attention. So you switch gears, read the email, and start crafting a response. Just as you're getting into the groove of it, *ding,* someone pings you on Slack and asks you a quick question. The temptation to check those messages is strong, but hold up! Don't fall into that trap. Instead, reduce that context-switching!

"Context-switching" between tasks refers to the act of switching your focus and attention from one task to another. It often occurs when you rapidly shift between different activities, projects, or contexts within a short period. While some people believe that multitasking increases productivity, research suggests otherwise. Psychologists have used task-switching experiments to test how detrimental or beneficial this behavior can be.

In experiments published in 2001, Joshua Rubinstein, Ph.D., Jeffrey Evans, Ph.D., and David Meyer, Ph.D., conducted four experiments in which young adults switched between different mathematical tasks. Their results showed that for all tasks, the participants lost time when they had to switch from one task to another. As the tasks became more involved, more time was lost. Notably, the more unfamiliar a task was to the participant, the more time it took to complete. Although switch costs may be relatively small, they can add up when people switch repeatedly back and forth between tasks. So multitasking can seem efficient in the moment, but may actually take more time in the end. And diverted attention might lead to increased sloppy mistakes and errors.

This scenario is all too common in our workdays. It's human nature for people to assume that what's important to them must also be a top priority for everyone else. A quick question here . . . a text . . . and a favor there. But, when these interruptions happen repeatedly during the precious morning hours when you're trying to do work, it derails your productivity for the whole day. It can be tempting to react to the influx of emails and texts right away. But I've learned the hard way that splitting my attention during my peak focus hours means I get less done overall. Then I'm stuck trying to think deeply or be creative during the late afternoon when I'm already drained. Each time you context-switch, your brain has to recalibrate, refocus, and find its footing again.

Now that I've made my point, here comes the million-dollar question: What if there was a way to offload these tasks to someone who not only excels at them but also relishes doing them? What if you could effectively "buy back" your time? Would you jump at the chance?

It's time to delve into finding the right kind of help. Your tribe can be sourced from three major pools: your personal life, your professional life, and potential outside hires.

EMBRACE "WE" INSTEAD OF "ME"

All right, let's get something straight here. The world likes to tell us that we have to be this one-person powerhouse, a modern-day Hercules pulling off every task single-handedly. Listen, that's just not feasible. No doubt, it's fabulous to have that "I got this" spirit. But as humans, we're wired for connection, for shared experiences, for that ride-or-die crew we call our "tribe." From all the way back when our ancestors were out hunting and gathering right up to us organizing a car pool for our kids (how times change, huh?), humans have been all about that team effort. We've been dividing and conquering since day one. Our strength isn't just in our individual hustle, it's in our collective power. It's in our community.

Back in the early years of Blavity, I was knee-deep in the beginning stages of growing the company. My heart throbbed with the excitement of our expanding reach, yet my plate was piling high with tasks. Among those, one was particularly daunting for me—hiring. Who knew that finding people who could breathe life into your vision would be such an epic quest? Creating job descriptions, standardizing pay, sourcing candidates, and going through thousands of applications—it was a lot. But there I was, juggling it all.

Enter Jackie, whom I met in a San Francisco nightclub for Jonathan's going away party when he moved to New York. With a heart as big as her smile, and a personality that could charm the birds from the trees, Jackie and I were instant friends. A few months later, she was at a crossroads, transitioning from her role as an administrative coordinator, and eager to dip her toes into the exciting pool of recruiting.

One day, we were hanging out in Oakland while I crashed on her couch to avoid paying for expensive San Francisco hotels. I had had a long week of meetings, and over some iced coffees, I found myself unspooling my hiring worries. I remember her listening attentively, her face serious, nodding at the right moments. And then, as if struck by a lightning bolt of inspiration, she made an offer that would change the trajectory of Blavity forever.

Jackie offered to help me with hiring. It wasn't about money, but rather a chance for her to flex her networking muscles and showcase her natural knack for connecting people. She offered to be my people-finder, talent-spotter, and hiring fairy godmother. To put it simply, Jackie had my back.

Over the next eighteen months, Jackie sourced and onboarded six of our foundational team members. Her warm personality, ability to articulate Blavity's mission with genuine passion, and talent for assessing potential were like a magnetic force pulling in the best fits for us. Each person she brought onto the team wasn't just a warm body filling a seat, they were skilled, motivated, and aligned with our mission. They understood the vision and were ready to walk this journey with us.

Fast-forward nine years and I'm still in awe of the longevity and impact of those hires. They've been with us longer than most, each contributing significantly to the growth and success of Blavity. Jackie, meanwhile, has catapulted her natural skill into a six-figure income, now hiring for the best tech companies and start-ups in the world. And to think, none of this would have been possible if Jackie hadn't stepped up to share the load with me.

That's the power of shared responsibilities. That's the magic of a tribe. Sometimes, the help you need is sitting right next to you, sipping an almond milk cold brew, just waiting for an opportunity to shine.

So, let's talk about your tribe. It's that precious group of folks who've got your back: your family, your besties, your colleagues, your mentors, and even your neighbor you wave to once a week. They are your collective, a go-to team that can help you share the load.

Now, here's where the art of negotiation comes in. We've established that not everything has to be handled by you. However, transferring these tasks to others involves clearly articulating what you need, and recognizing that something you dread is potentially something someone else enjoys. Just like a team at work, fostering a well-balanced tribe at home will create more ease.

For instance, perhaps you have a friend who lives for throwing over-the-top events and you couldn't host your way out of a reusable grocery bag. Most certainly you could trade one of your specialized skills in return for their help in planning your kid's birthday party. Or maybe you have a colleague at work who's an incredible designer and would be happy to take on a new logo for your side hustle in exchange for some of your time helping them build better financial models for their work budgets.

When I was preparing to relaunch my WorkSmart coaching program, I knew I wanted to test digital ads to reach more ambitious professionals. The only catch was I didn't have advertising expertise. Enter Lorell, a prospective client with her own marketing agency. I offered her a heavily discounted rate to join the new WorkSmart cohort in exchange for managing our ad strategy and design. It was a win-win—I gained her marketing firepower for the launch while she got premium coaching and networking to grow her business.

HOW TO SWAP WITHOUT LOSING YOUR PRECIOUS TIME

I know some of you may be thinking, "Trading skills sounds great, but I'm not sure I have any valuable traits to barter with." Listen, we all have unique talents, so don't sell yourself short! But I hear you, and hiring help outright may seem out of reach financially. The essence of skillful trading is all about recognizing and capitalizing on your natural strengths. And, best of all, it's free.

It's about making exchanges that light you up, not wear you out. Most important, it's about fiercely guarding your reclaimed time, ensuring it's spent on what truly matters. In the vast universe of talents, each of us possesses a unique set of skills that come effortlessly. Whether it's the ability to craft a compelling narrative, show up for your friends, sew a homemade Halloween costume, spontaneously say yes to a flight deal with no notice, or solve complex mathematical problems, these talents are innate to our being and skills. Recognizing and acknowledging these skills is the first step in the journey of artful trading. By understanding what we excel at, we can offer these skills in exchange for others that might not come as naturally to us.

HOW TO FIND YOUR "THING" TO BARTER

Here are a few ways to identify which skills you may excel at.

Bask in the Compliments: Throughout our lives, we receive compliments, often brushing them off out of modesty. However, these words of praise aren't merely fleeting moments of kindness. They are indicators of our strengths and natural talents. When someone admires the way we manage a project or the creativity we bring to our social media feed, it's a testament to our abilities. Embracing these compliments allows us to understand our value and the unique contributions we bring to the table.

Be the Go-to Guru: There's a certain sense of pride that comes with being the person others turn to for advice or expertise. Whether it's friends seeking guidance on a particular topic or colleagues asking for assistance, these moments actually highlight our expertise in specific areas. Where are you the Go-to Guru in your family or friend group? It's an affirmation that our knowledge and abilities are not only recognized but also sought after.

Revel in the Ease: You know that task everyone dreads but you secretly enjoy? Maybe it's editing videos, setting up new home appliances, or decluttering closets. These are prime trading materials!

Leveraging your skills through strategic bartering can be paradigm-shifting. But we have to be sure it's done right so those hard-won free hours don't slip away. Let's talk about guarding your time while still benefiting from smart trades.

First, think big picture. Bundle your offerings for more leverage, like providing social media management in monthly packages, not hourly stints. Don't just figure out one night when you can babysit for a friend, choose a few dates to schedule ahead of time. Aim for trades that are truly worth your precious time.

What type of help would make the biggest impact for you right now? Here are a few things you can consider requesting from your tribe that aren't task-oriented but create a shared collective that will result in your saving time.

- An accountability partner to help you stay focused on goals
- A networking buddy to meet people and exchange ideas

- A writing group to give you feedback and encouragement
- A babysitting co-op to trade childcare with other parents
- A weekly, rotating dinner with other friends and family to lighten the load and your spirits

The essential element here is a clear understanding and communication of needs and expectations. This way, you're not just delegating tasks, you're building relationships, fostering mutual exchanges, and most important, buying back your precious time. By becoming adept at negotiation and delegation, you can better manage your resource of time, paving the way to more freedom to do the things that drive you closer to your growth goals. So, start analyzing your tasks, identify potential helpers in your tribe, and begin the conversation. You might be surprised at the opportunities you discover.

Choose your tribe wisely. The essence of a successful barter lies in the mutual respect and reliability of the parties involved. Kind of like a group project in high school, you never want to be the one left doing all the work. It's crucial to be discerning about whom you trade with. Partner with individuals who recognize the worth of your time and skills and are equally committed to honoring their end of the bargain. Trust and reliability are the cornerstones of such exchanges. By being selective, you ensure that the trade is beneficial and that you're not left feeling shortchanged. To help, make sure you set clear ground rules up front about scope, availability, timelines, and more. Manage expectations early to prevent misunderstandings down the road. Remember, you're not on call 24/7.

Lastly, remember to leverage time-blocking. I want you to designate time in your calendar for the bartered tasks or projects so that it doesn't bleed into other priorities. Stay intentional about scheduling exchanges.

LET'S REVISIT YOUR WEALTH CODE

Now that we've fully exhausted the easy ways to reorganize your tasks and get some help from the people already in your sphere, you've likely realized there is a limit to what others will do for you for free, no matter how much they love you or want to help. Let's dig into how we're going to find the money and how to pick up the remaining tasks from your Operating Tasks list.

In order to transform your life, you need to invest in it. There is only a small distance that bartering, optimizing your calendar, and negotiating with your partner will take you. You should be willing to pay for convenience and to take things off your plate—no matter how small a contribution you can make and take. Before you skip this section because you feel too broke, have responsibilities at home, are in too much debt, or don't have any wiggle room in your discretionary income, I want you to bear with me here. You picked up this book because you wanted to stop being the person who just takes what the world gives them. You want to be someone who is creating their own destiny. So before we shut the door on what you can't afford, let's ground ourselves and use a few tactics to determine what is within our reach and who we need to hire.

HOW TO FUND YOUR FREEDOM

To assemble your own team, you must embrace some temporary discomfort—to liberate resources for your pillars of purpose. Let's crunch your numbers. What expenses might you trim, even briefly, to fund the help you need while fully immersed in purposeful work?

Start by taking a magnifying glass to your monthly expenses. We often spend from habit rather than intent. The daily triple-shot latte. The newspaper we never read. Biweekly trips to the barber. Premium cable with unwatched channels. Alone, these feel trivial. Together, they constitute a small fortune we might redirect. I've developed a habit of asking each director and card holder at Blavity to audit subscriptions and services every six months, canceling whatever no longer serves us. In my personal life, I haven't owned a car since age twenty-three, opting instead for walkable neighborhoods near public transit or Ubers if going a longer distance. This has eliminated a need for a car payment, insurance, and the mental load of vehicle maintenance and driving.

When examining your expenses, it helps to categorize them into needs, wants, and everything else in between. Focus first on trimming discretionary purchases in the "wants" or "nice-to-have" categories before attacking essential needs.

Dig into credit card and bank statements to tally up subscriptions, memberships, and regular leisure activities. For example—the gym membership you don't use, apps you could do without, credit card fees. These tend to blend into autopilot spending we barely notice.

Examine needs closely too for savings opportunities. Groceries, transportation, housing—small cuts or downstream changes here add up dramatically over time. Could you downgrade vehicles, commute via public transport once a week, or get a temporary roommate to cut rent?

Beyond daily expenses, reexamine lifestyle choices that drive bigger-ticket costs. Could your next vacation substitute a road trip for overseas flights? Is a four-bedroom house truly necessary if the kids leave home soon? The hundreds saved each month quickly compound into capacity to hire help where needed most. And the mental bandwidth preserved from logistical excess? That, too, fuels far more meaningful outputs.

The key is determining which spending adjustments impact your quality of life minimally for maximum upside. This requires ruthless examination of each line item—mixed with creativity toward lifestyle changes that enhance purpose. Yet, I want you to challenge yourself to live a little more frugally for a set period—maybe six months. Committing to financial changes can be uncomfortable. But remember, growth often requires stepping out of your comfort zones. The savings from this period can be your ticket to hiring the help you need.

The money you save and allocate now is an investment in your future self.

WHY PHONE A FRIEND WHEN YOU COULD HIRE AN ASSISTANT?

As we delve deeper into the realm of delegation, it's time we focus on an often-unsung hero in the journey of achieving greater productivity and having more unrestricted time—the assistant. Assisting roles are varied, and each type comes with a unique set of skills, budgets, and duties. I recommend that you start here with evaluating whom to hire in your life because different types of assistants can manage entire categories of tasks outlined in your CEO Tasks versus Operating Tasks exercise. But with so many assistant types available, how do you choose?

Let's break down the different types of assistants and help you figure out which one might be the best fit for you based on your Operating Tasks and your delegation categories.

1. *Administrative Assistant or Virtual Assistant*

Virtual assistants or administrative assistants are typically more junior in nature and can follow clear structures or operating procedures to get things done. They can respond to emails, schedule meetings, do data entry, manage customer support, or handle appointments. They might be a great fit if your Operating Tasks list is filled with repeatable daily tasks that are essential but time-consuming. They also can be remote, even abroad, typically resulting in more affordable hourly pay.

2. *Family Assistant, Nanny, or House Manager*

Family assistants are the superheroes of the household, balancing a mix of personal and household responsibilities. They might help with picking up the kids from school, arranging playdates, or even assisting with homework. Some family assistants were previously nannies and were trained in childcare. They might also take care of household chores, meal planning, grocery shopping, and errands.

If you have multiple young children and need care forty or more hours a week, a nanny may also be the way to go. Nannies typically don't help around the house beyond the scope of childcare duties, so really ask yourself whether you need a nanny or a family assistant.

A house manager can be a part-time person who helps you manage all of the random tasks of maintaining a home, everything from scheduling cleaners, to landscaping, or overseeing a renovation project. If you live in an apartment or have a partner, a house manager may not be the right fit for you. When I bought my first house, I had a part-time house manager for a year to help with the random midday deliveries of furniture, manage the unpacking, and even simple things like find an electrician to fix a wiring issue. If your Operating Tasks list includes a lot of family-related chores or errands and if you have children, this may be the right type of assistant to welcome into your life.

3. Personal Assistant

A personal assistant (PA) tends to be a broader role, encompassing a variety of personal tasks. They can handle everything from scheduling appointments, to booking travel, packing for trips, managing personal emails, managing gifting, running errands, helping create personal content, or even managing your social media accounts. A PA can be your right hand, helping you manage your personal life so you can focus on CEO Tasks. A PA can be part-time for a few hours a week or full-time if your schedule is intense. Personal assistants typically aren't a replacement for nannies and tend to be dedicated to the efficiency of just one person in the household.

4. Executive Assistant

Executive assistants (EA) are focused more on business and administrative tasks. They are seasoned professionals who manage your schedule, book business travel, prep you for meetings, handle correspondence, and manage projects. They can be a crucial strategic partner, helping you manage and prioritize your professional tasks. While an EA can take a number of daily tasks off your hands, their real value lies in their ability to proactively implement strategic changes to your daily focus, so that you fill your day with only the work you can do. EAs are typically full-time but you can have a part-time executive assistant or split one with someone else at work. If your Operating Tasks list is dominated by business-related tasks, an EA could be your go-to.

Selecting an assistant demands that you examine those Operating Tasks dragging you down. Effective delegation isn't about total off-loading, but strategic liberation of energy for higher aims. The right assistant lifts enough burdens to grant you critical mental space while managing what you delegate.

But striking that balance hinges on clearly defined roles aligned tightly to specific needs. Before browsing job posts, review your Operating Tasks list. Determine which duties create the greatest barriers between your current reality and your next-level goals. What assistance *right now* would drive the biggest leap toward your wealthy vision?

Three key questions add clarity:

- Can required tasks be executed remotely, or does a physical presence matter?
- What's your readiness level in sharing business or personal information?
- Which tasks demand specialized expertise beyond your own?

The objective: not blanket task elimination, but focused liberation from those blocking your unique ability to contribute. Even part-time or specialized assistance can drive disproportionate results. A virtual assistant tackling remote business tasks, for example, paired with a family assistant addressing household and personal needs.

Hiring represents more than off-loading what you loathe, but rather, investing in the environment for you to accelerate toward your wealthy vision. It's a commitment to purposeful growth, rather than stagnating in permanent helplessness. Properly understood, delegation unlocks the capacity to pursuing higher callings only you can achieve, if you had just a bit more space to breathe and focus.

CULTIVATING YOUR COMMUNITY

When I got serious about prioritizing my Relationships pillar, I realized I needed help. I needed a clearer definition of what I was looking for in a relationship because I just wasn't finding it on my own. Unfortunately, I lacked real-life examples. Most of my girlfriends were still single, eagerly yearning for their own life partners as they approached their early forties. My married friends had been partnered up since their twenties and couldn't offer much insight into the dating world. My parents, God love them, were no help either. They met when they were in high school and Dad courted my mom all through college! Adorable, yes, but my high school sweetheart ship had long since sailed away.

I was on my own. One evening, I found myself ordering books on how strong women should approach marriage, looking for stories on femininity, and downloading all the relationship podcasts I could find. When real life turns up empty-handed with advice, it's time to seek out the next best thing.

Nights and weekends became sacred spaces dedicated to immersing myself in gooey relationship content that ranged from crunchy to cheesy. Although some might consider it a little intense, these resources provided me with the space and confidence to dream up my own version of a fairy-tale romance. After a few months of studying, I felt equipped to craft my ultimate romantic vision. In a declaration of affirmations, I outlined in my journal what my Relationships pillar fulfilled would feel like.

> *It feels good to have a man who will pick up dinner after a long day.*
> *It feels good to have a man who rubs my feet when I'm tired.*
> *It feels good to have a man who sends me knowledge and information.*

*It feels good to have a man who cares about his family
and his mother.*

*It feels good to have a man who is consistent and unmovable
and shares his love patiently.*

*It feels good to have a man who listens and is invested in
sharing his thoughts on my career.*

*It feels good to have a man who is emotionally secure about
who he is.*

*It feels good to have a man who protects me and wants to
keep me safe.*

It feels good to have a man with whom I can feel free.

I wrote down exactly how I wanted my day to be, waking up next to my partner—how it felt, how it smelled, and what it looked like. In fact, I even went as far as googling quotes online and setting a lock screen on my phone that boldly stated, "Ten years from now, make sure you chose your life; you didn't settle for it." I had notes and reminders that said things like "Just because you want it to be a yes doesn't mean it is. Everyone defaults to a no until God is clear it's a yes." I know this sounds super cheesy, but hey, you gotta do what you gotta do. These simple reminders served as daily anchors, keeping me focused and determined on my path forward. If you have a hard time connecting to your wealthy vision, try using affirmations to train your mind to recognize the opportunities available to you now that align with your desires. This mental practice offers a glimpse into the fulfillment that is destined to unfold.

The books, online courses, and affirmations became my companions on this journey. They provided me with valuable lessons and frameworks to clearly define what my vision of a thriving Relationships pillar looked like. Most important, they gave me the vocabulary and framework to actualize my desires.

This wasn't just about partnership. It was about manifesting my biggest life even without accessible tools or advisers. The virtual coaches I discovered played pivotal roles—shaping mindsets and urging action from afar through teachings that deeply resonated with me.

While not physically present, these thought leaders pushed me to dream boldly, challenge old patterns, and design a thriving Relationships pillar. As I reflect, I'm grateful for their push toward a meaningful relationship without compromising what I truly wanted in a partner.

Infinite learning is available 24/7 through thought leadership blogs, podcasts, courses, and books. Geographic barriers and local resource constraints need not limit accessing wisdom from those ahead of you on the path.

DO YOU NEED A MENTOR OR AN ADVISER?

While the world-class thought leadership available online provides fuel for growth, even the most robust digital coaching cannot replace the catalyzing power of in-person one-to-one connections. As you build your pillars, carefully selected personal advisers and mentors can profoundly accelerate your ambitions.

There exists a key distinction between advisers and mentors, and understanding this enables us to access precisely the right guidance our journeys require. Too often I see people conflate these roles into one amorphous cocktail, diluting their unique powers. It's time to appreciate their differences so you can reap the specialized value each provides at distinct phases.

A mentor is like having a wise and experienced guru by your side. They've been there, done that, and have the battle scars to prove it. These are the people who have walked the path you want to walk and achieved the kind of success you dream of. They are the ones who can share their hard-earned wisdom, listen to your challenges, and inspire you to reach new heights.

Mentors also tend to be people who stay with you for long periods, like college professors you keep in touch with after graduation. Consider former bosses whom you can call to consult about whether to accept a dream job offer at a lower salary or stay put at your current role that pays more. Look for religious guides or spiritual mentors who can guide you in more abstract ways like finding your purpose or calling. Oftentimes, mentors won't provide an answer; they'll ask questions and help navigate your decision-making by serving as a mirror of your true desires. Mentors are like soulmates, you aren't going to get that many in your lifetime. They are people with whom you have a real connection. That doesn't happen often. So, when it does, hang on to it.

Now let's talk advisers. These folks are like your secret weapons, but they're not in it for the long haul. They bring specific expertise and knowledge to the table and then they're out. Personally, I have had only a few mentors in my life but constantly have a trove of three to five advisers in rotation depending on what life adjustments I'm trying to make. This makes total sense! I think of advisers as the superheroes of their respective fields, ready to swoop in and save the day with their specialized skills. Remember Adam, my wealth management adviser from the beginning of this book? He was one of my first paid advisers I invested in to help manage my personal finances and I've never looked back. Sticking to your fitness plan? Growing your business revenue? Advisers are the people who've got the answers. Unlike mentors, advisers may not have personally walked the exact path you're on, but they know their stuff. They are typically domain experts who can provide you with practical recommendations and tactical advice, and they help you navigate tricky situations with goal-setting and execution.

Whether you hire them, buy their course, or consult with them on a project basis, their job is to offer you targeted insights and provide clear solutions to your problems. Feel like you don't have a strong network? Turn to the internet. It's the ultimate leveler and frankly you have no excuse not to leverage it. Do your research to find advisers who can help accelerate your vision, tap into the brains of the sharpest minds and the most powerful experts in whatever field you need help with. It's all there, waiting for you to grab it and run.

THE GIANTS AMONG US

As the world was slowly emerging from its COVID cocoon in 2021, I found myself at a crossroads with Blavity. I had big visions of expanding our horizons into the world of live events, specifically music festivals and concerts. The idea was exciting, but the path was studded with potential land mines.

Namely, I had no clue how to organize a music festival! I had been to plenty of music festivals, but never tried to put one up myself. What was I thinking? How could I suddenly master the art of booking festival talent that could drive ticket sales? And how was I going to come up with the cash necessary for such a mammoth undertaking?

One evening, as I was mulling it all over, a thought struck me. Well, I suppose it was more of a thought of a person that stopped me. A close friend of mine was a managing partner at Wondaland Records, the powerhouse behind musical sensations like Janelle Monáe and Jidenna. If anyone could shed light on how to approach this new business, it was Mikael. Of course!

So, under the dim lights of a quintessentially overpriced restaurant in L.A., I laid out my vision for the next phase of Blavity Media, including my big idea to infuse music into our brand. My friend did not mince words. Speaking with the wisdom of someone who had been in the trenches, Mikael gave me a candid view of the industry. He dished all the dirt on festivals that seemed successful but were financially drowning and highlighted others that were printing profits. It wasn't going to be easy, but with a trusted adviser by my side, I knew I could make this unlikely dream a reality.

With Mikael's guidance, Blavity's journey into the world of music began. We started by introducing a musical element to AfroTech and, after two meticulous years of research and diligence, I acquired RNB House Party in 2023, a touring party series focused on city-dwelling millennials, marking our third acquisition. Throughout this wild ride, Mikael was my rock. He connected me with industry consultants, helped me navigate the age-old question of "build or buy," and even shielded me from potential financial pitfalls with overpriced brands we could have bought.

Oftentimes when you're looking for guidance in your life, you're actually looking for an adviser, not a mentor. So why do people get these two confused? Well, sometimes it's because they assume that a mentor can provide all the answers. They think, "Hey, if I have this wise mentor by my side, I'll have everything I need to succeed." But that's not always the case. Mentors can offer guidance and inspiration, but they might not keep up with the current moment or have the subject matter expertise, practical strategies, or innovation to help you outline *how* specifically to get to where you're going.

For either a mentor or an adviser, you've got to seek out someone who has blazed the trail before you. Tap into the people who have the knowledge and experience you crave. It could be someone in your industry, a leader you admire, or even a total badass outside of your field. But here's the key: They've got to align with your values and goals.

You need both mentors and advisers—people who are invested in your future and can help you stay on track for the long haul, and others who can give you a quick boost to get you from point A to point B.

HOW TO FIND YOUR GIANTS

Take a moment to reflect on your journey so far. Who are the giants in your life? These giants can come in various forms, like seasoned professionals, industry leaders, wise elders, or even close friends and family members who have achieved

GOING ALONE VS. SEEKING HELP

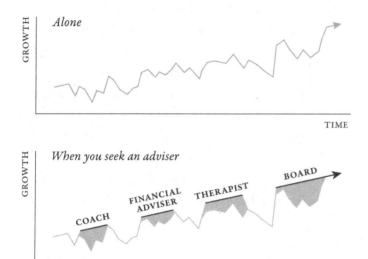

remarkable success in their own right. Giants are those individuals who have the knowledge, experience, and wisdom to help you see things you can't see for yourself. Check your contacts on LinkedIn, or even people you know personally but maybe haven't considered how their professional experience or careers may help you navigate your next move.

Here are some examples of giants who can help you in your journey based on the pillars you're prioritizing.

1. **Career and Professional Development Adviser:** Whether you're looking to climb the corporate ladder, switch industries, or negotiate a better job offer, this adviser specializes in helping you move through the complexities of your career. They can offer insights on networking, personal

branding, résumés, and job search strategies with industry-specific knowledge. For example, if your focus is Stability or Wealth, you might seek advice from a career coach who can help you identify the skills you need to build and the scripts and strategies to negotiate your next move.

2. **Financial Adviser:** When it comes to your Wealth pillar, a financial adviser can be a game changer. They can help you create a solid financial plan, make smart investment decisions, and optimize your wealth-building strategies. Whether it's planning for early retirement, managing debt, or building generational wealth, a financial adviser will be your financial guru.

3. **Nutritionist, Therapist, or Fitness Coach:** Your Wellness pillar is all about taking care of your mind, body, and spirit. A wellness coach can guide you in creating a holistic approach to your well-being, including nutrition, exercise, mindfulness, and stress management. There are even sleep therapists! They can help you set goals, develop healthy habits, and hold you accountable along the way.

4. **Relationship and Life Adviser:** Relationships are a crucial part of our lives, and an adviser specializing in this area can help you navigate the ups and downs of personal connections. Whether you're looking to improve your romantic relationships, strengthen friendships, or enhance family dynamics, someone who can provide insights, communication strategies, and emotional support can be a game changer. People like matchmakers or therapists who focus specifically on healthy relationship dynamics can help you introspect and make changes that help you get where you want to go.

5. **Subject Matter Experts:** Sometimes, our hobbies and passions revolve around specific subjects or areas of interest. For example, if you're passionate about astronomy, gardening, or even learning a new language, seeking guidance from online lessons or taking community college classes can deepen your knowledge and enrich your experience. These advisers can provide resources, recommend books or programs, and offer hands-on guidance to help you expand your skills and expertise.

These are just a few examples of the types of advisers you can find based on your pillars. Engaging with these advisers will often involve a financial commitment, either through hourly fees or a retainer agreement. This investment, while sometimes a stretch for your budget, is a step toward your personal growth and development. The key is to identify the specific area you want to focus on and seek out advisers who have expertise and can guide you on the right path. In my own journey, I've realized that seeking help from the right experts can be revolutionary. Now, having an adviser doesn't mean you suddenly get their years of hard-earned experience downloaded into your brain, *Matrix*-style. And it's not about stealing their wisdom, it's about using their insights to dodge the potholes and hit your goals faster. It's leveraging their know-how to make fewer dumb decisions and get where you want to be without the unnecessary drama. From pushing myself to the brink with personal trainers who've made me question my sanity to meticulously tracking my macros on a phone app, I've learned that the wisdom of others can propel me forward.

As a CEO, I've hired executive coaches to help me be a

better leader. These coaches and books became my advisers, challenging my assumptions and helping me unlock new levels of leadership excellence. Their insights and feedback were like a compass, guiding me through the murky terrain of decision-making and strategic thinking.

As I transitioned from founder of a small start-up to CEO of a growth-stage company, the complex world of finance and business operations often left me feeling like I was reading hieroglyphics. I didn't go to business school and I certainly am not an accountant, yet I was determined to bridge the knowledge gap. I dove headfirst into online classes and devoured books on financials for mid-cap businesses. Armed with newfound knowledge, I could confidently engage in meaningful conversations with my finance team, understanding the language and concepts that had once seemed like a foreign dialect.

Seeking help from experts is a smart move. It's a recognition that we can't be masters of everything. But here's the catch: Seeking guidance is only half the battle. The other half lies in our active participation. It's not enough to simply collect advice and insights. We must put them into practice, integrating them into our daily lives and taking responsibility for our own growth.

WHAT TO LOOK FOR IN AN ADVISER

You want to find an adviser who has worked with people like you, with similar goals. This will help you truly live. It's the same reason that companies that are about to get listed on the stock exchange (initial public offering or IPO) add people to their board or management team who have gone through a few successful IPOs. Or if you're looking to improve your fertility, you'd go to a reproductive endocrinologist, not an internist or even a general ob-gyn. You want the pro who deals with your scenario every day, not someone who treats it like a rare sighting.

I didn't stumble upon my financial adviser by chance. I found Adam through conversations with another media founder who had just gone through two acquisitions, was reprioritizing his time to focus on finding love, and wanted to make sure he was making smart financial decisions for his future. Hey, that sounded like me! Adam's expertise was advising entrepreneurs and founders who were pre-acquisition or during a liquidity event (selling their shares on a secondary market or on a public market).

You see, the right adviser is someone who specializes in your specific needs. If I had gone to a regular financial adviser referred by my parents or my friends who had traditional nine-to-five jobs, my situation would be an outlier in their portfolio. You don't want to be a unique case for your adviser. I wanted to be average or even below average! I don't want my adviser guessing or stretching for me. I want them saying, "I've seen this ten times this year already, and here's what we've done. Here are the different choices based on your preferences." You want someone who can guide you confidently because they've seen your scenario play out multiple times before.

Also, do your due diligence and look for a track record of

success. Look for testimonials from people who share your circumstances. You want an adviser who can relate to your journey and offer tailored advice that aligns with your goals.

ADVISER RED FLAGS TO AVOID

Not all advisers are created equal. There are some red flags you need to watch out for to ensure you're making the right choice.

First and foremost, be wary of advisers whose financial or moral incentives don't align with yours. You want someone who genuinely has your best interests at heart, not someone who's just in it for their own gain. If you sense any ulterior motives or conflicting priorities, run in the opposite direction. Your adviser should be focused on helping you achieve your goals, not using you as a stepping stone for their own success.

Another thing to avoid is anyone who promises overnight wins or claims they can get things done in the blink of an eye. Let me be clear: The good life takes time, effort, and consistent action. There are no shortcuts or magic formulas that can guarantee instant results. So if someone is selling you a quick fix or making outrageous promises, it's probably too good to be true. Look for advisers who understand the value of hard work, persistence, and long-term growth.

You'll know when you find the right adviser because it feels like unlocking a whole new level of potential. They become your sounding board, confidant, and biggest cheerleader. They can see things in you that you can't see in yourself, and they push you to reach heights you never thought possible. But keep in mind that advice without action is like a car without gas. It ain't going anywhere. So take those insights, those lessons, and put them to work. Because it's in the doing, the failing, and the trying again that knowledge transforms into wisdom.

Don't rush the process or settle for anything less than the best. Take your time, do your research, and trust your instincts. I want you to let go of any reservations or doubts about inviting people into your life to help you live your design. Whether it's in the realm of fitness, voice lessons, rock climbing, or any other area of your life, allow yourself to be guided by those who possess the knowledge and experience you seek. The ultimate responsibility lies with you. Take ownership of your growth like the CEO you are, apply the lessons learned, and transform that wisdom into action.

Let's dig in and start to identify and connect with advisers and giants who can significantly help you live your life's design. By working through the prompts provided, you will gain insights into the areas of your life where guidance is needed and learn how to proactively seek tools and advice.

EVALUATE YOUR AREAS FOR
ACCOUNTABILITY OR IMPROVEMENT:

a. In what areas of your life do you feel you need guidance or advice?

b. How can you proactively seek out tools or advisers to help guide you or hold you accountable to progress in these areas?

c. Reflect on the difference between a mentor and an adviser in your life. Do you have the right balance of both?

ADVISERS:

a. List the names of people who could potentially be your advisers. What qualities or experiences do they possess that align with your goals?

b. Identify areas in your life where you need advice and search online to find those who have expertise in those areas.

c. Reflect on a time when advice, a tool, or mentorship has had a significant impact on your life. What did you learn?

TAKE ACTION:

a. Make a commitment to yourself.

b. Block off time on your calendar to engage with advisers.

c. Document thoughts, ideas, and questions in your journal and tie your goals or vision for what you want to achieve to the help of your mentors and advisers.

One of the biggest ways you're going to make major moves to meet your goals, and see the fruits of your vision, is by partnering with the right people. Whether they are manning the ship so you can focus on charting the course or sitting at the lighthouse just a radio signal away, giving you the perspective you need to reach your destination safely, your team is going to get you there faster, smarter, and without a doubt, more joyfully.

6

HIT YOUR GOALS LIKE A START-UP

The bustling clatter of the hotel breakfast café faded as I gazed out the windows, heart racing. It was 2016, and less than twenty-four hours ago, I had looked out at the sea of shining faces filling our small, rented conference room at the San Francisco Centre. We had just wrapped the first-ever AfroTech—the start-up tech conference I envisioned, spotlighting talented Black innovators and entrepreneurs.

Somehow we had manifested the impossible. We were 50 percent over the 250-attendee venue capacity and received warnings from the fire marshal. As a first-time Black female founder, I had expected skepticism and empty seats. But as we stood thunderstruck watching Black founders, engineers, and tech professionals flood the sign-in tables, the potential dawned on me—we could catalyze something special here. Pride and exhilaration coursed through me.

Let me tell you, nobody, I mean *nobody*, expected to see

Black folks hustling into a tech conference back in 2016. But it was my dream to flip the script. I envisioned turning the tech scene into the new cool, transforming the stereotypical nerds into celebrated heroes for their innovation and successes. Our aim was to shift the narrative from the struggle of being Black in tech to the potential power within our collective stride. We weren't just dreaming of surviving the tech world, we intended to conquer it, soar into C-level positions, establish colossal ventures, and create a financing titan for our community's leading innovators. Wild ambition? Maybe. But a vision worth chasing? Absolutely. I was determined to turn this vision into reality, even if we had less than $400K rattling in the bank. I was willing to invest $135K to build the first iteration of AfroTech.

After the first year of the AfroTech event's roaring success, we could have played it safe with the incremental mindset and allowed for slow growth, from 375 attendees to a modest 700. Technically we still would have been successful with that growth in attendees. But that's not how visionary innovators operate. As the Blavity team buzzed recounting the event over coffee the next morning, my mind zoomed ten steps ahead. I locked eyes with my co-founder Aaron—no time to play small. If we significantly expanded our vision, imagine how we could light up opportunities for minorities in tech. Forget incremental. I said, "Bring me a pier! I want food trucks lining the harbor, I want free swag raining down. I want more DJs. Let's triple this next year!" I knew the momentum from our success could help us leapfrog ourselves and we took a risk and more than tripled the budget to

$500K. I felt him steady himself before breaking into a smile. "Challenge accepted."

The gauntlet was thrown down for our tiny but scrappy team. We had twelve months to make the exponential possible through sheer will like the first time. Our real work started. I spent the week after the event writing out a high-level plan and putting together a more experienced team who could get us there. Aaron immediately got to work on new, even bigger pricing and sales decks to win over sponsors again. He would steer the revenue engine to match our expanded vision. It was on me to build it, so every week for twelve months leading up to the event, I dedicated 3 P.M. to 6 P.M. every Monday to a recurring hold on my calendar for building this vision, whether it was research, meeting with prospective vendors, or reading through Crunchbase to see who our speakers could be.

In deciding to triple the event's size, we were making a step change, a significant leap from what *was* to what *could be.* When sponsors balked at the budget or timelines that felt unreasonably tight, I leaned on the vision to keep myself convicted. Our growth was not incremental but explosive, and it paid off. Come the second year of AfroTech, we had skyrocketed to become the largest Black tech conference in the nation. We breezed past veteran media organizations like Black Enterprise and others who had half a decade's head start in the field.

Most important, we changed the trajectory for minority founders and tech professionals forever. For too long, senior executives at big tech companies had cited a "pipeline problem" to explain their lack of diversity—there just weren't enough qualified minority candidates to hire, they claimed. I knew that after AfroTech reached scale, they could no longer lean on that excuse. We showcased an abundance of phenomenal Black and Brown founders, engineers, designers, and leaders. Attendees left inspired about opportunities to create and contribute using technology.

Our unapologetic celebration of excellence blew open the doors to Silicon Valley. We proved the talent was there by putting it center stage, right in the middle of the top companies in the world. The brilliance and potential had always existed; we provided the platform for the world to witness what was possible.

As CEO, I don't play small. I'm here to set the vision for our company and determine the speed at which we're gonna dominate the game. Are we aiming for a mind-blowing $200 million in revenue within the next five years? Or, are we plotting an exit that'll give ten times the return to all of our investors and shareholders? The direction I choose is crucial, but it's the Step-change Growth goals that separate the winners from the wannabes.

THE STEP-CHANGE GROWTH METHOD

The Step-change Growth method is an ambitious goal-setting strategy that pushes you out of your comfort zone. It addresses the gap between your everyday life and long-term vision by setting bold targets for meaningful change.

To get started, you must first set a specific, quantifiable

outcome that currently feels like an enormous leap forward in your life but is still oriented toward your bigger vision. Maybe it's a new job that earns $10K more in salary, hitting ten thousand steps a day, or bringing in eight new clients to your consulting business. Then you should set a clear deadline of six to twelve months, and outline the key things needed to make it happen.

So many people stroll through life, convinced they're destined for a little better than average, that they couldn't and shouldn't strive to achieve anything extraordinary. They play it safe with goal-setting, reaching for low-hanging fruit and quick wins that feel satisfying in the moment but don't make any real strides toward a vision. These are the same people who look at the high achievers and think, "Well, they must have some secret genius or exclusive access that I lack." That's not you. You know better by now!

I'm sure you've done goal-setting exercises before in your life, and you may have used methods like SMART (Specific, Measurable, Achievable, Relevant, and Time-bound) Goals.

While SMART Goals do have their place, I see far too many people get hung up on the "A" (achievable) aspect and become too conservative with their timeframe or even the goal itself. While I agree that being realistic with your goals is necessary—y'all aren't headed to the moon anytime soon—I often see the fear of setting lofty targets hold people back from pushing their limits and striving for greatness. In contrast, a Step-change Growth goal-setting strategy encourages you to push past what you can even imagine to be achievable. This type of goal-setting method isn't for the faint of heart. It demands that you go beyond your comfort zone.

WHAT DOES STEP-CHANGE GROWTH
LOOK LIKE IN PRACTICE?

Step-change Growth is a significant milestone, especially one that results in a big improvement or leap forward. A step-change function in math represents a sudden, discrete jump from one level to another at a specific point in time. There is no gradual ramp—it instantly steps up or down. Similarly, Step-change Growth goals are designed to create a "step change" in progress by pushing for a significant leap forward rather than incremental gains.

For example, if someone has been used to earning $50K per year, setting a Step-change Growth goal to increase income to $75K in six months would represent a major step-change function upward. Just like in a mathematical step-change function, there is no gradual buildup. The person is instantly stepping up their earning capability to a new level through the achievement of that ambitious goal.

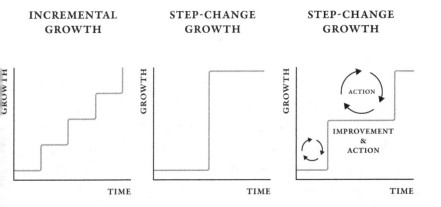

INCREMENTAL GROWTH   STEP-CHANGE GROWTH   STEP-CHANGE GROWTH

Step-change Growth is how we defy expectations. It's all about setting audacious goals that make even the most ambitious folks raise an eyebrow. We don't just think big, we think massive, astronomical, out-of-this-world big. We take our visionary dreams and break 'em down into actionable goals for each six-to-twelve-month period. We're not here to play it safe or move at a snail's pace. By embracing Step-change Growth goal-setting, we're tricking our brains into believing that massive leaps forward are not only possible but basically inevitable. Throughout this book I want you to reset your mind to think in terms of exponential growth, to push beyond what you once thought was possible. Step-change Growth is the opposite of incremental growth, which tends to be slow and steady baby steps toward change. An incremental mindset focuses on making something better, while the mindset of Step-change Growth is to make something different. It's all about instantly establishing a new normal, a new baseline. Then you can jump off that for the next goal.

Let's start with the science. Researchers have proved that when you set goals, you're actually rewiring your brain, optimizing it to achieve greatness. This is because your brain has something called neuroplasticity—it can grow and change in response to stimuli—which means the act of goal-setting literally alters the structure of your brain in order to meet your end target. This was first shown in a study of female multiple sclerosis patients at the University of Texas, which found that MS patients who set ambitious wellness goals had fewer and less severe symptoms than a control group. These challenging goals had a significant effect on their physical and mental well-being.

But here's the kicker. It's not just any ol' goal that gets your juices flowing. Nope, we're talking about setting goals that scare the crap outta you and are directly tied to your Purpose Principle. You know, those fearless, stretch-your-limits kinds of goals. Turns out, those are the ones that light a fire under your butt and kick your motivation into overdrive. Another study found that people who committed to an ambitious goal, in this case reducing energy consumption by 20 percent, actually ended up saving energy. People who committed to an easier goal, reducing consumption by only 2 percent, ended up consuming the same amount as before the study started.

See, here's the deal: Small, safe goals might give us a cozy, warm feeling inside, but they won't push us to new levels. No. It's the bold, gutsy goals that light a spark within us. They push us to step outside our comfort zones and unleash our true potential. In some cases, they apparently even get us to save on our energy bills! But the study didn't just look at the effect of setting ambitious goals, it emphasized the importance of *progress*. Aside from the difficulty of the goal, a second variable of receiving feedback was considered. The participants who set the most ambitious energy reduction goal *and* also received feedback during the study far outperformed the group by saving the most energy. The researchers concluded that the positive impact a challenging goal can have is dependent on feedback—in other words, acknowledging and appreciating progress is motivating.

So, my fellow CEOs: We're gonna use the Step-change Growth goal-setting method, even if it scares the living daylights out of us. We're going to keep our vision for life at the top of our minds and identify the opportunities along the way to make leaps in consistent progress. Because it's in that progress that we find true fulfillment, joy, and a sense of accomplishment that's off the charts! It's time to aim high.

As the CEO of your life, with each step forward, you grow and learn, becoming better versions of yourself along the way. This can be achieved by taking the time to focus on the fundamentals and investing in personal growth, even if it means slowing down in other areas. It could be learning another language so you slide closer to your vision of moving abroad and living in Spain. It could be getting a computer science certification so that you can transition into a higher-paying technology job and get closer to your dream career making six figures while working remotely.

STEP-CHANGE GROWTH CASE STUDIES

Netflix is an excellent example of a company that didn't settle for incremental growth, but instead set its sights on bold, exponential growth through massive industry disruption. Reed Hastings co-founded Netflix in 1997, as an alternative to brick-and-mortar video rentals. While it started with a classic subscription model delivering DVDs through the mail, that business was always intended as a stepping stone. Even with millions of happy mail-order customers, Reed knew that incremental growth wasn't going to cut it. He wanted exponential Step-change growth and started building the streaming business. Most CEOs would have been satisfied with stopping at the successful disruption of their competitors, as he did with Redbox and Blockbuster.

Yet, Hastings had a bigger vision and knew progress required sacrificing short-term gains for long-term, game-changing growth. He needed to be willing to cannibalize the cash cow DVD biz to slingshot Netflix into the future. So, while DVD profits funded the company's transition, Hastings as CEO fostered a culture singularly focused on streaming and winning on the digital battlefield. It was a bold bet with no guarantee of payoff. Fast-forward to today, through a series of all-in moves and next-level strategy, Netflix now rules supreme with 220 million global subscribers—and they're just getting started. Reed knew success wouldn't come through playing it safe and steady, and neither should you.

Remember, this kind of risk-taking isn't reserved for the elite C-suite, celebs, or billionaires. These sorts of big swings are available to anyone, they might just look a little different on a smaller scale. Take the following examples to illustrate how Step-change Growth can come to life in different contexts.

The Screenwriter

Let's say a writer is using Step-change Growth goal-setting to focus on Passions right now. It's time; they've finally decided to finish their screenplay. Traditional gurus might recommend writing for twenty minutes a day and gradually increasing writing time, without an end date. But what if instead they could set a goal to write one thousand words a day or more, regardless of how long it takes them? Or they could even challenge themselves to write an entire act in one week, hire a writing coach to hold them accountable, and aim to have the first draft of their screenplay within one month. Now, that's a Step-change Growth approach to moving the needle toward their vision in a big way.

The Corporate Star

Let's say a mid-level marketing employee is focusing on their Stability and Money pillars. They are working at a company that builds maternal health products. They are passionate about the mission and have a vision to climb the ranks and one day become a decision-maker. They want to make a difference and more money.

PATHWAY A:

At the end of twelve months, they want to negotiate a 10 percent raise by excelling at their job and building a stronger relationship with their supervisor. They also want to start shadowing people in the product development division so they can understand the business better.

PATHWAY B:

At the end of twelve months, they want to get a 20 percent raise by developing technical skills and switching to a new job internally. They want to build stronger relationships with senior executives and have quarterly skip levels (a meeting with someone who is two levels higher) with a C-level executive at this company. This will help them better understand the strategy of how the company is moving forward.

Which pathway do you think will help them reach their vision of becoming a wealthier decision-maker faster? Which one do you think will be more likely to end in that promotion from their boss? Pathway A will produce growth using an incremental approach, but Pathway B uses a step-change method to set a goal that aligns with the vision *and* pushes them much further in the same amount of time.

The Athlete

Imagine a person who wants to get in shape, so they are focused on their Wellness pillar. They want to look and feel healthier, and they also used to be a college track star and miss running. Normal goal-setting would have them exercising for an hour, three times a week to drop the pounds. But a step-change approach will encourage them to train for a marathon, hire a coach, follow a disciplined workout and food routine, optimize nutrition, and achieve peak physical fitness in time for the race. Not only will they tone their muscles, but they'll reconnect with a past passion with a feeling of accomplishment.

Step-change Growth is about taking a more ambitious approach to achieving your vision, one that requires more effort, focus, and commitment, but also has the potential to yield greater rewards and a sense of accomplishment.

WHERE TO GO WHEN YOU PLATEAU

When you're on the journey to unlocking new levels, it can sometimes feel like you're stuck in a rut and that your pace toward progress has slowed. It can be frustrating and discouraging, but I'm here to tell you that hitting a plateau is actually a good thing. While you're in a period of Step-change

Growth, settling into maintenance mode or a plateau after a rapid period of growth is a sign of you hitting a stride at your new normal. This oftentimes may feel like you're in a daily cycle of sameness and that you're operating in flow with your day-to-day. It can last a few weeks or even a year. Do not be alarmed! It doesn't mean that you've stopped growing. On the contrary, it's the exact moment in which you're building toward your next leap forward.

STEP-CHANGE GROWTH

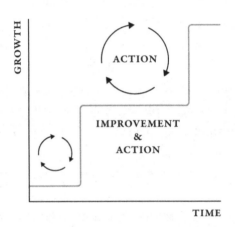

Too often we focus all our energy and attention on the steep step up, but in reality, the difficult thing is to sit on the flat part. Experiencing a plateau is a sign that you're being consistent with the new daily actions and behavior pushing you forward, staying committed to your goals, even when things get tough. Embrace the friction and the stress that come with stretching yourself to new levels. That friction is a signal that you're growing and that you're on the right track. So, stay disciplined in the actions you're taking, and follow through on the commitment that you made to yourself.

Progress is typically not a straight line to the top. The upward incline that was once motivating you may level out. But that doesn't mean you should throw in the towel. No, my friend, that means you need to buckle down and keep pushing yourself.

IGNORE VANITY METRICS

You know that friend who's always ticking off goals but somehow not making any real progress? The one who gets a thrill from gaining more followers, or launching a shiny new personal website, only to bask in the sweet dopamine hit that comes from crossing things off the list. Here's the rub: They can't really measure the impact of those goals. Sound familiar? Maybe you've been that friend (no judgment—we've all been there!), but it's time for a change.

You can't dream up a dazzling new vision for your life and then get sidetracked by surface-level achievements that don't tell the real story of impact and growth. It's like mistaking fool's gold for the real deal. So let's explore why these vanity metrics are sneakily sabotaging your journey to greatness and how you can steer clear of them for good.

Vanity metrics focus on goals that make you feel good in the short term but don't really matter in the grand scheme of things. They are a distraction. It's like when you're obsessed with getting a certain number of likes on a social media post.

Sure, the likes might make you feel good for a minute, but they're not really getting you any closer to your ultimate goal or purpose in life.

The problem with vanity metrics is that they can distract individuals and even entire organizations from their vision. By focusing solely on these surface-level metrics, you may miss out on more meaningful, long-term objectives. For example, a movie studio executive could be overly focused on media attention for an exciting publicity stunt, but fail to put energy into driving audiences to theaters and ultimately end up with an opening weekend flop. Those sneaky vanity metrics can give you a warm illusion of success, which might just lull you into cozy complacency, stroke your ego, and cause you to miss out on fantastic opportunities to learn and grow.

I see this a lot when I meet young start-up founders who are proud to tell me about all the pitch competitions they have won. Winning a pitch competition is a vanity metric. It's a signal of social proof but not the ultimate goal. The intention of an early-stage start-up is to get a huge uptick of customers or to find product market fit. You don't start a company just to be the best pitch competitor in the country, right?

This mindset is also evident in the corporate world, where individuals are fixated on titles rather than what the role offers. Let's say you're a director at a large consumer company looking to climb the corporate ladder. Are you only focused on getting a promotion or a certain job title? Or are you more concerned with building your skill set, expanding your network, and adding value to your company?

Some candidates refuse to consider a job opportunity if it

means a perceived step back in their career ladder. However, job titles don't carry much weight in the grand scheme of things. What's more important is the ownership, responsibility, and compensation associated with the role. Would you rather hold the title of vice president among a sea of three hundred other VPs, or be a director who reports to the C-level executives? I think the answer is pretty obvious.

Sure, a promotion or job title might give you a temporary ego boost, but in the long run, it's not going to get you where you want to be. Instead, focus on the things that actually matter, like gaining new skills, taking on new challenges, and building strong relationships with your colleagues and superiors.

Ultimately, vanity metrics can be a slippery slope to finding success. They can distract us from our objectives and give us a false sense of achievement. While it may feel good to hit a certain number of followers or update your LinkedIn with a new C-level title, these metrics ultimately don't define our success or progress toward our long-term purpose. By ignoring vanity metrics and focusing on what matters to us, we can prioritize the things that will help us achieve our lifestyle goals and pillars.

How do I know if my metrics are just vanity metrics? Well, ask yourself these four questions:

1. Does this metric actually get me closer to my ultimate goal?
2. Am I focused solely on the numbers or am I looking at the bigger picture?

3. Is this an external validator or is it something that will help me unlock my growth goals?
4. Does this metric align with the Pillar that I'm focusing on, or is it just a distraction?

As you move through the Step-change Growth goal-setting process, focus on what's going to impact your personal bottom line here and now. Take a beat and ask yourself if you are getting caught up in vanity metrics that are holding you back. Remember, success is not just about making 30 Under 30 lists, it's about creating a meaningful impact. My advice to you is this: Focus on what will truly move the needle toward your big-picture purpose. Don't let the lure of short-term success distract you from the long-term target.

BRIDGING THE GAP BETWEEN TALK AND ACTION

After one too many nights of takeout despite my healthy eating visions, I realized my nutrition goals were all talk, no action. My pristine vision of wholesome home-cooked meals and plant-based bliss eroded daily while I faced fatigue deciding what's for dinner. How does this happen? I'll admit, on my journey toward optimal wellness, even I can find myself saying one thing and doing another. After a long, stressful day, even though my vision is clean eating and keeping sugar to a minimum, it's far too easy to declare I need to "treat myself" and order a huge bowl of pasta for delivery. In the moment, it satisfies the emotional need and craving. But I feel disappointed in myself afterward for giving in again to momentary impulses that undermine my overall health aims.

Turns out, I'm not alone. Though we often equate procrastination with laziness, it's actually a bit misunderstood. Psychological research reveals that procrastination is less of a character flaw and more of a way to cope with challenging emotions like insecurity, self-doubt, inadequacy, anxiety, and more that often accompany certain tasks. In a 2013 study, psychology professors Dr. Fuschia Sirois and Dr. Tim Pychyl found that mitigating procrastination is more about focusing on managing bad feelings around a task or obligation than taking the action itself. It could be something surface level, like not wanting to muster the energy to wash the car, or the negative emotion could stem from something deeper like a fear of failure. And, of course, those negative thoughts only compound over time, pulling you further away from what you want to do. It's a vicious cycle of feeling bad about not following through, which only propels procrastination even further. So don't feel bad about putting things off; your inaction is likely not because you're lazy, flaky, or incapable. There's something deeper going on, and this section of the book is all about using frameworks to help you do the work so you don't fall into the trap of just talking away about what you're going to do.

The best way to get the gears turning toward a wealthy vision for yourself is to follow up on the promises you make. Saying what you want to change is the easy part, but taking the steps to action is much more difficult. This is what I call the Say/Do Ratio. Without action, dreams remain simply that—visions without manifestation. I've seen far too many people have their big talk drained by everyday demands, unable to bridge the canyon between intentions and outcomes.

WHAT DOES YOUR SAY/DO RATIO LOOK LIKE?

Monitoring your Say/Do Ratio is critical. What percentage of your aspirations translate into concrete steps forward? Can you identify places where you might be falling short? Here's a cheat sheet on how to identify the "all talk" you want to steer clear of when aiming to reach new levels.

Talkers don't want to be uncomfortable. When presented with the opportunity to stay out late with friends four days a week or go to brunch, a wannabe isn't going to miss a chance to blow off responsibilities and kick it.

Talkers don't take financial risks. They expect an increase in their income for just doing their job and not taking on more responsibility. They want an investor to give them money for their new start-up company without putting their own skin in the game or investing their own cash to build out the first version of the product.

Talkers care about their image and others' perception of their success. They may have a fancy business card or a slick landing page designed by a professional, but where's the product, the app, the customers, the website, or any real experience to back up their claims? It's time to stop putting CEO, founder, or "creator of" in your Instagram bio and start doing the real work.

Talkers lack focus and direction. They jump from one project to another without a clear plan or strategy, and they struggle to prioritize their tasks and responsibilities. As a result, they often fail to make significant progress in any of their projects, and their work lacks depth and impact.

Talkers don't seek constructive criticism. They have a fixed mindset and are resistant to feedback, believing that they already know everything they need to know. As a result, they miss out on opportunities for growth and improvement, and their work may suffer as a result.

Talkers don't take ownership of their mistakes. They are quick to blame others or make excuses when things go wrong, instead of taking responsibility for their actions. They fail to see the value in learning from their mistakes and may repeat the same errors again and again.

Let's break free from the chains of a static mindset. If you're stuck in a pattern of talking more than doing, it's likely that your work life, business, wellness, and passions are at a standstill. You may find yourself with unclear goals that aren't guiding you in the right direction. But when you shift your mindset and become a doer, you're choosing to take the necessary steps to create a brighter future.

Step-change Growth demands a pragmatic approach to reaching your big life goals. Over the next week, note when your actions deviate from your stated aims. Don't judge the disconnect, but consider what need is fulfilled in that momentary deviation that your vision isn't meeting. Get curious, not critical. It requires a greater level of effort, focus, and commitment, but the potential rewards and sense of fulfillment are limitless. Just imagine what it would feel like to achieve your Step-change Growth goal in just six months. Are you prepared for the success that awaits you? Do you have the capacity, the time, and the energy in your life to handle it? In the upcoming chapters, we'll explore ways to make this a reality.

Keep your focus on what truly matters, stay true to your purpose, and don't get distracted by superficial measures of success. By implementing this refreshed perspective on goals, I want you to embody what a life "true" to yourself is, and not the life that others expect of you. Let's aim for that big, audacious vision for your life with everything we've got!

USING SPRINTS TO INCREASE YOUR MOMENTUM

In the fast-paced world of Silicon Valley start-ups, speed is everything. Companies live or die based on how quickly they can deliver product innovation and improvements. But with limited resources and tight deadlines, how do you rapidly develop and launch new features without compromising quality? Enter sprints—the secret weapon for going fast without crashing. Typically reserved for moving businesses to the next level, sprints can offer wisdom if implemented in your own life as well.

I first discovered the power of sprints early in my product management career at Intuit, working on an app in the Small Business division called Snap Payroll. The product was a handy tool for small business owners that helped alleviate the drudgery of manual payroll tax calculations, wrapping it up into an easy-to-use, in-your-pocket freemium app. Cool, right?

Young, eager, and just a smidge overconfident, I was a junior product manager trying to learn how to wade through this chaos, one ticket at a time. You know that image of the lonely lighthouse keeper, tirelessly sending out beacons of light into the stormy night? Well, that was me, but replace the beacon with support tickets and the lighthouse with my tiny cubicle.

With each day, I gained the trust of my manager, Colin, who finally decided to offer me a bigger paddle for this ocean we were trying to cross. I was tasked with creating the first draft of product requirements for the app that would take our offering nationwide. This gig was my chance to prove I had the chops, and I was ready to knock it out of the park. I was teamed up with a UI/UX (user interface, user experience) research whiz kid, and together we were tasked with creating new templates for the app as we expanded our capabilities and demographics.

So, how were we going to pull this off? We brought in a secret weapon called "the sprint," borrowed from the agile method, which is a project management approach that involves breaking a project into phases and emphasizing ongoing collaboration and iteration. In the world of agile product management, a sprint is like a mini-marathon. You set a very specific goal, pull together a list of tasks to achieve that goal, and then it's go time. It's like stepping on the gas and turbocharging your project. Instead of doing the slow dance of one individual task at a time, we would group tasks together and tackle small batches. Each sprint was a power play to accelerate our progress and keep us on track to hit our ambitious expansion goal.

This isn't to be confused with the Step-change Growth

goal. Those are big milestones that move you forward that aren't necessarily time-bound. Though it would be nice to reach them sooner than later, the element of a short, finite timeline is really what sets a sprint apart.

Back to this new product we were building. For our payroll app, Colin developed a twelve-month road map for expanding our product nationwide. But rather than proceed state-by-state, we used two-week sprints to launch in strategic regional batches. I worked alongside the UI/UX designer to research payroll requirements for each of the target states included in the upcoming sprint and create tailored templates. We had to balance ambition with realism—grouping three to four states at a time so our engineers could deliver on both quality and speed.

While grueling, when executed effectively, sprints delivered phenomenal momentum. The focused intensity helped us enter hyperdrive while removing all unnecessary distractions. We reflected with a retroactive and celebrated victory at each sprint's conclusion, boosting morale and energy for the next push.

So there I was, a newbie in the tech world, sprinting alongside seasoned pros! It was daunting, exciting, and a little bit terrifying. But there's nothing quite like the thrill of sprinting in Silicon Valley, fueled by complimentary green tea and a dream. That's where I learned the power of the sprint, and let me tell you, it's a method I've never stopped using both in my work and personal life. Sprinting is something I revisit time and time again when I'm feeling stuck on a goal that I've set. It's a method I teach each of the entrepreneurs I mentor to help them build up a momentum of success. I use it at my company when it feels like the team is working hard but we're not seeing significant strides or increased benefits to our customers.

SPRINT DIAGRAM

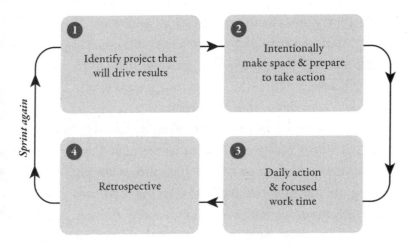

Since then, I've utilized agile sprints to drive everything from product launches to improving my listening skills and beyond. The guidelines I bring with me for every sprint?

- Establish the timeframe for the sprint. I recommend two weeks.
- Set specific, measurable goals and commitments for each sprint.
- Maintain laser focus to cut out extraneous efforts that don't impact your outcome.

- Assemble a lean but mighty sprint team with clear roles or do it solo.
- Prepare and provide resources to quickly unblock progress.
- Cheer on even small wins to build momentum.
- Retrospect to continuously improve your sprint processes.

Two weeks. Fourteen days. Three hundred and thirty-six hours (but who's counting?). That's all you've got, and it's plenty. With the right preparation and commitment, sprints enable you to accomplish in days or weeks that which might normally take months. The exhilarating pace is totally addictive, like a continuous shot of espresso.

This, my friend, is where we take what we learned from the world of Silicon Valley product management and apply it to the bumpy road of our own lives. The sprint is not just about coding quicker or launching a product faster. In this game, there's no room for stagnation. It's all about growing, learning, and then growing some more. It's about grabbing your life by the wheel, stomping that gas pedal, and leaving the plateaus behind.

SPRINTING ANYWHERE AND EVERYWHERE

So how do you use a sprint in your life and identify when to sprint? Let's revisit the concept of Step-change Growth. Remember how we identified areas for potential growth? Well, it's time to narrow that down to a specific sprint you can tackle in fourteen days.

A sprint is a short, focused burst of energy and effort aimed at achieving a specific goal. It's like saying, "Hey, I'm going to

WHY WE SPRINT

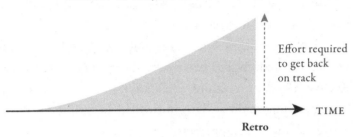

ONE END-OF-PROJECT RETROSPECTIVE

Effort required
to get back
on track

TIME

Retro

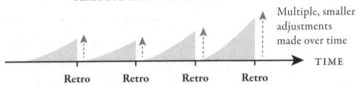

PERIODIC GROWTH SPRINTS

Multiple, smaller
adjustments
made over time

TIME

Retro   **Retro**   **Retro**   **Retro**

give my *all* to this one thing for these fourteen days." It's not about juggling ten balls at once. It's about prioritizing one ball and giving it your undivided attention. "But, Morgan," I hear you saying, "I've got a life to live, kids to raise, a job to do. How am I supposed to find time for a fourteen-day sprint?"

A valid concern, but with the data you've uncovered about your habits and routines, you should have carved out at least two extra hours per day. Guard that time fiercely for your sprint. Wake up early, stay up late, add a work block on a Saturday morning, or delegate tasks—do whatever it takes to protect those two hours for fourteen days. Sprints take sacrifice. I don't want there to be any excuse. Will it be rigorous?

Of course, but you can do a hard thing for two weeks. This is how we're going to use it. I promise you that once you dive into a sprint, you'll be surprised at how much you can achieve when you're really focused.

The key is picking a single measurable goal and removing *all* other distractions. For two weeks, just go all in on this one objective. Give it everything you've got. No multitasking or spreading yourself thin. With undivided attention, you'll be shocked at how much progress you can make.

A Wellness sprint could be committing to a clean diet and daily exercise. A Passions sprint could involve finishing that painting that's been half-done for months. If it's a Money sprint, you might be focused on bringing in a certain number of new clients. Or if you're getting ready to pop the question, you could be in an "engagement ring fund" sprint mode, saving every penny. You get the picture.

The key is tailoring the tasks and focus to produce maximum progress on a specific objective in a short period. Remember, we're not aiming for perfection here. We're looking for growth. So don't beat yourself up if everything doesn't go exactly as planned.

VISUALIZE YOUR SPRINT
USING A KANBAN BOARD

One of the key tools to organize sprints that I was introduced to as a product manager was a kanban board. The term "kanban" translates to "visual signal" or "card" in Japanese. Kanban boards help to visualize work, limit the work in progress, and maximize efficiency to accomplish your goal. They are used in tech companies to help clearly define the work that needs to be done, the status of what is in the backlog of work to come up, and what has been completed.

Trying to juggle ten to fifteen tasks during your sprint without a clear system often leads to frustration and failure. This approach originated in Japan and was first implemented in the manufacturing sector by Toyota. Now we can use it to bring order to our personal sprints too!

In tech we used kanban boards to organize all of the product tasks that needed to be done, and anyone has the authority to add a feature request, report a bug, or flag an issue to the backlog for consideration. It was a phenomenal tool for collaborative thinking that engaged an entire team. More heads were often better than one.

In the spring of 2022, I found myself in the midst of organizing my first private retreat for a select group of thirty to fifty entrepreneurs. The retreat, a combination of networking, brainstorming, and rejuvenation, was a passion project of mine. For years I had built a small community of Black entrepreneurs in my advising program and I wanted to create a space for some of my most successful CEOs to come together. But with my day job, other business ventures, and the daily dance of life, the enormity of the task often felt overwhelming.

Organizing the retreat wasn't just about booking a venue or sending out invites. It was about curating experiences and making sure every entrepreneur left with more than they came with—be it knowledge, connections, or memories.

From selecting the perfect venue in Nashville, coordinating with speakers, and planning the menu to ensuring every tiny detail was in place, the list of things to do was endless.

One evening, as I sat amid a pile of notes, emails, and a very unorganized spreadsheet, I realized I needed a better system. I considered the kanban board from my product development life. Would it work in a non–product development context?

I started with a large whiteboard, sectioning it off into three columns: "To Do," "In Progress," and "Done." Each task, no matter how big or small, was written out. From hiring an event coordinator and reviewing hundreds of applications to even selecting the background music for dinner, everything found its place on the board.

When I had free time, I'd pick three to five tasks, move them to the In Progress column, and set about bringing them to fruition. It was a visual representation of progress, a testament to the fact that I was inching closer to my goal. On days when unexpected meetings cropped up, or when life threw a curveball, I could quickly glance at the board, pick a task that fit the time I had, and get to work. It eliminated the paralysis of choice and the overwhelming feeling of not knowing where to start. As weeks turned into days, and the retreat drew closer, my board became a sea of tasks moved to the Done column. It was no longer just a tool, it was a story of my journey, late nights, challenges overcome, and small victories celebrated. Because it was such a success, we still do the retreat once a year.

CORE PRINCIPLES OF KANBAN

Visualize Work: By visualizing your tasks, you can more clearly see the status of the tasks and understand the flow better.

Limit Work in Progress: By limiting the number of tasks you're working on simultaneously, you can focus better and complete tasks faster. Kanban teaches you the art of focus. It's a gentle reminder that while juggling might be a cool circus trick, in real life, it often leads to dropped balls.

Manage Flow: Monitor, analyze, and optimize the flow of tasks to improve efficiency.

Make Process Policies Explicit: Clearly define the rules for how tasks move from one stage to another.

Feedback and Continuous Improvement: Always look for ways to optimize and improve the workflow. At its core, kanban isn't just about getting things done. It's about understanding your flow, recognizing your patterns, and crafting a life where progress is constant and stagnation is a foreign concept.

ZOOM OUT TO ZOOM IN

In day-to-day life, many of us are caught in the whirlwind of perpetual motion. We're constantly on the move, racing against time, trying to fit more into our days. But as I've often said, motion doesn't necessarily equate to progress. Building momentum in life isn't about perpetual motion but purposeful movement.

In a culture that idolizes pushing yourself as long as humanly possible, sprints remind us of the power of short, focused bursts of energy. It's about giving your all to a specific task or goal for a set period and then taking a moment to rest, reflect, and recalibrate. You can do multiple sprints back to back if you want to speed up progress or you can do them every few months whenever you feel stuck.

As we wrap up this chapter, I want to leave you with a thought. In your quest for progress, don't be seduced by the chaos of perpetual motion. Embrace the power of purposeful movement. With sprints and kanban by your side, you won't just move, you'll move with intention, clarity, and precision. And that, my friend, is the true essence of mastering your method.

7

HOW TO PACE YOUR LIFE

For two years straight, I might as well have lived in the air. Between 2018 and 2019, my life was a blur of airport lounges, hotel rooms, and the hum of airplane engines. Every other week, I found myself in a different city, zipping in and out of meetings, always on the move. My suitcase was perpetually packed, ready for the next business trip.

The adrenaline of closing advertising deals, the satisfaction of a successful presentation, and the thrill of being in a new city every few weeks was a total rush. But with the excitement came tunnel vision. I was so laser-focused on the work that I never actually saw the cities I was so happy to visit. New York, D.C., Miami, Dallas—they all blended into one another, a mishmash of skyscrapers and conference rooms. It got so bad one time that I literally couldn't remember the hotel room number by the time I got off the elevator, only to find a jumble of plastic key cards in my purse.

One evening, as I was boarding a flight leaving LAX, I remember thinking about how I couldn't wait to get home and have a "real" weekend with a bit more balance. I was so intent on compartmentalizing my life—work trips were for work and weekends in Los Angeles were for relaxation and fun—that the idea of mixing the two seemed impossible. But, before the wheels touched down at my destination, I had a chance encounter that changed my perspective.

I found myself seated next to a woman in her midforties with a sparkle in her eye. As the plane took off, she turned to me and shared that it was her first time going to Washington, D.C. Her excitement was palpable. She spoke animatedly about her itinerary, which included museums, the White House, and walking the National Mall. She had a whole trip planned out, down to the last detail.

As she spoke, I felt a pang of envy. Here I was, having been to D.C. two times in the past month for political meetings, as we geared up for coverage of the 2020 presidential election, and I hadn't taken the time to see anything on her list. I had been so caught up in my work, and the rush to return home, that I had missed out on the magic of our nation's capital! I realized that in my quest to compartmentalize my life, I had been robbing myself of the balance I was so determined to find.

That conversation was a wake-up call. I started to see my work trips in a new light. Instead of rushing in and out of cities, I began taking the time to explore. I'd grab dinner with a friend in Chicago, visit a museum in New York, or take a walk along the beach in Miami. Instead of leaving a meeting and heading straight to the airport, I would pick a later flight so I'd have time to grab dinner at a local restaurant. Despite a hectic schedule, I trained myself to integrate work and personal life by finding moments of joy and relaxation.

In my years as a business coach and adviser, I have had hundreds of interactions with ambitious individuals, entrepreneurs, and go-getters through various platforms—one-on-one calls, retreats, and even casual coffee conversations. If there's one question that recurrently arises, it's this: "How do you find work-life balance?" I candidly acknowledge that for a considerable chunk of my life, I didn't have it. There were times in my life when balance wasn't even within my line of sight, but I did consistently figure out ways to find moments of balance while building toward my dreams.

In this chapter, we'll unravel a truth that may seem counterintuitive yet is profoundly liberating. Many believe that to make dreams come to life, one must engage in relentless toil in pursuit of success. In reality, it is the harmony of work and life that crafts true success. This delicate dance between ambition and well-being is not static, it evolves with the seasons of life. There are times when the scales may tip more toward fast-paced hard work, and periods of slowness when your Relationships, Passions, and Wellness pillars must take precedence. In the previous chapter you learned how to sprint, and now we're going to focus on mastering the pace of your life. Not every season of life will be written with the ink of sixty-hour workweeks; some of the most crucial, memorable, and impactful times of your life will flow from seasons when you actually worked less and used that time to reinvest in everything else.

As we delve into the strategies that shape a well-paced, balanced life, remember that balance itself is personal and dynamic. It's not a one-size-fits-all formula but a tailored rhythm that suits the flow of your current circumstances. This chapter is your guide to discerning when to push forward with vigor and when to breathe deeply, stepping back to ground yourself. It's about learning to own your schedule and relationship with work so that you have the freedom of time to actually invest.

We'll explore how to set boundaries that protect your time for people, passions, and joy, which, in turn, fuel your productivity and enhance your capacity to achieve your vision. You'll also discover how to leverage the power of a weekly schedule to be a consistent rubric for balancing your pillars.

By the end of this chapter, you'll have a tool kit for navigating the ebbs and flows of life's demands, ensuring that you remain steadfast in pursuit of your goals without sacrificing the essence of what makes the journey worthwhile. You'll emerge with a renewed understanding that the strongest foundations for success are built not just on the stones of hard work but also on the soil of a life lived in equilibrium.

OVERWORKED AND OVERWHELMED

The concept of work-life balance isn't some hot new trend that sprouted overnight. It has been a pressing concern for people in the workforce for decades, evolving right alongside changes in societal norms, technology, and workplace practices.

Quick history refresher: In the late eighteenth century, the Industrial Revolution brought about drastic changes in work structures, including longer hours and the proliferation of factories. During this period, balance between work and life was virtually nonexistent. Laborers toiled for up to sixteen hours a day in factories and mills, and the concept of "life" outside of work was a privilege enjoyed by a few on top of the food chain.

However, post World War II, there was a shift in perception. The forty-hour workweek was becoming the norm, giving birth to the modern concept of work-life balance. Yet, even then, work and life were seen as separate entities—work was less about identity and more a means to an end. People went to work and then came home to enjoy dinner with their family, have an evening cocktail, and go to bed. Work and life still occupied separate spaces physically and mentally. You clocked in, you clocked out, end of story. People would spend an evening tuning in to their favorite radio or TV show, and then, get this, they actually slept! No midnight emails, no video calls at the crack of dawn, no trying to finish work from the day because you were stuck in too many meetings.

The digital age has strained this compartmentalized notion of balance. With the advent of the internet in the late twentieth century, a new set of challenges began to blur the line between work and home. Being constantly connected via smartphones and laptops has increased expectations around response times. According to a 2019 report by Asurion, the average American checks their phone ninety-six times a day, about once every ten minutes. Emails pile up after hours and video calls straddle early mornings and late nights. The boundaries that previously kept work contained within the office have dissipated. While technology has enabled more flexibility, it has also led to an "always-on" culture. Unplugging is no longer a given as work bleeds into nights, weekends, and vacations.

This constant connectivity takes a toll. In France, it is literally illegal for companies with more than fifty employees to send emails on the weekend, in order to delineate between work and personal time. But in many countries, being reachable 24/7 is an increasing expectation, even as policies paying lip service to work-life balance proliferate. Despite adequate vacation days and flexibility programs, many feel pressure to minimize time off. In 2023, Pew Research Center discovered that almost half of U.S. workers—yes, 46 percent—who have the option of paid time off aren't taking all of it. Isn't that wild?

As a CEO, I've actively had to counter societal pressures driving overwork. We ended unlimited vacation because employees actually began taking less time off than before (when our goal was the opposite) fearing judgment or the volumes of work that would be waiting for them upon return. We've also asked employees to disable notifications outside working hours and indicate on their calendars when they are unavailable for a quick huddle. But these moves required going against the grain of what's traditionally allowed by most employers.

The reality is that modern work environments prioritize business demands above all else. Reward systems incentivize longer hours and quicker response times. There is an underlying expectation for employees to be reachable and working. Let's face it: The modern work environment isn't designed for balance. It's designed for employees to be overworked and to drive profit for the business. Employers want more out of you for less. They dangle the carrot of "work-life balance" with perks like flexible hours and remote work, but at the end of the day, the scales are always tipped in their favor.

In my experience as an adviser and people manager, I find that people most often bring up their work-life balance at times when they are engaged in work they don't deeply enjoy, giving them the sense that they lack sufficient time for the pillars they really care about, like Freedom, Relationships, and Passions. It usually comes up when they're stuck in jobs that mentally suck the life out of them. They feel robbed of time for things that matter most.

Resentment brews toward bosses and systems and "the man" for creating a system that requires them to work forty to sixty hours a week just to enjoy a couple of weeks' vacation and to pay the rent. The cycle continues—we keep grinding through each week only to start again, lacking long-term direction. Time flies by, the vision for a life we enjoy relegated to the back burner.

Picture our current lifestyle: the week is a blur of work, and the weekends? They're often just a catch-up session for rest and chores. Suddenly, it's Monday again, and we're left wondering why time flies away so fast, leaving our cherished dreams and ambitions lingering in the background.

But let's flip the script for a second. When was the last time someone complained about their work-life balance while they were enjoying a heartwarming family dinner, getting lost in a hobby they adore, or traveling to a destination they've always wanted to visit? I bet my left Gucci shoe it is literally never. That's because the real puzzle isn't about balancing work and life as separate entities, it's about integrating them in a way that enriches our entire existence.

WORK-LIFE BALANCE IS BULLSHIT

Let's cut the BS. The concept of work-life balance itself is not even feasible. It implies that work and life are like two kids on a seesaw, unable to be balanced. Forget the old myth of work-life balance. It's a mirage, an unattainable ideal that sets us up for perpetual dissatisfaction. The truth is, life isn't a neatly segmented pie where work and personal life occupy equal, static slices. It's time to embrace a more dynamic, realistic approach to integrating work and life.

Consider this: Life is a series of seasons, each with its unique rhythm and demands. There are times when your career will take the front seat, propelling you toward financial stability or significant impact. Then there are moments when you'll slow down professionally, to savor personal milestones or rejuvenate your spirit. This ebb and flow isn't a failure of balance, it's a natural, healthy rhythm of life.

Let me say it louder for the people in the back. Work and life are not separate! Reject the notion that work and life are adversaries in a zero-sum game. They are interconnected facets of your existence, each enriching the other. Your professional endeavors can fuel personal growth, and your personal experiences can enrich your professional contributions.

Unless you're independently wealthy, your work is a vital part of your broader life journey. This means you need to start either incorporating your life more into your work, or simply looking at your job from a different, more positive perspective. Maybe you don't like your job because society tells you it's cool to hate what you do from nine to five, or you think you should be getting paid more to work less. Sometimes I meet with employees who love working at Blavity and the company culture but literally hate their job responsibilities and description. For example, I've had people who joined the company in our HR department but knew deep down they wanted to be a content creator. I've seen people ask to be promoted into management to make more money, but they really didn't want the stress of managing people, being responsible for their team's work, or performing administrative tasks, and now have less time to do the work they love.

So what's the solution? Do we resign ourselves to a life of perpetual burnout and dissatisfaction? Not a chance! It's time to redefine what balance means to you, individually. It's more about changing your mindset, not your job. (It's possible!) It starts by challenging societal norms and preconceived notions of what work should be. It's about aligning our work with our core values and seeking opportunities that allow us to thrive.

I believe that you should be seeking Work-Life Integration or Life-Work Integration, and if you don't fall into one of these two categories then it may be time for you to make a change.

Work-Life Integration

A doctor through and through, my father is a walking example of what Work-Life Integration looks like. We're a family woven together by the threads of medical practice, generations bound by the Hippocratic oath. He isn't simply a doctor; he is an enthusiast, a scholar, a relentless advocate. Workaholic? No, he is more of a work devotee. He derives immense fulfillment from his academic pursuits, particularly in the realm of pediatric sickle cell disease research.

Growing up, I had a front-row seat to his passion. My morning commutes to high school weren't filled with sleepy silences or NPR, they were soundtracked by the hum of global research conference calls. I'd listen to my father pore over protocols, mentor his colleagues, and collaborate with principal investigators on groundbreaking grant proposals for the National Institutes of Health. I grew up to the rhythm of these calls, a symphony of medical jargon and determined voices. At first, I resented the constant calls and weekend work hours that intruded on family time. But as I matured, my perspective shifted. I realized true work-life balance wasn't my father's goal. He sought integration rather than a rigid separation of work and life.

His career was intertwined with his spirit of service and humanity. Helping his young patients filled him with purpose and meaning. In turn, that sense of fulfillment fueled him to go the extra mile at work. His work nurtured his soul as much as it nurtured the children.

Our dinner table was no different. It was a forum where patient stories unfolded, case studies were dissected, and medical miracles were shared. The dinner table was more than just a place for us to eat, it was a classroom where my father, whom I occasionally call "Professor Dad," instilled in us a sense of awe for the work he did. You couldn't help but be rooting for the families, mentees, and kids under his tutelage.

The most memorable of these lessons in Work-Life Integration came during the summer camps my parents organized for kids who are living with sickle cell disease. Sickle cell disease primarily impacts the Black population in the United States, and because of the symptoms, many children have strokes or other physical challenges that make going to a normal summer camp almost impossible. It was here that I saw the full scope of my father's dedication. He wasn't merely treating a disease, he was giving these children a semblance of a normal childhood, creating a space where they could forget their pain and just be kids. At this camp, kids had counselors who were older teenagers or young adults with sickle cell disease, nurses were on staff to help manage any small pain episodes without a hospital visit, and patient education was integrated into the camp curriculum. It was an act of humanity that extended far beyond the realm of normal medical practice, with no incentive besides the desire to see his patients smile.

I learned at a young age that aligning work and life isn't about perfect equilibrium. It's possible to have your professional path nourish your values, passions, and spirit. My father's work integrated seamlessly with who he was at his core. When your career stems from your inner purpose, it ceases to feel like a burden. This type of Work-Life Integration requires embracing work as part of your wholeness, not an oppositional force.

Life-Work Integration

Steve Jobs once said to college students during a commencement speech, "The only way to do great work is to love what you do. If you haven't found it yet, keep looking. Don't settle."

Love me some Steve, and I don't disagree. However, I do think this is unrealistic for a lot of people, like if you're a first-generation college student or someone who really has the odds stacked against them with systemic limitations and structural failures. Yes, some people are lucky enough to do work they care deeply about, such as my father, but it's totally okay if that's not where you are right now. More than okay.

It's crucial to remember that taking a step back isn't a step down. It's a step inward, a moment to reconnect with what truly matters to you. It's about finding that sweet spot where your work and your life don't just co-exist, but they enrich each other. It's okay if your job isn't your lifelong calling right now, or ever, honestly. You can and will still find fulfillment. There are so many areas of your life to find your true purpose that don't involve being on the payroll.

If this sounds like you, then I want you to focus on Life-Work Integration instead of Work-Life Integration. This means making everything else the priority and integrating work to support your vision. This year, one of my employees decided that they were going to sublease their apartment and travel to a different city every month. Since we work remotely, they decided to prioritize their passion for travel and make work fit into their adventure. Life-Work Integration means your life takes priority.

There are times when your job is just that—*a job*. And that's okay. So, how can you leverage your job to work for *you* and your life? When I kept my consulting gig at Intuit while launching Blavity, I was integrating work into my life. My passion was Blavity, but it wasn't realistic for me to fully make that transition, and that was okay. In fact, it was actually ideal. I was able to focus my best energy on building a brand and community instead of worrying too much about a source of income.

The way our society views "work" is a big part of the issue. If work is just a paycheck, a means to an end, it's always going to feel like a chore that we have to balance against the good stuff. So, instead of following Steve Jobs's advice to find work that you're passionate about, I want you to shift your perspective and see work as something that finances your passions and engages your interests. Find fulfillment in the hobbies you have, the adventures you go on, and the people you help because you have the financial freedom to do so.

The goal of Life-Work Integration is to prevent an unfulfilling job from negatively dominating your whole life. Protect your time and energy. Seek small ways to shape your experience or find the exit route if needed. Prioritize aligning work to fit into the life you want to live in this season.

Things you can do in the job you currently have:

- Focus on the positive aspects of the job, even small things, and reflect on what you've gained and learned. How are you using your job to help you get closer to your vision? Is it bankrolling those tennis lessons you always wanted? Are you learning a new skill at work that will pay off one day when you take the leap as a full-time entrepreneur?

- Set clear boundaries and compartmentalize to protect your personal life from negativity or stress from work. For example, remove work email from your phone and communicate that to your team members. If necessary, renegotiate with your current job to fit your life.
- Cultivate a rich life outside of work filled with hobbies, learning, and relationships. Don't let your job define your entire existence.
- Explore creative ways to incorporate more meaning into your work, like helping co-workers, performing small acts of service, and mentoring interns.
- Use paid time off, flex scheduling if available, and full vacation allotment to regularly rejuvenate.

If you feel like you need a change:

- Consider lateral moves within the company or negotiating changes that better suit you. See if you can pivot your roles. Ensure the job description you are targeting reflects what you *want* to do, not what you think you *need* to do to follow a standard corporate progression.
- Be open to new professional paths that align with your passions and strengths if the current job is draining your soul. The job market today ain't what it used to be for the generations before us. Now we've got more choices to tailor our careers to our lifestyles and values.
- If changing jobs, allow your values to guide the search versus just income potential. Seek integration.

You deserve a life that fuels your freedom to live fully. You are not your job. Your life's worth isn't determined by how many hours you put in, how many deals you close, or how many promotions you get. Modern society has conditioned us to believe otherwise. We're made to feel that if we're not constantly producing, achieving, and outdoing ourselves, we're failures. Resist this philosophy at all costs and renegotiate with yourself how your life and work can exist in harmony with each other, so you can wholeheartedly enjoy your life.

No matter which bucket you fall into, Work-Life Integration or Life-Work Integration, we have to also improve our relationship with time, your irreplaceable asset.

YOU'RE THE BOSS OF YOUR TIME

When you adopt a rigorous view of your time, things start to change around you. The people around you start to fall in line. The whole world transforms. In order to start to find the harmony and rhythm of the life you crave, it's critical that you find more time that can be used to reinvest in your goals and life pillars outside of work. Time, once spent, is gone forever. You've heard this before, but it really is that simple. So let's get into how to use your relationship with time to your benefit instead of feeling like it's something you're constantly running out of.

Like many entrepreneurs, I used to believe that the key to success was relentlessly pushing myself to do more. More meetings, more trips, more investor pitches, more sales—

more hours, more hustle, and, ultimately, more money. In the early years of my business, I equated success with being constantly available, responding to every email within the same day, and dedicating every spare moment to checking off tasks on my to-do list. While this intense dedication and un-wavering focus undoubtedly contributed to my accomplish-ments, it also hindered my ability to transition from founder to CEO, which was crucial for allowing my company and its employees to flourish.

My "brute force" mentality initially played a significant role in transforming my vision, which began as a simple idea on a whiteboard in my San Francisco living room, into a thriving, profitable company. But this mindset also limited my ability to adapt and grow as a leader. I was so focused on the minutiae of daily tasks that I struggled to recognize the bigger picture and identify where I, as the CEO, could truly make a difference.

It wasn't until I consciously chose to slow down, reassess my priorities, and align my to-do list with my emotions and high-impact projects that I began to witness remarkable changes in my spirit, my daily joy, and my company's growth. By intentionally removing nonessential items from my calen-dar, I created space to reflect on my role as a leader and un-derstand where I could drive the most significant impact.

Through this process, I discovered the value of mindful productivity—a philosophy that guides my behavior to get right with the goals and pillars I am prioritizing. Mindful productivity is the belief that your schedule and time should reflect your emotions and energy levels. Mindfulness means slowing down and taking time to digest, think, breathe, and be intentional about your actions and thoughts. The key word here is "intentional." It's something that you should be doing throughout your day. Mindful productivity allows you to have more space and be more present. While it may not be the ideal approach for everyone, it has allowed me to set boundaries that maintain a healthy integration of my work and life, bringing happiness and fulfillment to my personal life, while still enabling me to concentrate on the critical projects that propel my company forward.

WHAT IS MINDFUL PRODUCTIVITY?

It's so easy to get caught in the trap of constant busyness without intention. Now, let's debunk a common misconception. When I talk about energy management and mindfulness, I'm not suggesting that you *only* need to add an extra hour of meditation to your morning routine or memorize a list of deep breathing exercises. I'm suggesting that you begin to see mindfulness as an integral part of your life, in and out of work. Being mindful of your energy means going off autopilot mode, and taking the time to appreciate the little things by staying observant of your mental state. This doesn't require that you stop what you're doing or lose momentum.

Mindfulness in the context of Work-Life/Life-Work Integration is about getting in tune with your emotional state, your natural rhythms, and discovering your optimal flow state to maximize output. "Flow," a term coined by Hungarian-American psychologist Mihaly Robert Csikszentmihalyi, is a highly focused mental state conducive to productivity. You've likely experienced flow and didn't even know it. Whenever you've felt like you lost track of time while concentrating, when you were "in the zone," that was a flow state. Mindfulness in your day can increase the opportunities for you to enter a flow state, which is not only where you'll find the most output, but also the greatest enjoyment in the task itself.

With that in mind, incorporating mindfulness into your productivity will actually lower your stress so that you're not overwhelming yourself. It will help you quiet that inner critic who judges you harshly, whispering, "Why are you doing that? You know that was the wrong move." In fact, it will instead hand the mic over to your inner cheerleader yelling, "Hell yeah! You're on a roll!"

How do you become better positioned to eliminate the stress and emotional guilt that comes with not getting everything done on time? There's no need to choose between working and spending time with yourself, your friends, or your family. Let me give you a guide to matching your energy with your productive zones so that you can have less friction and guilt in your daily routine.

MAP YOUR ENERGY PEAKS AND VALLEYS

Remember those CEO Tasks and Operating Tasks lists you completed? Go grab them and put them in front of you. Let's revisit. You might be on your way to delegating some of those Operating Tasks to someone else or still managing them, but either way we're going to use these lists as a base to separate your high-energy tasks and low-energy tasks. Most likely, your CEO Tasks will be high-energy, but audit these lists.

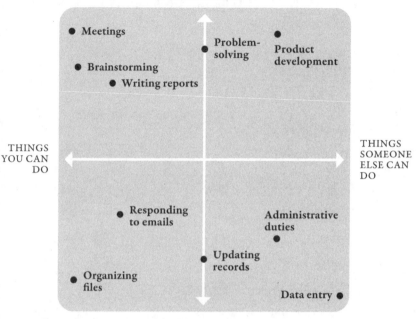

High-energy tasks require more focus, creativity, and mental stamina—think problem-solving, brainstorming, or writing reports. Low-energy tasks, on the other hand, are less demanding—like responding to emails, organizing files, or performing routine administrative duties.

Now that you've got a handle on your energy patterns and task categories, it's time to map them out. Take all that busywork that bores you to tears—answering emails, doing laundry, data entry—and stick it squarely in the times when you drag. Don't even think about tackling the big, creative projects when you can barely keep your eyes open. Save those babies for when your brain is popping. And don't forget to

TASK SCHEDULING BASED ON ENERGY LEVELS

	MOTIVATION		
	Low	*Medium*	*High*
EARLY MORNING (*Peak Energy*)			
Exercise			😊
Problem-Solving			😊
Brainstorming		😊	
LATE MORNING (*Peak Energy*)			
Writing Reports		😊	
Meetings		😐	
Important Project		😐	
EARLY AFTERNOON (*Low Energy*)			
Break			😊
Answering Emails		😐	
Organizing Files	☹️		
LATE AFTERNOON (*Low Energy*)			
Administrative Work	☹️		
Revising Work		😐	
EVENING (*Rest Period*)			
Break		😐	
Taking a Class		😐	
Hanging Out with Family		😊	

pencil in walking breaks, watercooler gossip, and other fun stuff. Your brain needs a rest every now and then. You're not a robot, even if Becky from accounting thinks you are. Put exercise on the calendar—no excuses!

Be transparent about your schedule and energy peaks with your partner, colleagues, and team. While it may not be feasible to completely overhaul your daily schedule, open communication can lead to compromises and accommodations that help you work more in tune with your natural flow. My team knows that I'm an early bird and if they need me to approve anything within the next twenty-four hours, it needs to be in my messages or inbox by the time I wake up or else it will have to wait until the next morning. You'll be surprised how much people will respect someone who is self-aware and has the self-confidence to clearly communicate how to get the best work from them. While this may require some negotiation and practice, trust me, it's worth the effort to renegotiate and free yourself.

As the COVID-19 pandemic began to subside, I made the decision to keep our company fully remote. You see, before the world turned upside down, my employees had been politely knocking on my door, asking for a four-day workweek, compressed workdays, or permission to work remotely on Fridays. Why, you ask? Well, life had become a juggling act, with school pickups, caregiving, and the ever-rising cost of homeownership driving people farther from our downtown Los Angeles office.

It was crystal clear that I needed to find a way to accommodate these requests. Our workforce was practically begging for more flexibility to get their work done and reduce the stress in their lives. The pandemic had forced us all into a remote work experiment. Fast-forward to today: Our employees have traded cramped offices for cozy home workspaces where they can take leisurely strolls in the middle of the day, burn the midnight oil, shift their hours early or late, or preschedule emails and messages to maintain the illusion of a traditional workday (I see you, night owls). Many now have time for afternoon school pickup for their little ones, moments that previously required a great deal of negotiation and the prying eyes of child-free colleagues. By making this change, we have been able to remain competitive in the marketplace and attract top senior talent who are looking for a workplace where they can live life beyond the weekends.

This grand transformation didn't just affect our employees' work selves, it rippled through their personal lives too. No longer shackled by rigid schedules and commuting nightmares, they found themselves with more time to nurture relationships, pursue hobbies, and build healthier routines. After all, isn't that what life's all about? And how much better do you think they're performing at work when they're invited to be whole people? A lot.

While remote work and flexible hours have become increasingly popular, many still find themselves needing to adhere to a more constrained schedule. There's nothing wrong with craving structure. There are plenty of ways to apply the art of working in rhythm with your flow, even within the confines of a nine-to-five job.

By standard definitions, productivity is related to the volume of output with the highest level of efficiency. But many people often conflate productivity with busyness and quantity. I challenge you to consider productivity as output created in less time, using the least amount of energy, fueled by more joy—all while maintaining a high quality. That's the true definition of being a productive person. Ideally, you slow down to speed up, and then get the results you want.

THE BALANCE BLUEPRINT

Not so long ago, I woke up feeling off-balance with my pillars. I had spent the past three days waking up on my cellphone, ordering takeout for dinner, and just in my zone grinding and prepping for an upcoming board meeting (I wasn't sprinting, this was just a rough period) where I was proposing a serious reorganization of the company. I barely remembered what the inside of my gym looked like. I drank a double espresso every day. And, worst of all, I had very little awareness of what was happening in the lives of my friends and family outside what they posted on Instagram. The weekend was knocking and I had zero plans, except maybe more work. I was spiraling, and I could see where it was headed. So what did I do? A little self-intervention: booked a salon appointment and hit up my girls for a dinner night to break the cycle.

I have a rule that I live by called the "Balance Blueprint." This is a framework I continually revisit to make sure my days and weeks are balanced. Think of it as a cheat sheet to life, ensuring I don't tip over the edge. It's my way of sprinkling some sanity into my weeks. It's oriented around the Six Pillars, which, again, are Money, Stability, Freedom, Relationships, Passions, and Wellness.

Balancing my Six Pillars throughout the week is a key strategy that helps prevent burnout, ensures I have enough space to put in the necessary hard work, and gives me guardrails to stay focused on my goals. The Balance Blueprint is essentially an ideal outline of what I want any normal week to look like, what habits I want to have, and how I want my time to be distributed throughout the week. Even though some of your pillars will be on the back burner, it is still important to make time and space to maintain them.

This road map helps me stay grounded in my daily joys while still pursuing the larger vision that I've designed for my life. Like any smart strategy, the Balance Blueprint isn't a set-it-and-forget-it situation. Every Friday afternoon I challenge myself to audit the last seven days and readjust as needed for the upcoming week, removing meetings that don't matter, scheduling self-care appointments, or making notes in my calendar to run to the grocery store. The Balance Blueprint is a small but powerful way to hold yourself accountable. As I said earlier, we have to get brutally honest about where we are now to get to where we are going.

MY SEVEN-DAY BALANCE BLUEPRINT LOOKS LIKE THIS:

Money: Getting meaningful work done to push the business forward. Not overspending on takeout. Have gone to Trader Joe's for groceries.

Stability: Feeling secure, without anxiety about work, my relationship, or society. No employee drama. The house is clean and organized.

Freedom: Getting seven to eight hours of sleep. A simple routine that avoids having meaningless meetings or calls on my calendar. Ending my workday between 5 and 7 P.M., despite time zone differences with colleagues.

Relationships: Having at least one meal a day with my partner. Texting and connecting with at least one friend or family member per day.

Passions: Reading a book for a few hours, listening to a podcast while on a walk, or working on a painting.

Wellness: Going to the gym at least once, charging and using my Apple Watch's health apps, choosing matcha tea instead of espresso, and not eating dairy.

Your Balance Blueprint should encompass a whole week, not one day. If I tried to do all these things in one day, I'd fail miserably. But getting to the gym once a week? Sending a text to a friend once a day? These all feel very doable!

DESIGN YOUR BALANCE BLUEPRINT

What does your Balance Blueprint look like? Your perfect week is a glimpse into the life you want to lead and the kind of person you want to become. It reflects what's most important to you, what brings you joy, and what you want to prioritize in your life. By getting clear on what this looks like, you'll be able to reverse engineer it into your present reality. Consider each of the Six Pillars of your perfect week: Money, Stability, Freedom, Relationships, Passions, and Wellness.

BUILDING YOUR BALANCE
BLUEPRINT: AN EXERCISE

MONEY

Start by thinking about how you're *spending* your money, not how you're making it. Are you splurging on luxurious experiences or are you saving for the future? Are you investing in yourself or in others? What do your daily spending habits feel like? This will give you a good idea of what your priorities are in terms of money and what kind of life you want to lead.

STABILITY

Do you want a predictable week or do you prefer new things, projects, people, and/or opportunities presented to you? Perhaps you want a sense of stability in your personal life, but also the freedom to be spontaneous and try new things at work. Write down how you would like to experience stability during your week and what that means for you.

FREEDOM

Consider how much freedom you want in your perfect week. Do you prefer complete freedom to do whatever you want, or would you rather have structure? Perhaps you want a balance of both, structure in the morning and evenings of freedom. Or consider a batching lifestyle where you negotiate with your boss that you're going to work ten-hour days Tuesday through Friday so that you can take Mondays off to relax and spend long weekends with family or passions.

RELATIONSHIPS

Next, think about who you would spend time with during this week. Are you surrounded by close friends and family, or do you prefer to spend time alone? Maybe a bit of both. Are you building new relationships in your city or strengthening old ones that you want to rekindle? This will give you a good idea of the kinds of relationships you want to cultivate and what kind of community you want to be a part of.

PASSIONS

Consider what you might do outside of work and how you might feel over the course of a week. Are you engaging in activities that bring you joy and fulfillment (but don't generate money)?

WELLNESS

Evaluate how you allocate time for your physical and mental well-being. Do you want to have time blocked off each day to attend exercise classes or would you prefer to adjust your work meetings to be calls so you can walk while you talk? Do you have a daily meditation time on your calendar or are you committed to speaking with a therapist?

DESIGN YOUR SCHEDULE FOR MINDFULNESS

No matter what your work or offline life looks like, you are in control of your schedule. And hear me out: The more you can control your schedule, the freer you are to find opportunities to be more mindful. When you don't have to think about what's next, you can focus on the moment. Why not do that legwork for yourself up front?

You might be reading this and thinking, "Morgan, having a detailed calendar isn't exactly a groundbreaking concept." And yes, I understand that. I acknowledge that this may seem like a mundane suggestion. But, in my experience as a mentor to start-up founders and entrepreneurs, I have found that a detailed calendar is one of the most powerful tools for transforming your daily actions and aligning your behavior with your growth goals. Pretty much every high performer has some sort of to-do list management mechanism, whether you email yourself tasks or keep track of your to-dos in a notebook.

Despite the undying loyalty to these running registers of

promised tasks, at the end of each day, they reveal a sickening truth. The list of uncompleted tasks has grown longer, not shorter. It's a cycle that repeats day after day, month after month, and sometimes even across entire careers. A harried blur of never getting enough done, despite the promise of a technique that's supposed to make you more productive. However, what might feel a little revolutionary is that I want you to shift your thinking from being a task-list master to being a schedule designer.

As soon as I hear someone's revenue or life goals, I ask them to share their calendar with me. What would I see if I opened your calendar right now? Would I see time blocks dedicated to your pillars? Would I see consistent spaces for mental and physical wellness? Would I see blocks of one-hour meetings back-to-back during your workweek? A calendar is one of the most transformative tools that can provide valuable insights (remember your data) into your daily intentions and actions. Bear with me as we go back to collegiate fundamentals of self-management. I guarantee you the reason you haven't been able to accomplish your goals or make more time for your pillars is because you've been operating with a fixed mindset, thinking, "I don't have enough time." Let's adopt a growth mindset together. Say it with me now: "I have enough time for everything I want to do."

When I was a freshman in college, I was a part of a merit-based scholarship program called Ervin Scholars—a four-year scholarship and cohort of students who had exhibited a commitment to social justice and academic excellence. This program is how I met two of my co-founders, Aaron and Jeff. Each year, a few weeks before the start of semester, our scholarship program would gather to reconnect after the summer break and prepare for another year of academic excellence and self-discovery. We participated in leadership workshops, met incoming freshmen, and set our goals for the year ahead.

The most transformative part of these gatherings was creating a detailed routine that covered every half hour of a typical seven-day week based on our goals and class schedules. All one hundred of us would sit in a room with calendar worksheets and plan out our days from the moment we opened our eyes until we collapsed onto our twin beds in our dorm rooms. There were a few requirements:

- You must sleep for at least eight hours a night.
- You must plan when you will eat three meals a day.
- You must schedule exercise or a wellness activity three days a week.

Incorporating this deceptively simple habit into my life changed the way I approached time management and productivity. It allowed me to prioritize the most important aspects of my life and ensure that my well-being was never compromised in the pursuit of success. It made me believe I had enough time.

A well-planned calendar goes beyond simply scheduling meetings and appointments. It represents a conscious effort to take control of your time and ensure that every moment is spent with purpose. By thoughtfully allocating time for both work and personal activities, you can strike a healthy balance and maintain a sense of well-being.

	MON	TUE	WED	THU	FRI	SAT	SUN
5 AM							
6 AM							
7 AM							
8 AM							
9 AM							
10 AM							
11 AM							
12 PM							
1 PM							
2 PM							
3 PM							
4 PM							
5 PM							
6 PM							
7 PM							
8 PM							
9 PM							
10 PM							
11 PM							
12 AM							

Take a moment to consider your current situation. When reading this book, where are you? Did you deliberately set aside time to rest and read (or listen)? Is this book something you picked up at the airport and read instead of listening to music on the plane? Did you decide to read it on a Sunday afternoon while your laundry is in the washing machine? Did you plan or spontaneously choose to read it?

Consider how much of your day is taken up by the impulses of your mind, overriding the intentions of your calendar. You see, the secret to enjoying life often lies in planning for it. Sure, happiness can occasionally sneak up on you, but if you truly want a life filled with joy, it's essential to take matters into your own hands. You have to make a full commitment to plan your bliss. It isn't something that just happens to you, it's something you actively create. It's time to shift your mindset from that of a passive recipient to one of an active participant in your own happiness. Embrace the idea that, while there will always be external factors, you have the power to influence your own well-being.

So, let's continue on this journey with your calendar and become a master scheduler, shall we? The goal here is not to eliminate spontaneity, but to create a balance between proactive planning and flexibility, allowing you the space to be present in whatever you're doing at the moment.

THEME YOUR DAYS

To increase your chances of staying mindful and focused in the moment, I recommend assigning themes to your days. Designating days for specialized activities—Meeting Mondays,

Writing Wednesdays, and so forth—engraves time for vital projects otherwise sacrificed in the urgency of the moment. By theming your day you'll guarantee you have at least two to four hours dedicated to making progress on your Step-change Growth projects and overall vision. Whether you're an entrepreneur or stay-at-home mom or you're navigating corporate life, you can aim to theme your days for a better use of your time.

In my capacity overseeing multiple business lines, themed days provide structure amid my competing hats, guaranteeing forward progress across each arena. Leadership meetings occupy Mondays. Tuesdays we dive deep on our events and talent vertical. Wednesdays we analyze our media holdings. Thursdays I keep unscheduled, opening space to convene teams on arising needs and impromptu conversations. Fridays fuel my personal passions—writing, public speaking, and painting.

This concentration of similar tasks massively reduces the mental tax of toggling between wildly different responsibilities day-to-day. Our working memory can only juggle so many context switches before our mental bandwidth starts suffering. Grouping like activities limits that churn while still ensuring that diverse projects progress. Aside from that, establishing set days for certain work makes it far simpler to decline distracting one-offs. When a request comes in or a new opportunity arises on your designated writing day, you can easily redirect the request. "Tuesdays are my writing days, so I need to keep my creative focus. But I could put something on the calendar for Thursday!" Now you have both upheld your theme day and scheduled that call without compromising either. If you are in a corporate nine-to-five role and are thinking, "Right, I'm just going to tell my manager I can't attend a client call because it's my writing day," I hear you. For those who have less autonomy over their schedule, adapting the concept of themed days to enhance productivity might involve starting with small, manageable changes within your existing constraints. By carving out specific times for tasks like email, project work, or meetings, you can introduce a semblance of structure akin to themed days. It's also beneficial to communicate with your manager about your goals for improved focus and efficiency, suggesting a trial of this modified approach that aligns with your responsibilities and team expectations.

Theming enables easy rescheduling by offering predefined containers for certain types of meetings or tasks. Rather than blindly moving items around, you have target days aligned to specific functions. This cuts down overstuffed days while evening out your workload across weeks. The calendar becomes your ally in optimization rather than merely a record of commitments.

Block Out Time for Step-change Growth Goals

Now that you've themed your days to align with the workflow, let's get down to business. On your schedule, allocate generous blocks of time for working on your Step-change Growth goals uninterrupted. These are the big-ticket items that propel you forward in your personal and professional life, so give them the attention they deserve. For instance, if you're working on a new product launch, dedicate several hours on Thursday afternoons to brainstorming, strategizing, and executing your plan. If you're focused on developing your new skill in graphic design, dedicate time to perfecting your craft through an online course or program.

Schedule Personal and Relationship Commitments

If your Relationships pillar is a top priority, make sure to pencil in blocks for your loved ones and personal commitments. Whether it's a standing Saturday morning breakfast date with your partner, a weekly call with your parents, or a monthly book club gathering, make sure to include these essential interactions in your calendar. By scheduling them in advance, you demonstrate that these relationships are a priority and ensure that you're nurturing them alongside your professional responsibilities.

Incorporate Daily Tasks and Self-care

Next, schedule time for exercise, meal breaks, commuting, and other day-to-day tasks. These activities may seem mundane, but they're crucial for maintaining your physical and mental well-being. For example, block out thirty minutes each morning for a workout, followed by breakfast. Additionally, schedule short breaks throughout your day to stretch, scroll Instagram, meditate, read, take a walk, or simply relax and recharge.

Front-load Your Week to Prevent Blockers

To keep your week flowing smoothly, schedule important interactions, such as meetings and check-ins, earlier in the week. This will help prevent potential blockers and ensure you have ample time to address any issues that may arise. For instance, schedule a Monday morning team meeting to discuss priorities, challenges, and progress, so everyone starts the week on the same page and with a clear understanding of their responsibilities.

Take a moment to consider what is expected of you in the coming week, and build time into your schedule for your own preparation. I use my Friday afternoons and Monday evenings as time allocated for preparation. This may include researching for an upcoming client meeting, brainstorming ideas for a marketing campaign, or practicing a presentation for a conference. By setting aside time for these activities, you'll be ready to dazzle and perform at your best when the time comes.

Expect the Unexpected

Are you always derailed by midafternoon because requests are coming in from email, or do you have to go pick up your kids and get stuck in traffic? Use your calendar to build in time for the unexpected so that you're not playing catch-up or feeling behind. Unplanned slowdowns are pretty much guaranteed in any given week. They are unavoidable and that's actually part of life, so plan for them. Add thirty-minute blocks of free time or transition time that can be used for catching up on unexpected requests or tasks. These are labeled "buffer" in my calendar.

How you work is as unique as your fingerprint—it's something that should be celebrated, not hidden away in shame. Our society often values a one-size-fits-all approach to productivity and scheduling, but the truth is that each person's path to success looks different. As you embark on your own journey of personal and professional growth, I invite you to allow the philosophy of mindful productivity to dictate your daily behavior. You may find, as I did, that slowing down and focusing on what truly matters when you need it most in the day can lead to increased success, happiness, and a more fulfilling life. Stop forcing yourself to do tasks when you're running low on steam.

As we've discussed, different seasons will demand different things from you. Some pillars will be pulled to the forefront more than others at various times. This will influence what "balance" means for you depending on the goals you're working toward that lead to your vision. It won't always look like an even split between all Six Pillars. It's important to remember that your perfect week may change over time depending on how much you are prioritizing certain pillars in your life. As you grow and evolve, so will your priorities and desires. That's okay, it's all part of the journey. The most important thing is that you take the time to visualize and prioritize what you want in life.

PAY ATTENTION TO FREE TIME

As you build your Balance Blueprint and design your schedule for work or life integration being your priority, I want you to recognize that despite your efforts, you will ultimately still have some unscheduled time. So, what are you doing in your free time? Some people are blissfully running errands without their toddlers in tow, and others are taking a midday siesta. But, ultimately, free time is the ability to do whatever you want, when you want to do it.

On any given Saturday morning or any evening after work, how are you spending your time? Are you hustling to get to the gym for your class? Are you cheering your kid on at their tennis match? Are you volunteering at a community center? Are you scrolling Pinterest to figure out the perfect mantel decoration for Halloween?

Freedom for me today looks like ending my meetings at 4 P.M. and spending a few hours reading or having time to learn something new. Our choices outside of work or school are incredibly telling when it comes to figuring out how we are naturally allocating our time. It tells us where our defaults are today so that we can have a picture of what we need to change tomorrow. These are the beginning steps of designing your map—seeing where you are now so that you can move toward the final destination. Balance is attainable, but perhaps not the way it's been sold to us before.

THE JOURNEY CONTINUES

As we close this section of the book, I want to leave you with a powerful thought: Own your pace. Throughout these pages, we've explored various methods to master the art of timing in life. It's about knowing when to push the pedal to the metal and when to ease off the gas, making those decisions confidently and on your own terms. Whether it's sprinting toward your goals, gaining more time back, using data to work smarter, or leveraging your network to bypass potential pitfalls, the key is to navigate your journey with intention and purpose.

We're about to embark on my favorite part of the book. It's one thing to have a clear vision and robust frameworks, but there's often something elusive that can keep us from advancing to the next level. This next section is dedicated to uncovering and overcoming those barriers, to rewriting the rules in every aspect of your life, for every season you encounter.

Remember, this book isn't just a one-time read. It's a tool, a companion in your journey, meant to be revisited as you grow and evolve. Some of you might need to pause here, to put into practice what you've learned before moving forward. Others may be ready to dive into the next section headfirst. So, take a deep breath, reflect on your journey so far, and when you're ready, let's step into the next exciting phase together.

PART 3

MASTER

YOUR GROWTH

There comes a season in everyone's life when the winds of change begin to stir. Perhaps the fire of a once-powerful passion has begun to flicker, or maybe you've scaled the highest peaks of your goals with nowhere left to go. It could be as simple as successfully realigning your life around priority pillars and now you want to shift into the next phase. The reasons may vary, but they all lead to a crossroads where you have to consider moving on from your current vision and toward something new. These final chapters pose key questions and provide guiding principles to help you master your growth—for the long haul.

We'll also confront the challenges head-on. You'll likely face resistance, both from within and from others, as you move away from the tried and true. But remember, the most rewarding victories often come from the toughest battles. By building resilience, embracing flexibility, and developing a growth mindset, you'll turn potential roadblocks into stepping stones.

Pause for a moment and assess the state of your passion for life. Do you wake up each morning with a sense of excitement and enthusiasm? Are you eager to tackle the challenges that lie ahead, or do you find yourself dreading the day, feeling drained and uninspired? Your level of joy and fulfillment is a powerful indicator of whether it's time to embrace change. If the drive within you has dimmed or disappeared altogether, it may be the universe gently nudging you toward a new path.

This is the part of the book where we answer "What's next?" You've done the hard work, and it's time to both revel in the rewards and keep your eyes cast forward for the next opportunity. A wealthy life can't be sustained without constant protection of what you've created and effort to keep evolving and improving.

Now is the time to revisit your priority pillars and evaluate how well your current vision and goals align with them. Are you still in harmony with your core values, passions, and aspirations? Have your priorities shifted or evolved over time? It's important to be honest with yourself and recognize when your current trajectory no longer serves your highest purpose. Aligning your life with your priorities is crucial for long-term fulfillment and success. If things aren't gelling well, it may be a sign that it's time for a redesign. Yep, you might have to start the whole thing over again. In fact, I know you will. That's the whole point!

Life is essentially a series of trade-offs. You trade your time for money at work. You trade your free time for the joy of raising a family or pursuing a hobby. Recognizing this truth helps you to achieve a semblance of balance. Having it all doesn't mean cramming everything into your day. It means strategically choosing what you're focusing on at any given time. Maybe this year you're concentrating on climbing the career ladder. Perhaps next year your focus shifts to starting a family or auditioning for a local theater production. Remember, it's not just about celebrating the small wins—those are great, but we're here for something bigger, something bolder! We're talking about that jaw-dropping, life-changing goal that makes you want to dance in your living room. It's about creating a vision so vibrant and so incredible that it transforms your whole world. And let me tell you, that kind of progress doesn't just fall into your lap.

In this section, I'll walk you through how to follow your intuition in seasons of change, quiet the noise, and listen to your inner voice. I'll empower you to trust your instincts to make courageous decisions and embark on a journey rich with evolution and upward growth. Knowing how to balance the hard work with big joy allows you to embrace the unknown with faith and confidence in your own inner wisdom.

8

THE POWER OF DECISIVENESS

It was a brisk fall morning as I prepared for a meeting with one of our top AfroTech clients; for the sake of anonymity let's call them Techifiy. A senior executive girlfriend who works at Techifiy gave me a call, "sister to sister," before the larger meeting to give me a heads-up that some of the people internally at Techifiy didn't want to renew their partnership with our company. Apparently, they were unhappy because we didn't give their speakers a mainstage spot (which isn't for sale) or list them as a top partner over other companies (that paid more than they did).

In other words, she was politely giving me a nudge to budge a little with some of our constraints so we could get the deal done. I appreciated the tip, no doubt. It's always good to know what you're walking into, right? So I jumped into this meeting, armed with this new info, but here's the thing—I didn't budge on our policies. At our conferences, no company, no matter how big or how much they're paying, gets special treatment. That's just not how we roll.

Now, you can imagine, this didn't exactly make me the most popular person back at Blavity. My sales team couldn't wrap their heads around why I'd pass up what seemed like easy money. Here's my take: Compromising our integrity for a quick buck? That's a slippery slope. The speakers Techifiy wanted to push weren't really cutting it. Their time would have turned into more of an ad for Techifiy than a valuable talk for our community. And if there's one thing I stand by, it's that our speaker lineup has to bring real value, not just be a back-scratching exercise for a company.

So, yeah, I guess that decision made me look like the tough one, the hard-ass, but you know what? I'm okay with that. In this game, you've got to stick to your principles and make a decision, even if it ruffles a few feathers.

Look, I'm not going to sugarcoat this for you. If you want to get anywhere in life, you need to stop being an indecisive, wishy-washy person. Seriously, the faster you can make decisions, the quicker you'll get to where you want to be. It's that simple. When you're trying to do something new and groundbreaking it's critical that you figure out how to get better at taking calculated risks. Most people are terrified of making the wrong choice. They'd rather spend hours, days, or even weeks agonizing over every little detail than just picking a path and going for it. And you know what? That's a surefire way to stay stuck exactly where you are.

Think of momentum as the fuel in your journey as a high achiever. Society might have you believe that every step needs to be meticulously planned and safe. But let's challenge that. In reality, especially on an unconventional path, it's that forward motion—the result of being decisive—that keeps you going. It's like learning to ride a bike: You can't build momentum if you're always stopping to check if you're doing it right. Sometimes, you've just got to pedal and adjust as you go. This momentum, born from your decisiveness, is key in keeping you from stalling or veering off course.

This is your dream and your life journey, even if it looks different from your friends' lives or society's conventions. No one will feel the rewards or struggles in quite the same immediate way as you. So you have to get more comfortable tuning out the noise and making the calls that you believe are right, not what others will easily understand or sign off on. It's easy to get caught in a loop, trying to make the "perfect" decision. While it's important to be thoughtful, there's a fine line between careful consideration and being paralyzed by analysis. Here's a different perspective: Rather than aiming for perfection in every decision, embrace the learning that comes from quick, well-informed choices. This mindset is about breaking free from the trap of overcaution and embracing a more dynamic way of navigating your path.

DECIDE LIKE A CEO

How many times have you waited for something because you couldn't decide what you wanted and then missed an opportunity as a result? The flight price changed before you bought your ticket, the promotion at work went to someone more decisive because you hesitated to express your interest, and the girlfriend of your dreams left because you couldn't commit. (Okay, maybe that's a little extreme! But you get my point.) If you don't make a decision, the decision will get made for you and indecisiveness will damage your ability to move faster and smarter toward the opportunities that knock on your door. By recognizing these costs, you can begin to shift your mindset and embrace the power of decisiveness.

To hit your Step-change Growth goals, you have to be prepared to take advantage of the opportunities that come your way. Successful leaders don't waste their precious time hemming and hawing over every single decision. They understand that time is money, and dithering over every little detail can be costly, both in terms of resources and morale. By being decisive, they demonstrate confidence and direction, inspiring those around them to follow suit.

If you're truly going to be the CEO of your life, you have to improve your ability to make smart and quick decisions. Let's stop wasting time writing up the perfect pitch deck before showing anyone, and stop scheduling "pick your brain" coffee chats, just so you can get emotional reassurance that you're doing the right thing. The faster you can make decisions, the quicker you'll start seeing results. And the more results you see, the more motivated you'll be to keep pushing forward. Ultimately, it's what separates the goal-reachers from the goal-seekers.

THE SCIENCE OF EFFECTIVE DECISION-MAKING

Do you already have an idea of what kind of decision-maker you are? Consider the concept of being action-oriented versus state-oriented. Action-oriented people are focused on forward momentum. They always get things done, whether on their own, by delegating to others, or by working collaboratively in a team. They typically have a high batting average with follow-through and don't just make decisions. They implement them. Conversely, state-oriented people are focused on their emotions, which often leads them to be seen as indecisive. It's a challenge for them to commit to their choices and not second-guess all the time. Frequently, they act with hesitance and jump ship on their commitments.

Which one are you? Be honest! Because the science says that state-oriented, indecisive people aren't actually worse at making decisions than naturally action-oriented decisive people. Research shows that the capacity and ability to be an effective decision-maker are available to all people, no matter if you're naturally action-oriented or state-oriented.

In other words, no excuses! Even if you are currently a state-oriented person, you absolutely have the ability to become decisive. The secret ingredient? It's simpler than you might believe. It's confidence!

The real difference in someone who's kicking ass, checking off to-dos, and bringing their vision to life has nothing to do with where their focus lies, but with their level of conviction. Action-oriented people have been shown to possess more confidence than those who are state-oriented. Ultimately, the confidence to make decisions begets the ability to make decisions. If you're always second-guessing yourself . . . stop! Instead of focusing on trying to be more decisive, try to spend more time building your confidence, and badass decision-making skills will naturally follow. So how do you decide . . . how to decide?

THIRTY SECONDS OR LESS RULE

For a leader, making fast yet thoughtful decisions is a crucial skill. I aim to decide most daily matters in thirty seconds or less. This threshold forces me to listen to my intuition and prevents me from overthinking minor issues. If I cannot decide within half a minute, that signals to me that the decision likely requires more consideration.

CEOs and executives know that their time is precious. So when presented with a choice, they quickly weigh the options, risks, and potential outcomes. If much uncertainty or complexity exists, they hold off temporarily to gather more input. However, simple or repetitive issues get handled rapidly to maintain momentum.

I find that a thirty-second rule works well for my day-to-day responsibilities and requests. It allows me to zoom through inconsequential items on my plate. And it ensures I apply focused energy toward more difficult discussions by delaying the final call. As issues escalate to me, my team expects decisive guidance. This framework allows me to provide quick verdicts when possible and flag sensitive topics that need patience.

With practice, you strengthen the muscle to make sound judgments efficiently. Ask yourself: Does this decision hold major consequences? Do I possess enough context to feel certain? Can I logically defend my choice if challenged? If you can confidently answer yes, trust your instinct and decide. But if doubts exist, or you lack key perspectives, place it into a more robust framework like the DRIP method.

THE DRIP METHOD

Imagine you're at a crossroads in your personal life. Maybe you're considering a big move, a career change, or even starting a family. These aren't small decisions, they're the kind that can change the trajectory of your life. So, how do you approach them? I want to introduce you to a method that is as adaptable as it is effective—the DRIP method—Define, Review, Imagine, Pick.

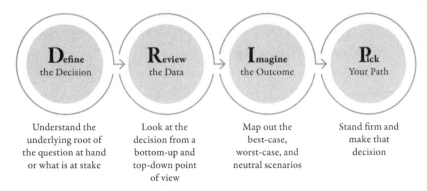

Define the Decision	**R**eview the Data	**I**magine the Outcome	**P**ick Your Path
Understand the underlying root of the question at hand or what is at stake	Look at the decision from a bottom-up and top-down point of view	Map out the best-case, worst-case, and neutral scenarios	Stand firm and make that decision

This approach can take a mere three minutes or extend to several weeks, depending on the complexity and significance of the decision at hand. Here is how it breaks down.

Step 1: Define the decision.

When you're faced with a bigger decision, the first thing you need to do is to really hone in on what the decision is all about. This sounds straightforward, but it's surprising how often we can miss the mark if we don't take the time to dig deep.

Sometimes, when a decision feels particularly tricky, it's not just because of the options in front of you. It's because there's something more, something deeper that you haven't quite put your finger on yet. This is where you need to do a bit of soul-searching.

Start by asking yourself some key questions: What exactly am I deciding here? Is it just about the apparent choices in front of me, or is there a bigger underlying issue that I need to address? For example, if you're struggling with a career decision, is it really just about choosing between job A and job B, or is there a deeper question about your career path, your values, or your life goals?

Understanding the root of the decision involves peeling back the layers. It's like being a detective in your own life. You're looking for clues, patterns, anything that can help you understand what's really at stake. This process might involve reflecting on your past decisions, your long-term goals, and what truly matters to you.

Step 2: Review the data.

When facing a decision, we need to shed light on the issue from multiple perspectives. Look at the decision from a bottom-up and top-down point of view. I like to think of it as adopting both a worm's-eye and bird's-eye view.

The **bottom-up view** involves immersing ourselves in the details—gathering and analyzing data from a variety of sources, both qualitative and quantitative. It's about understanding the specific, tangible elements that will impact your decision. I want you to research and gather and analyze data from multiple sources. Evaluate how each piece of information contributes to the broader decision. This might mean reading reviews online, asking advisers or your tribe for their perspective, or reviewing historical data you've been tracking. If you're thinking about moving, research different cities or neighborhoods. What's the cost of living? What are the job opportunities like? If it's a career change, dive into what skills you might need, or the financial implications of such a shift. This step is all about the details.

Then, we shift to a **top-down view,** which involves stepping back to see the larger picture. From this vantage point, we look for patterns and macro trends, and we even consider our pillars or Step-change Growth statements. This perspective helps us see beyond the immediate and apparent, connecting our decision to any unintended consequences that may be around the corner. This isn't just about what's happening now, it's about understanding how current trends can shape the future—your future.

Take a step back and look at the larger trends in your industry, society, or life in general. For instance, if your long-term goal is to grow your business, what are the emerging trends in your market? How is consumer behavior changing? What technological advancements could impact your business in the next five years?

Apply this to your personal life as well. If your long-term goal is to achieve a certain lifestyle, consider the trends in your personal development, relationships, and health. How have you grown over the past years, and what patterns do you see emerging? Understanding these can guide decisions that align with your personal growth and life goals. By understanding these macro life trends, you can align your decisions to not just be relevant today but also remain relevant in the future.

Focusing on patterns related to your long-term goals allows you to essentially future-proof your choices. This approach ensures that the steps you take today are not merely reactions to current events, but deliberate actions that lead you toward the future you envision for yourself and your life's work.

Step 3: Imagine the outcome.

Armed with all the necessary information, it's time to outline your potential courses of action. This involves carefully balancing optimism and pragmatism, and being mindful of personal biases.

Importantly, I also consider the opportunity cost of each path. The opportunity cost is the value of the next-best alternative I would miss out on by making a certain choice. Think of it like being at a crossroads where each path leads to a totally different adventure. Choosing one path means you can't experience the others—at least not right now. That's what opportunity cost is all about. It's like the price tag of the road not taken.

So, imagine you're weighing up whether to spend your evening working on a new skill for your job or chilling out with a new hobby. If you go for the skill-building, what you're giving up is the relaxation and fun of your hobby. And if you choose the hobby, you're missing out on the career benefits that new skill could bring. Sometimes, putting actual dollar figures or goals on these choices makes it clearer. Like, "If I learn this skill, I could be making X amount more in a year," or "If I spend time on my hobby, I'm gaining X hours of stress relief."

But opportunity cost isn't just about money or a career. It's about life. Every choice you make shapes your future in some way. Say you decide to work late nights this month to get your side hustle off the ground. The opportunity cost? Maybe it's missing your kid's soccer games or time with your friends. Fast-forward a few years and think about how you'll look back on these choices. Will you be high-fiving yourself because the extra income you made helped you get closer to retiring early, or wishing you'd done things differently and invested more time with people important to you?

Beyond opportunity cost, I mentally map out the best-case, worst-case, and neutral scenarios. Every path echoes into the future, so I visualize how each outcome could play out short term and long term.

As you write out these mini-future stories, contemplate questions like:

- What future versions of myself might thank or fault me for this impending decision?
- Best case: If everything clicked into place perfectly, what would the impact be over time?
- Worst case: What regrets might I have looking back? If

things totally tanked or I ended up hating this path, what negative outcomes might persist?

- Neutral case: If it ends up being just okay, not amazing or terrible, what's the scenario here?

Evaluating trade-offs through the lens of opportunity cost and potential scenarios provides the creative friction needed to make thoughtful decisions aligned with my core values and goals. This imagining step urges me to have the courage to analyze all perspectives.

Step 4: Pick your path.

Make the decision! You've dissected the issue, gathered your arsenal of information, and mapped out the scenarios. Now stand firm and make that decision. It's about taking all that you've learned, weighed, and anticipated, and turning it into a decision that resonates with confidence and clarity. After the decision is made, move on. Stop thinking about it. Remember, this isn't just about choosing a path, it's about forging ahead with conviction.

BE AWARE OF YOUR BIASES

When you're going through the DRIP method and imagining the outcome of a decision or doing your research, being aware of personal biases is crucial. We all like to think we make rational, objective decisions based on careful analysis of the facts. But unfortunately, human psychology gets in the way more often than we realize. Our brains rely on mental shortcuts and ingrained ways of thinking that can undermine logical reasoning—without us even noticing. These are known as cognitive biases.

As you explore big life decisions and changes to the rules by which you live, it's important to understand how cognitive biases impact the way you process information, assess risk, and envision future outcomes. Common traps like confirmation bias, anchoring bias, and availability bias can quietly send our judgments down problematic paths. Let's chat a bit more about different types of cognitive biases and how they sneak into our everyday lives.

First up, there's **confirmation bias**. This one's a real trickster. Basically, it means we humans tend to notice and believe things that match what we already think is true about the world. In cognitive scientist Daniel Kahneman's acclaimed 2011 book, *Thinking, Fast and Slow,* he dives deep into how our minds work, including the concept of confirmation bias. Confirmation bias contributes to exaggerating probabilities because when you accumulate evidence in your mind that supports your hypothesis, you can think something is much more probable than it actually is. It makes our mind kind of ignore or make excuses for stuff that contradicts those beliefs. You can think of it like having blinders on that only let you see what you already believe. Say you think your favorite coffee shop has the best coffee in town. You're more likely to notice and remember all the times you had a great cup there and conveniently forget the times it was just meh. This bias makes us cherry-pick information that backs up our existing beliefs and ignore what doesn't.

Then there's **anchoring bias.** Think about when you go shopping and see a shirt marked down from $100 to $50. You think you're getting a great deal because your mind is anchored to that original $100 price tag. In reality, the shirt might not even be worth $50. We do this all the time, not just with prices but with first impressions, initial ideas, or the first piece of advice we get.

Anchoring bias was first identified by psychologists Amos Tversky and Daniel Kahneman. They did studies that showed if you give someone a completely random high number before asking them to estimate something numerical, they'll guess a number higher on average. And vice versa with random low numbers! Crazy, right?

An anchoring bias is a fascinating psychological phenomenon. Let me give you an example.

Imagine you're at a charity auction. Before the auction starts, the auctioneer mentions that, last year, a similar item sold for $5,000. Even though this information is arbitrary and may not reflect the actual value of the item being auctioned this year, it sets an "anchor" in your mind. So, when it's time to bid on the item, you might find yourself starting your bidding around that $5,000 mark, or at least being influenced by it in determining your maximum bid. This happens even if the item is actually worth significantly less. The initial figure of $5,000 skews your perception and judgment, leading to potentially higher bids than if no anchor had been set.

In other words, in negotiations, the first offer often sets the tone for the rest of the discussion, regardless of its fairness or logic. This is why savvy negotiators often start with an extreme offer—it shifts the entire frame of the negotiation.

But where this gets dangerously relevant is in big personal

decisions and rewriting your life's rules. It's easy to anchor on to early criticism from others, past failed attempts, or even your own first viscerally fearful reaction. Those initial impressions stick and start to disproportionately color your evaluation of options.

Suddenly even objectively viable paths can get dismissed if they don't jibe with the anchoring points cemented in your mind already—around risk, difficulty, time, and cash money required. Stuff that scared you at first pass now subconsciously scares you consistently, blocking sound judgment!

And frankly, people breaking the rules of life probably don't anchor enough to other people who have unconventional success stories that should expand our sense of possibility. The status quo and what we were taught growing up about the "right way" or "risky things" often unfairly anchors our thinking on what "seems reasonable."

Anchoring can worsen your decision-making ability unless actively counteracted. Now that you've learned more about this specific type of bias, I want you to practice noticing when your assessments seem irrationally glued to arbitrary reference points that may be initial impressions stamped into your brain. Easier said than done of course; we all fall victim to the pull of the anchor. But awareness helps us not get quite so stuck.

The **availability bias,** also a concept introduced by Tversky and Kahneman, is a mental shortcut that plays a big role in how we make decisions. It's about how our brains tend to give more weight to information and examples that come to mind easily, whether because they're recent, dramatic, or emotionally charged. Basically, anything that's memorable.

Now let's see how this plays out in real life. Let's say a certain diet is all over social media, endorsed by celebrities and influencers. It's everywhere, so naturally it starts to feel like the perfect solution for everyone. But just because this diet is the most visible and talked about doesn't mean it's the best or only option for your personal health. The availability heuristic can make us overlook other, potentially more suitable nutrition plans that aren't as prominent in the public eye.

Then there's how this plays out in your beliefs around relationships. Imagine your close friend just had a rough, messy breakup. It's a big story in your social circle, so it's fresh in your mind. When you think about starting to date, this recent breakup looms large, and you start to overestimate the chances you will go down the same path as your recently heartbroken friend. You're not thinking about all the happy, healthy relationships out there, you're focused on this one negative example because it's so vivid and recent.

In both cases, the availability heuristic can lead us down a path where we base our decisions on what's most easily recalled rather than what's most accurate or beneficial. It's a reminder to look beyond the most immediate or dramatic examples when making decisions and to seek a more balanced, comprehensive view.

When embarking on a journey toward a life that's unconventional, successful, and harmoniously balanced, you need to become adept at spotting and countering biases. Think about it this way: We all have certain tendencies and preferences that shape how we view the world. These biases are like filters on a camera lens—they can subtly alter the picture we see. So how do you fight it? Actively question your initial thoughts and assumptions. Why do you think a certain out-

come is more likely? Is there data to support it or is it just a
feeling? Being critical of your own assumptions is key to
overcoming bias. Remember, biases aren't inherently bad—
they're just part of being human. However, when you're striv-
ing to live a life that's both unconventional and successful,
being aware of these biases and actively working to mitigate
their influence becomes even more important. By doing so,
you can make decisions that are more grounded in reality
rather than skewed by subjective perceptions. This approach
will help you align your decisions more closely with your
Step-change Growth goals and priority pillars.

THE DRIP METHOD IN ACTION

Okay, now that you're aware of your biases, let's get some
practice with the DRIP method. I've used this method time
and time again to help me make decisions big and small. In
year two of Blavity, I faced a critical personal decision—whether
to split my time between leading at Blavity and attending a
prestigious business school full-time or staying full-time
working on the company. I had just spent years working re-
lentlessly to get Blavity off the ground as CEO and we were
gaining traction, but I could easily see that one of my limita-
tions for growth was the lack of a "good ol' boys" network
and stamp of approval from a major institution. Business
school tempted me with the potential to expand my network
with VCs and leadership skills to bring back to the company.
However, stepping away would distract me from day-to-day
operations when we needed all hands on deck. To make this
career-defining choice, I applied the DRIP method.

Define the decision: I was facing the decision of whether to enroll in a top MBA program or continue focusing solely on growing my start-up full-time. This decision would significantly impact the trajectory of my career and what my life would look like for the next few years.

Review the data: I already had over three years of experience running my tech start-up as CEO. I had to be super careful with the data I was looking at. It's easy to get swayed by those big, flashy success stories of MBA grads. I really pushed myself to look beyond the most obvious or emotionally charged info, pulling in a wide range of insights—from real start-up growth figures published by universities to the actual impact of business school networks. It was all about getting a complete, unbiased picture specific to my situation, not just the loudest or most common narratives out there. While business school could provide networking and structured learning, data shows most graduates end up at large firms, not running their own companies. Likewise, many successful founders are forging their own paths without an MBA. I also compared potential earnings—I could match the salary I'd likely make by year three post-MBA by growing my company, without taking on student loans.

Imagine the outcomes: Best case, business school accelerates my network with investors and potential future business partners. I'd also grow skills to grow the business faster and perhaps make fewer mistakes along the way because I have better frameworks for decision-making. But the opportunity cost also meant stepping away at a crucial time and racking up debt. Business school would provide skills but distract me from operations for two years.

I started to look at alternative ways to build a network and gain access to great teachings and did more research on accelerators. I looked at Y Combinator, the top one in Silicon Valley, applied for their office hours, and I started to ask around about 500 Startups, another high-touch accelerator that could amplify our growth with mentors, fundraising help, and product feedback.

Pick your path: I decided not to apply to business school and instead joined 500 Startups's accelerator. For three months, a few team members and I commuted to Mountain View for the program. We rapidly iterated on product-market fit with user interviews and adviser strategy sessions. I expanded my network with venture capitalists and top entrepreneurs. Post-program we doubled our key metrics and closed our million-seed round after the demo day pitch. Applying to 500 Startups versus business school was absolutely the right near-term decision.

The intensive accelerator provided targeted start-up growth support compared to a broader business school curriculum. And participating kept me hands-on as CEO during a crucial growth period, while rapidly expanding my leadership skills and network. The DRIP framework was invaluable for evaluating these very different options quickly and not second-guessing my decision.

"DIFFICULT" = DECISION-MAKER

Making these tough choices, standing your ground, it sort of brands you with a certain label. Some folks—I'm talking about investors, clients, those big shots in advertising agencies—they've taken to calling me "difficult." Why? Because I don't just nod along. I'm discerning and fiercely protective of my company's brand. I refuse to devalue our work or be bullied into submission by a large corporate entity. I don't play the subservient role well, and I don't get swayed by short-term gains at the cost of my long-term vision. I have an unbending commitment to my company, our mission, and the audience.

So here's a little insider tip for anyone chasing a dream: If people start calling you difficult, stubborn, or hard to work with, take it as a compliment. It means you're not willing to compromise on what's important. Embrace it. Being difficult often means you're not willing to settle for less than you deserve. You're not just allowed to be meticulous in your decision-making, you're expected to be. Being considered difficult is a key indicator that you know how to make a damn decision! You make decisions that other people don't like, but who cares? You're making decisions for *you*, not them. This is your show, your rules. You're in the driver's seat, and that's exactly where you need to be.

Many of us are conditioned to avoid conflict, conform to societal expectations, and take the path of least resistance.

This is not a mandate. It's not a one-size-fits-all rule for success. If anything, those who stand their ground, hold on to their vision, and remain unwavering in their point of view are often the ones who end up making the most significant impact.

Remember, you are the CEO of your life, you are rewriting the rules here, and like any good leader, it's crucial to keep in mind that everyone else in the room has their vested interests, perspectives, and limitations. They don't have the complete picture of your truth. It's your duty to steer the ship of your life in the direction you see fit.

Embracing a "take charge and don't look back" decision-making mindset can be applied to any aspect of life or any pillar. Let's say you're committed to a healthier lifestyle and decide to abstain from alcohol. Yet every time you meet your friends, they pressure you into having a drink, because your sobriety makes them uncomfortable. That's not your problem. You are under no obligation to compromise your well-being to fit into someone else's idea of "normal." Or consider this scenario: You're committed to improving your personal finances and choose to DIY your holiday gifts this year instead of splurging. Some may find it "cheap." But you know these gifts were made with love, thought, and a touch of creativity. More important, the decision to go DIY helped you stay on track financially.

As you navigate your path, irrespective of your field or situation, these lessons can serve as guiding beliefs. We all face crossroads in life and business where we must make big choices. You may be the CEO of a company, the head of your household, or the ruler of your own life. Regardless, making decisions can feel daunting. Deciding when to be stubborn or when to let things go is a nuanced process. It involves understanding your core values, the cost and impact of the decision on your larger life vision, and the benefits of remaining flexible.

BE MORE DECISIVE BY MAKING FEWER CHOICES

Now that you have a proven method to work through decisions, I'd like you to consider reducing the number of decisions that you make every day. Have you ever had a workday filled with back-to-back meetings and, by the end of it all, your willpower to make smart and healthy decisions is slim to none? Instead of going to the gym, you just head to the couch and watch TV, even though you commit to exercise at least three times a week. Instead of reading the draft proposal that your employee sent you for review and leaving detailed written comments and notes, you just do a quick skim and mark it approved. Sound familiar? This inability to make the right choice for your truest self is called decision-making fatigue.

I once caught myself in this exact scenario one Thursday afternoon at 4 P.M., feeling overwhelmed by a super detailed email proposal from one of my directors. As I attempted to digest it and craft thoughtful feedback, I could feel my eyes slowly glazing over. I started to write a response but quickly realized I probably wasn't in the best energy flow to think critically and provide my input. Instead of responding, I marked it as "unread" in my inbox and shut down my computer for the night.

The data echoes my own personal experiences. In an analysis of 1,100 parole board decisions, inmates with cases that were first in line to be presented to the board enjoyed a significantly higher probability of early release, compared to their counterparts in identical situations who appeared later in the day. Upon scrutinizing the data, it was revealed that the likelihood of a defendant receiving a favorable outcome was 65 percent at the beginning of each session. This probability plummeted to nearly 0 percent by the session's end. The primary determinant of whether the prisoners were released or not was the parole board's decision fatigue after assessing cases throughout the day.

Your willpower is like a muscle. And, just as the muscles in your arms can get overwhelmed when you constantly use them, so can your decision-making and willpower. Every time you make a choice, it's like lifting a weight. Do you know how your legs feel wobbly at the end of that Pilates class? Your brain gets tired, too. A fatigued mind will lead to uninformed decisions, passive opt-ins, and, worst of all, hesitancy. This is exactly the type of behavior we do *not* want to have while building momentum for our goals.

As a go-getter navigating the roller coaster of life, you're constantly making decisions, big and small. Did you know that by the time you hit the sack, you've made an average of 35,000 decisions in just one day? That's a staggering number! But even though you're well on the way to becoming the CEO of your life, you're not a decision-making machine (yet). So, let's start transforming your perspective on decision-making by asking yourself: What would the best, most wealthy, and most disciplined version of me decide if money was no object? To get your creative juices flowing, let's look at some examples of successful leaders who've mastered the art of decision-making.

A CASE STUDY: THE UNIFORM APPROACH TO DECISION-MAKING

What do Barack Obama, Steve Jobs, Mark Zuckerberg, Carolina Herrera, and Albert Einstein all have in common? They all donned almost the same outfit every single day. By adopting this "uniform" approach, they've significantly reduced the number of daily decisions they need to make, freeing up mental bandwidth to focus on more critical choices.

In an interview with *Vanity Fair* in October 2012, Barack Obama explained his rationale: "I'm trying to pare down decisions. I don't want to make decisions about what I'm eating or wearing. Because I have too many other decisions to make." He added, "You need to focus your decision-making energy. You need to routine yourself. You can't be going through the day distracted by trivia."

Do you find yourself spending precious minutes each morning rummaging through your closet, trying to decide what to wear? Maybe you don't particularly enjoy shopping or picking out outfits, but you still want to look put-together and feel confident. That's where the concept of a daily uniform comes into play.

As a founder navigating the happy hour jungle and pounding the pavement of San Francisco, I faced this dilemma. But lo and behold, I found solace in my trusty Blavity branded tee, black jeans, and the unyielding comfort of combat boots (especially given the amount of walking I was doing to save money on Lyfts). This uniform was the staple of Bay Area start-up gurus, and embracing the drudgery of daily sameness allowed me to reclaim five to ten minutes before evening soirees that I could use to strategize my entrance into the lion's den of Silicon Valley. By streamlining your wardrobe and embracing a go-to outfit, you can reduce decision fatigue and free up more time for other aspects of your life.

Is this extreme? Sure, but are there compounding impacts of saving five to ten minutes, five days a week, for twelve months? Absolutely. Just as financial experts advise you to skip one $5 latte a week to end up saving $260 per year, I'm telling you the same is true of time. Let's say you waste fifteen minutes a week just deciding what to eat (or more, let's be real) and an average of fifteen minutes (conservatively) picking out clothes, you're looking at thirty minutes a week you could save yourself. Annualized, that's twenty-six hours—over a whole freaking day!

Now imagine that instead of wasting time wading through the chaos of your wardrobe and blankly staring at an open fridge, you use those saved minutes to sharpen your skills, expand your network, or spend time on your Passions pillar. Convinced yet? Let's dive deeper into this uniform example and see what your daily look could be and how you can create one that works for you, whether you're a college freshman or corporate executive.

MASTER PREEMPTIVE DECISIONS

Reducing decision-making fatigue and making faster choices can also be achieved by anticipating situations and developing decision-making criteria in advance. By creating "if-then" scenarios, you can make choices proactively, rather than reacting to situations as they arise. This approach can save you time, energy, and stress. Scenario-planning is the process of considering possible situations and determining how you will respond to them. By creating a mental map of potential scenarios, you can reduce decision-making fatigue and make more informed choices.

If one of your priority pillars is Wellness and you've determined that healthy eating is a key thing you want to improve, establish a set of rules for different dining situations to help you make healthier choices. For example:

- If a salad is available, always order it and eat it first.
- If a salad isn't available, order a soup with protein.
- If soup isn't available, avoid white carbs and opt for whole grains or vegetables.

If you're working on your Money pillar, establish rules to help you make smart financial choices.

- If you're tempted to make an impulse purchase, observe a waiting period before buying.
- If you receive a bonus or unexpected income, decide in advance how much you'll save or invest.
- If you're considering a large purchase, have a predetermined set of criteria to evaluate its worth.

The compounded interest of saving time, now that you're better at making decisions and automating your life, will be exponential. In this crazy, fast-paced world where time is a luxury, those reclaimed moments become your secret weapon, allowing you to focus on what's truly important: forging meaningful connections, honing your craft, and feeding your passion. The ripple effect of these seemingly tiny time-saving actions can, over time, launch you into a level of success and personal fulfillment you might never have thought possible.

So when you decide to adopt these practical time-management hacks, you're not just relieving yourself of daily clothing conundrums. Oh no, you're actually embracing the art of being present, making sure every precious second of your life is spent chasing growth, purpose, and success. And that, my friend, is how you win the game of life.

MAKE YOURSELF MORE BORING

You've already gotten hours back in your life. How can we push even further and reclaim more time? Life's complicated enough. Why add extra layers? Simplify the small stuff. I want you to consider the daily routines and habits you have and identify areas where you can reduce the number of choices you make. The goal is to become more predictable and automate routine decisions, allowing you to dedicate your mental bandwidth to your priority pillars and save more time. Become more boring on decisions your brain has to make every day. I want you to become so boring that you have a routine that runs so smoothly it fades into the background, giving your mind the freedom and space to focus on the bigger, brighter, and more exciting aspects of life. Here's how you transform into the most delightfully dull version of yourself, and trust me, your brain will thank you for it.

Wake up at the same time every day. Yes, even on weekends. Why? Because your body clock loves predictability more than a cat loves a cardboard box. When the sun sets and the world whispers goodnight, that's your cue too. Same bedtime, every night. It's like a ritual, but with fewer candles and more Z's.

Take a look at your wardrobe. Find your color, your style. Maybe it's bright spring shades, maybe it's all navy with gold accessories. Whatever it is, let it dominate your closet. It makes your mornings less of a choice, more of a routine. And routines are like comfort food for your brain.

Consider making your daily meals consistent. Why not find that one breakfast that ticks all the boxes? A matcha latte and Greek yogurt with flax seeds, blueberries, and banana perhaps? Make it your morning staple. Same goes for lunch and dinner. A signature dish, repeated. It's like being a regular at a restaurant, but that restaurant is your kitchen. Efficient, easy, no daily menu dilemmas. Consistent sleep, a streamlined closet.

It's not just about being boring. It's about freeing up mental space for the big leagues—the stuff that really matters. And in the grand scheme of things, being a bit predictable is a small price to pay for a mind as sharp and focused as yours is going to be. This lifestyle isn't about removing all spontaneity, it's about creating a framework within which spontaneity can flourish. When the big decisions are already made— when to wake, what to wear, what to eat—you have more mental bandwidth for creativity, problem-solving, and, yes, even a little bit of chaos. I want to challenge you to give it a try. Pick one of these items and have the discipline to try it for seven days. I know, I know—it might feel a little weird at first. But trust me, once you start reaping the benefits of a more streamlined life, you'll be a boring convert in no time.

THE SEVEN-DAY BE BORING CHALLENGE

Breakfast: For one week, commit to eating the same breakfast every single day. It could be something as simple as avocado toast or a protein smoothie. At the end of the week, reflect on how it felt to have one less decision to make each morning. Did it free up mental space? Did it make your mornings feel a little less hectic? Eating the same meal every day at least once a day can save you a significant amount of time and mental energy. Bob Iger, CEO of Disney, reportedly ate the same meal every day, regardless of the meeting he was attending. I've personally seen it. One time I was in a group lunch meeting with Disney and we were all served the standard delicious catered meal, but Bob's chief of staff personally brought him some sort of protein grain bar.

The Capsule Wardrobe: Take a hard look at your closet and pick out a few key pieces that you love and feel great in. Challenge yourself to create a capsule wardrobe for the next week, mixing and matching these pieces to create different outfits. Set it aside in your closet so you know exactly where to look. Notice how it feels to have a more limited, but still stylish, set of options to choose from each day.

The Boring Bedtime: Lastly, set a consistent bedtime for yourself, and stick to it as closely as possible. Get your sound machine, put on pajamas, let go of your phone, and go to bed!

Keep a journal to track how you feel each day. Do you notice a difference in your energy levels? Your ability to concentrate? Your overall mood?

Give boring a chance. Start small and see how it feels.

The actual amount of time saved will differ for each individual based on their unique situation and the efficiency gains they experience from adopting these strategies. Yet the key takeaway is that implementing even a few of these techniques can lead to significant time savings, allowing you to dedicate more time to what truly matters.

Trust that over time, making decisions for yourself will feel easier and more natural. You'll still value input from those you respect but you'll retain clarity on determining the right path for yourself. That confidence in your own judgment will empower you tremendously in staying true to the new direction in which your life is headed. And on that note, let's get ready to tackle something that looms large for everyone: fear.

9

BE THE ROUGH DRAFT: A BETTER
RELATIONSHIP WITH FEAR

There's a peculiar kind of exhilaration that accompanies growth in your life. You're feeling stretched thin, like a rubber band on the verge of snapping. By now, as you've implemented new mindsets and strategies, you might be feeling anxious, uncomfortable, and downright fearful. Fantastic!

When it comes to facing our fears and pursuing personal growth, it's tempting to wait until we feel completely ready, until we've perfected our approach and eliminated all potential for failure. But the truth is, this perfectionist mindset can be paralyzing, keeping you stuck in a cycle of fear and inaction. To conquer your fears as you gallantly move your life in the direction of your dreams, you need to embrace the power of being a "rough draft," tackling your fears head-on, even when you feel imperfect or unprepared.

Think of facing your fears as the first draft of a brave new story you're writing. Like any rough draft, it might be messy, uncomfortable, and filled with uncertainty. But it's also a crucial first step, a bold leap into the unknown that sets the stage for living based on your new set of rules, vision, and Wealth Code.

When you embrace the concept of being a rough draft, you give yourself permission to be imperfect in the face of fear. Imagine life's going smoothly, everything's flowing, and then, suddenly, you hit a bump—your dreams are tugging you one way, but then your job or family responsibilities pull you another way. What you're feeling are the glorious growing pains of stepping out of your comfort zone. Take a deep breath and lean into it.

Fear. It sneaks in and turns up the intensity. It's the worry about what'll happen next, of making a bad decision, of things actually working out. Or that uneasy feeling about stepping out of your comfort zone that can cause you to sabotage yourself. Fear just makes everything feel more overwhelming.

But fear is just a part of the rough draft. When you're writing the first version of your new story, fear is the red pen that marks up all the areas that need attention and revision. It's not a sign that you're on the wrong track, but rather an indication that you're pushing yourself into the realm of transformation.

Now, I'm not talking about the obvious, stomach-churning terror that we associate with things like skydiving or public speaking. More often, it's the quiet, insidious kind of fear that disguises itself as rational thinking or practicality. That's the fear we're going to get better at tackling in this chapter.

It's the voice in your head that says, "Who am I to start my own business? I don't have what it takes." Or "I can't ask for that raise—what if they laugh me out of the office?" Or "I shouldn't express my real feelings—what if they reject me?"

Instead of letting fear paralyze you, let's learn how to embrace it as a natural part of the process. Every great story, every masterpiece, starts with a messy, imperfect draft. And just like a writer who keeps showing up to the page, day after day, you too can learn to face your fears with courage and patience.

There's a valuable lesson I've learned on my journey, especially during my high-growth phases in life. When you're knee-deep in anxiety and discomfort, you're probably *exactly* where you need to be. Remember, growth doesn't come from standing still. It comes from pushing your limits, stretching your boundaries, and learning to dance with the discomfort. I want you to hold on to this throughout your journey: *Be the rough draft as big fear begets big change.*

STRETCHING IN THE FACE OF FEAR

After three years in business, I was finishing integrating our first acquisition of an entertainment site called Shadow and Act. We were moving into our second office, the team was expanding, and the energy when you walked into the lobby every day was electric. Blavity Inc. was well on its way to transitioning from a small brand founded by a team of young Black kids to a real competitor in the digital media space. We were weeks out from our second AfroTech conference when I finished closing the acquisition of a travel and lifestyle company called Travel Noire. The company, led by a fiercely ambitious and visionary founder, Zim Flores, had become a beacon of diaspora travel culture. Travel Noire had hundreds of thousands of followers on Instagram and millions of comments from a niche-engaged audience. But, like many pioneering brands, it had also encountered its share of growth challenges. The company was having operational setbacks from scaling and was looking for a larger entity that could handle the ebbs and flows of the seasonal travel world and stabilize its cash flow.

My mind was buzzing with energy and anticipation as I entered the final stages of negotiation and diligence on the deal. We were about to take a bold leap of faith. It was not normal for a business less than five years old to attempt an acquisition, let alone two within eighteen months of each other. Yet I knew that this acquisition could be a transformative move for our company, allowing us to broaden our audience and deepen our impact. Travel Noire wasn't just an Instagram account and tour operator. It was a movement that inspired people of color to explore the world and share their unique experiences. We worked hard to close the deal and envision a new chapter for the brand.

What I didn't anticipate, however, was the labyrinth of operational issues that came with it after the contract was signed. The once-enticing opportunity quickly transformed into a multifaceted challenge. There were surprises in our post-acquisition integration, unanticipated costs, and execution risks of managing travel tours overseas that threatened to derail our grand vision of a profitable impact-driven media company. Where were these unexpected new resources going to come from?

My ambition had led me to acquire a unique business. But

as the reality of these unforeseen complexities set in, a shadow of fear crept over me. Fear of failure. Fear of disappointing my employees. Fear of embarrassing our company and Zim, and letting down our customers. In the face of these fears, I had a choice to make: Succumb to the pressure and retreat to the safety of convention, or rise to the occasion and prove that our unique approach could weather any storm. I chose the latter. I chose to lean into the uncertainty, to view each challenge as an opportunity to learn, grow, and innovate. I chose to lead by example, showing my team that we could adapt and thrive in the face of adversity.

I knew there was no way I was facing my fears alone, so I turned to my most reliable team members to form an internal war room that strategized, faced each problem, and adapted our plans in real time. We met twice a week to tackle each issue head-on, brainstorming, problem-solving, and systematically knocking out each surprise that came our way. But this wasn't just an effort on behalf of my immediate circle. I had to lean on a broader network too. When unexpected costs threatened to strain our existing operations, I rallied our investors and raised an additional $300,000 in less than six weeks. This influx of capital ensured that the operational surprise presented by acquiring Travel Noire didn't pull us under. And it was in this crucible of doubt and determination that I forged a deeper understanding of what it means to truly break the mold. It's not about avoiding the unknown—it's about embracing it with open arms. It's about having the courage to take risks. It's about the humility to learn from mistakes. It's about the resilience to keep pushing forward, no matter what obstacles lie in my path.

BREAKING THE MOLD

What holds you back? Fear of success? The unknown? Judgment of others? Rewriting the rules you're living by is a process of breaking through your fears and addressing them head-on. Many of us were raised in homes and environments where big risks were discouraged. Putting yourself out there comes with uncertainty, but it's an essential part of pushing through our limitations and achieving personal growth. Fears are inevitable, so it's up to us not to get rid of them entirely, but rather to proactively manage them into a background hum. Run down the list of excellence that has come before you: politicians, athletes, executives, and innovators. I'd be shocked if none of them had felt the friction and the pangs of fear. What accelerated them to greatness was their ability to push past the discomfort and see what lay on the other side.

There are two fears that we're going to dig deeper into:

1. Fear of Success and of Failure
2. Fear of Rejection

When we listen to these fears, when we let them dictate our actions and decisions, we end up undermining our own success. We procrastinate, we make excuses, we settle for less than we deserve. We keep ourselves small and safe instead of taking the risks that could lead to big rewards.

But here's the messed-up thing: We often don't even realize we're doing it. We convince ourselves that we're being responsible, or realistic, or protecting ourselves from failure. But in reality, we're just letting fear run the show. I want you to go on the offensive when it comes to your fears and use the tools from this chapter to build a foundation to address them.

Understanding How Fear Plays Out in Your Life

When I was in the process of raising our Series A round of funding in 2018, I'd been on what felt like an endless treadmill of meetings, speaking with every media investor who'd give me the time of day. The good news? We were gaining traction, and the funding round was going better than expected. The not-so-good news? Finding someone to lead the round, and to set the terms that all the other investors would follow, was proving to be a herculean task.

You see, many were ready to place a moderate bet, somewhere in the ballpark of $250K to $500K, hoping against hope that we'd defy the odds. However, the lead investor usually shoulders about half of the round, translating to an investment of roughly $3 to $4 million in our case. They'd take a seat on our board, becoming my partner in turning our fledgling venture into a scalable business model. It's not just about the financial risk, it's about committing to the time and effort, akin to a long, complex marriage.

Here's the elephant in the room: Attracting predominantly white, male investment firms to commit to a Black-owned company serving Black audiences, with a big, ambitious vision, was an uphill battle. While many acknowledged the potential market, personal uncertainties shrouded their confidence to the point where leading the round seemed like too much of a gamble. The rejections began to weigh heavily on me, and as our bank account dwindled, the sense of defeat started to settle in like an ominous cloud.

Fast-forward to that spring when I found myself at the huge festival South by Southwest, hoping to escape the all-consuming fundraising and soak up some energy from fellow founders. A few days in, I attended a Black founders happy hour at a local barbecue joint. I ended up sitting next to none other than Lo Toney, then a partner at Google Ventures (GV). Lo was, in a sense, a mythical creature in our circles— a Black partner at a high-profile VC: rarely seen but much talked about.

Lo casually asked how things were going with Blavity. Ex-hausted, I decided to bare it all. I told him about my struggles to find a lead investor, about the near-empty coffers, and about the term sheet I was hesitant to accept. He suggested I pitch to GV, to which my initial reaction was a disbelieving snort. GV, with only one Black founder in their portfolio, seemed light-years away. But Lo's next words sparked a glimmer of hope. "Well, if I can get you a meeting, can you make it to San Francisco next week?"

At this point, my sheer exhaustion from the process over-powered any influence that my friend fear was trying to wield and I quickly agreed. Later that night, as I scrolled through my emails in the quiet of my hotel room on Austin's out-skirts, there it was—a meeting invitation with John Lyman, a partner at GV. Suddenly, I was on the precipice of an oppor-tunity that could change everything. My brain wanted to run the other way and not respond to the meeting request, but I squashed my own impulse to self-sabotage and pressed ac-cept.

A few days later, I stepped off a plane in San Francisco, making my way to GV's office lobby. I ascended to the sixth floor and found myself seated across from John in a small conference room. No slides, no fancy presentations, just me, John, and the raw, unfiltered vision for Blavity. The exchange was enlightening. John grasped the scope of the opportunity swiftly, promising to mull it over and schedule another meeting with a broader set of partners.

And so, after a few weeks, I found myself back in San Francisco, crashing on a friend's couch in Oakland, and preparing for a second meeting. This time, the room held a more seasoned partner with extensive media experience and an associate whose technical expertise and personal connection to our core demographic added another dimension to the discussion. We conversed, exchanged ideas, and probed one another's thoughts. I felt a sense of accomplishment as I exited the meeting. There was a hint of potential success in the air.

But then, a twist: The final approval still needed a larger partner meeting, which made me apprehensive. I had always handled fundraising calls and meetings alone but questioned if I should do so with this larger meeting.

As a female founder, I understood that the world is quick to attribute your company's success to male co-founders, with the woman often typecast as a symbolic figurehead.

Let me draw your attention to a phenomenon that often goes unmentioned, lurking behind closed doors and in boardroom meetings: the subtle, yet pervasive, bias against women in leadership roles. My co-founders Aaron and Jeff are skilled, charismatic, and innately talented. Aaron possesses a magnetic personality that immediately attracts and engages, while Jeff's technical prowess adds depth to our team. Both are essential elements of our collective strength, a balanced trifecta of charisma, technical know-how, and strategic vision. Yet, my fear was not rooted in their abilities, but in a societal bias that might diminish my role as the operating CEO.

This bias exists on a subconscious level, often unintentionally. It manifests as a quiet underestimation of a woman's capabilities, a readiness to attribute her success to the men on her team, and a willingness to question her competence. Shaking hands with a new person at an event who assumes my male employee in sales standing next to me is the CEO and I'm his assistant. A supervisor automatically attributing a win to your male colleague who wasn't even on your project.

If you identify as a woman, you know what I'm talking about. It's a bias that whispers that a woman must have had help, must have been guided, or, worse, must have merely been lucky. This constant undermining can lead women to doubt their own success, question their skills, and second-guess their decisions. These biases create a hostile environment, forcing women to constantly prove their worth and justify their positions. It's a wearisome burden that chips away at confidence and breeds insecurity. It sows seeds of doubt where conviction should bloom, and it was precisely this bias that I feared might be at play if the investor joining our board overlooked my leadership capabilities with two of my male co-founders seated next to me.

The introspection on the cause of my fear was difficult but necessary. It forced me to confront my fear of success, fear of belonging, and fear of self-doubt. I had to remind myself that my success was not a fluke or a byproduct of luck or male assistance. It was a result of my hard work, vision, and determination. Why shouldn't I, too, be a top founder and have my Series A led by GV? Why shouldn't this room of partners feel comfortable, maybe even excited, about the fact that this company is genuinely led by a woman?

As I pondered my dilemma, I found myself at a crossroads: Did I showcase our cohesive teamwork by enlisting the support of my team? Or did I let my worry that I wouldn't be taken seriously overshadow what would be best for the company? It was about reaffirming my position and proving that my success was not a byproduct of my male co-founders' input, but a result of my capabilities as a leader, strategist, and innovator. It was about accepting the reality of these biases and still choosing to believe in my abilities, assert my worth, and command the respect and recognition I deserved.

I vowed to face my fears head-on. My worth, and our collective team's value, was nonnegotiable. I needed to put my fear of not being seen as a badass CEO aside. I knew the power in numbers was going to result in the best outcome. I had to trust that, even flanked by my male co-founders, I would still shine. Though I had the capacity to do it alone, I asked Aaron to join the meeting and requested that Jeff cut his Dubai trip short. I knew having my business partners by my side would help me not revert to old habits of self-sabotage. They both agreed, and we began preparing for what we hoped would be our final pitch. To manage my fears I openly talked to Aaron and Jeff about the possibility of a room full of men defaulting to them instead of me, the leader of this fundraising effort. Not through any fault of their own; it was something I asked that they proactively keep in mind as we managed the presentation and Q&A section.

Finally, the day came, a culmination of countless hours of hard work and determination. Sitting in that room, encircled by VCs at a long, impressive conference table, I was acutely aware of the gravity of the moment. The air crackled with anticipation, every eye on us, waiting to be captivated. We were ready to seize this opportunity with both hands.

We stepped forward with authenticity and confidence, our unity palpable. It felt like we were in perfect harmony, each of us playing our part in a well-orchestrated performance. Our presentation was more than a mere pitch, it was a vibrant tapestry we wove, showcasing our synergy and the strategic vision we held for the company.

Our meticulous planning paid off. We had devised subtle cues and strategies, ensuring that my voice, as the leader, remained the focal point of our narrative. This wasn't just about asserting my role, it was about reinforcing the idea that I was the linchpin of our vision. Every time I spoke, it wasn't just words filling the room, it was our dreams, our aspirations, our future.

After the meeting, we grabbed lunch at a nearby Mexican restaurant and the team disbanded. Aaron headed back down to Palo Alto and Jeff hopped on another plane to Dubai to rejoin his family vacation. I returned to my friend's couch, a sense of satisfaction washing over me. I knew I'd given it my all, leaving no room for regret. Even if GV decided to pass on the deal, it wouldn't be because I shied away from confronting my fear of success and dwelling in the "what-ifs." I walked away knowing I had stepped into the arena, faced the top partners, and done everything within my power to seize the opportunity for our growing company.

I headed back to L.A. a few days later and stayed glued to my inbox while continuing with my daily responsibilities, yet the air seemed to hum with the unspoken question: "Did we make it?" I could barely sleep that Sunday night knowing that within twenty-four hours we would hear back. Most venture funds make final deal decisions after their Monday general partners investment meetings. The answer came not in a whisper, but with the resonating boom of a gavel, sealing a decision. I received an email from John to get on a quick call, and he told me they were in! GV was going to lead our Series A funding round, and they wanted to invest an incredible $5.5 million into our company. With that investment, they placed their faith in our vision, capabilities, and me as the operating CEO. John joined our board. He brought with him not only GV's network, but his expertise, insights, and faith in our capacity. More than that, he was an ally, open and respectful, who recognized my role and worked in tandem with me.

In the subsequent six years, we established a transparent and respectful working relationship. There was no undermining, no bias toward me as a female leader, just an understanding of our respective roles as investors and founders and the shared goal of steering the company toward success. The GV deal was more than a financial win, it was a testament to our innovation and an affirmation of my leadership. The process allowed me to confront my fears, question societal norms, and emerge victorious, not in spite of being a woman leader, but because of it.

Fear. It's a four-letter word that has the power to stop us

dead in our tracks, paralyzing us with uncertainty and clouding our judgment. My experience with GV made me realize that fear isn't something that evaporates with growth; rather, it's a companion that runs alongside us, a shadow cast by our achievements and ambitions. It becomes especially potent when we're facing the prospect of pushing ourselves to new heights. This fear isn't necessarily a foe but a signal—an indicator that we're on the precipice of something significant. Instead of seeing fear as the enemy, it's so important to view your nervous partner as a best friend.

FEAR OF SUCCESS AND OF FAILURE

Who will you become if you win? What would happen if things actually work out? Have you ever envisioned the increased responsibilities that come from actually achieving your goals and dreaded the expectation of continuing to keep up that high-quality output? Yeah, that's fear creeping in.

As a CEO, I have often grappled with various fears that commonly emerge alongside new milestones in business.

Hitting one hundred employees? Enter fear: the pressure cooker responsibility of holding people's livelihoods in my hands.

Achieving $40 million in revenue while remaining profitable? Enter fear: That number was a one-hit wonder.

Receiving an email from a top VC requesting a meeting? Enter fear: Am I ready? Cue conveniently "forgetting" to respond because I was at a loss for words.

The most formidable fear I have had to confront actively in

my life is the fear of success. A lot of times, the fear of success is really just the fear of failure in disguise. But here's the thing—failure is not the opposite of success, it's a necessary part of the journey. External validation like awards and funding rounds stirred pride in me but also profound discomfort. As the business continued to grow and thrive, I was scared of the all-consuming nature that comes along with a profitable business. Would I have time for my identity outside of Blavity? For my loved ones and the ability to build a future family?

On the flip side, I was also scared that Blavity would become so enormous that if it failed, everything would come crashing down. Knowing that so many eyes watched our trajectory as an outlier Black-founded start-up company bred a subconscious pressure. If I stumbled after coming so far, I felt that it would reverberate beyond normal start-up business failure and potentially be a signal that investing in a Black consumer and audience was too risky.

My friend, fear of success, visited me every step of the way.

While being a Black female founder in white-male dominated spaces carried distinct challenges, my central fear of success traced more to perfectionism and control tendencies. External praise triggered imposter syndrome rather than pride in milestones achieved. Turns out playing the underdog felt way safer—people root for the little guy! And with scale arose heightened responsibility for staff livelihoods now dependent on Blavity's continued success.

Let's get clear on what the fear of success actually is. It's not about being afraid of accomplishing your goals or making a ton of money. It's about being afraid of *the consequences of success*—the added responsibility, the heightened potential for failure, the shifts it might bring to your relationships and your sense of self.

See if any of these sound familiar.

- You're convinced that even if you do achieve success, you won't be able to sustain it. You'll just end up failing and losing everything you've gained.
- You're constantly compromising your own goals and dreams to keep the peace and avoid conflict or judgment from people close to you.
- You procrastinate completing projects or reaching your goals because of the extra responsibility, recognition, or criticism you may face.
- You set unrealistically high standards for yourself and feel like anything less than perfect is not worth your time and effort.

So how do you manage it? Well, remember the team of people we put together earlier? Or DRIP, our decision-making framework? You leverage the tools you have around you to trick your brain into action. Fear loves company, and if you're hanging out with a bunch of people who are also afraid of success, who want to play by the rules, you're going to stay stuck. You surround yourself with people who are playing big and hold you accountable to playing big too. When you surround yourself with risk-takers, people who are pushing through their own fears and creating extraordinary lives, it starts to rub off on you. You start to see what's possible, and you start to normalize the belief that you can do it too.

FEAR OF REJECTION

Rejection, while often perceived as an overwhelmingly negative experience, is rarely as devastating as our brains imagine. However, research has revealed that social rejection can actually feel like physical pain because it activates the same regions of the brain. The more intense the rejection, the higher the pain response experienced.

The fear of rejection can show up in various aspects of life, causing self-doubt and self-sabotage and impeding growth. This fear can present itself in the form of evading social situations or remaining silent during meetings, driven by the dread of judgment or criticism. For instance, if you have ever hesitated to get a new colleague's number at a networking event because you "don't want to bother them," that's fear of rejection in action. This apprehension can breed self-doubt, stagnating both personal growth and career advancement.

Social psychology proposes that the opposite of rejection is social acceptance, which means that you feel wanted and included in groups. Social acceptance actually sits on a continuum where one side of the spectrum is merely tolerating someone's existence and the other is the active pursuit of connection. It's possible for someone to experience both social acceptance and rejection chronically—both of which can have major impacts on how they view the world and approach situations. Someone who's always felt accepted is more likely to never have a problem getting the dream job, the party invites, and the romantic partners. They haven't been rejected much, so there's nothing to fear. Conversely, those who have a history of rejection in certain or all areas of life are understandably fearful that it will keep happening, and therefore more hesitant to put themselves out there.

The need to belong boils down to keeping long-lasting relationships, which requires frequent positive social contact and mutual concern for one another. Because humans evolved in small groups, cooperative living was the main line to survival. In that way, the fear of social rejection is actually motivating! It helps prevent you from being left out of the group and not getting resources, like protection, food, water, and shelter. Or, in modern times, it helps make sure you get social support, money, and opportunity.

Have a look at this list and see if there is anything that makes your heart drop a little. If any of the following resonate with you, you may be afraid of rejection.

- You hesitate to share your ideas or proposals with clients or stakeholders, because you're afraid of being rejected or having your work criticized.
- You hold back from sharing your opinions or suggestions in meetings, online, or in public forums, because you fear being dismissed or ridiculed by your colleagues, society, or superiors.
- You stick to tried-and-true methods or ideas, because you're afraid of proposing something innovative or unconventional that might be rejected.
- You take on extra work or overwork on projects, even if it means sacrificing your personal life, because you want to prove your worth and avoid being seen as dispensable.

- You have difficulty speaking up for yourself, setting boundaries, or saying no to others for fear of disappointing them or losing their approval.
- You avoid attending industry events or reaching out to new contacts because you're afraid of being rejected or feeling out of place in professional social situations.
- You struggle with negotiating for more money because you fear being turned down, losing the opportunity, or being viewed as undeserving.

Rejection is a normal part of life, and everyone experiences it at some point. With that in mind, I want you to start viewing rejection as motivation to form these important relationships. You deserve to be included. You can be included. You *will* be included. If you're not, then you won't get a piece of the pie. Does that scare the daylights out of you? Let's start small.

One way to improve your resilience to social rejection is to gradually increase opportunities where experiencing it is possible. See someone's outfit at the gym you like? Ask where they got it. Checking in to a hotel and want a corner room? Ask them for it. Want a specific drink not on the menu? Ask the bartender. We often expect the worst, yet people are generally benevolent, flattered, and just as insecure as you—if not more so.

This deliberate practice, often referred to as "exposure therapy," can help desensitize us to the sting of rejection, build our emotional resilience, and create critical interpersonal connections that help bring you the social acceptance you need to succeed. As we become more accustomed to facing rejection, we can develop the courage to take risks and seize opportunities. How do you put this into action? Target the type of rejection you're most worried about and practice exposure at a pace you can handle. When things get complicated, remind yourself of the benefits of building a more robust mental muscle with rejection.

CREATE ROUGH DRAFTS

You know that feeling when you're completely lost in something you love doing? Maybe it's playing guitar, putting together LEGO, playing with puppies at the pound, or even just tinkering with some random DIY project. It's like the world around you just disappears and you're in this awesome little bubble of pure, unadulterated joy. That's your Passions pillar peeking through. It's a beautiful escape from the constant pressure to perform, to meet expectations, and to be "good enough." In this sacred space, you're free to explore, to experiment, and to simply be, without the fear of judgment or rejection.

Think of your passion projects as the rough drafts of your life's masterpiece. Just like a writer who fearlessly puts pen to paper, knowing that the first draft will be imperfect and messy, you too can approach your hobbies and interests with a sense of playful experimentation and self-compassion. When you're engaged in a hobby, you give yourself permission to just be. To play around and to suck at something without beating yourself up about it. Embracing our inner rookie is not just okay, it's essential for growth and mastery. In fact, environmental mastery, which is the ability to feel competent and able to manage a complex environment, is one of the six dimensions of psychological well-being established by psychologist and researcher Carol Ryff. We need to feel like we are in control of our surroundings and proficient in the contexts we create for ourselves.

This is why you probably recoil at the thought of being unskilled, but I need you to push through that feeling. I want you to accept that it's totally normal to be bad at something initially. In fact, it's a requirement. How can you fight back against those feelings of inadequacy? As I mentioned earlier, my preferred method is exposure therapy through practice. Here's the beautiful thing about the rough draft: It's not about perfection, it's about progress. Every time you show up to your passion projects, every time you allow yourself to be a beginner and embrace the messiness of the process, you're rewriting your own rules for what's possible within a new endeavor. You're learning, growing, and discovering new aspects of yourself that you never knew existed.

And just like a rough draft that gets better with each revision, your skills and confidence will grow with each imperfect attempt. You'll start to see *progress,* not perfection, as the true measure of success.

Now, this does involve *deliberately* putting yourself in situations where you're not very good at the skill or task at hand. So what do you say? Ready to be the rough draft?

Here's what I want you to do. Pick a hobby—tap into that Passions pillar you defined earlier and pick something! A quick reminder: A hobby, by definition, should have *nothing* to do with your achievements, external validation, or expertise. While many people can become very skilled at hobbies, it is not a requirement to start or engage in one. It also doesn't matter if you remain terrible at it forever. If you embrace the rough draft and keep showing up, you start to build incredible resilience. Hobbies are great places for practicing the not-so-great feeling of fear.

In my advising programs, I frequently inquire about my clients' lives beyond the confines of their work and family commitments. Unsurprisingly, many have lost touch with the enchantment of hobbies and leisure activities that once brought them joy. To delve deeper, I often ask them to reminisce about the pastimes they relished during their college or high school years—perhaps gaming, cycling, or playing basketball. Personally, I used to lose myself in painting and attending art classes. However, as I matured and embarked on my entrepreneurial journey, I ignored pursuing my real passions. I had also started following many other artists who had turned their passion for painting into a career, and there was a voice in the back of my head that said I could never be as good as they were because for me it was just a hobby.

But I told that voice to beat it! I went to the art store and bought paints, brushes, and canvases to fill. I knew I wouldn't be a fine artist at first, or maybe ever, but that wasn't the point! When I pick up a brush, I remind myself I'm painting for me, not for anyone else's approval. Art has become a space where mistakes aren't failures, but, as iconic fine artist Bob Ross used to say, "happy little accidents" and opportunities to learn.

Leaning into activities where I'm a novice has been tremendously liberating. Mastery isn't the goal—joyful self-expression and discovery are the rewards. It's helped quiet my inner critic. I let go of control and perfectionism and make room for self-compassion. I tap into unbridled creativity versus polished performance. Don't let not being the best at something stop you from doing it or enjoying it. I like to purposely put myself in situations where I know I am the least qualified person in the room. As an adult, a positive place to start is with all the forsaken hobbies or activities you once adored, feeling the weight of the belief that you're no longer proficient enough.

Rekindling your love for a long-lost hobby or embracing a new one can not only strengthen your resilience to your fears, but it also has the added benefit of reigniting your passions and fostering a sense of balance in your life. Science has proved that leisure and recreational activities offer a preventative remedy for adversity, coping strategies for stress, and a way to push past challenging moments in life. Seeking experiences that produce happiness and pleasure will not only increase the value or impact of leisure in your life, but they will also increase your capacity to use recreation as a tool to increase mental and physical health and well-being. It'll help the fears dissipate in other areas of your life.

When you permit yourself to engage in activities without the pressure of rejection, you create space for exploration, experimentation, and learning. What if, by embracing the notion of being unskilled, you create an opportunity to unleash creativity and evolve in ways previously unimagined? Whether it's painting, taking a software class online, or trying to learn a new language at forty years old, embrace the experience of being imperfect. Remember, engaging in something you think you're "bad" at doesn't need to have any end result other than simple pleasure.

Take the pottery class without future-scaping into a world where you are so good you start an online store, leave your job, and have a ceramics empire. Just try to make a bowl and laugh at yourself as you go. Picking up a hobby does not make you, in any way, obligated to turn it into a small business or grow a following on social media. No one needs to see, or even know about, what you do for pure pleasure. My hope for you is that as you flex your fear-fighting muscle through your hobby, you'll cultivate a deep sense of self-acceptance, resilience, and courage that will permeate every aspect of your life. For more practice fighting fear and embracing imperfection, visit MorganDeBaun.com and join my free online hobby challenge.

TAKE CONTROL OF YOUR FEARS

In 2019, I received an invitation to the Lobby conference in Hawaii—an exclusive invite-only (not to mention very expensive) event shrouded in mystery, often whispered about among the Silicon Valley elite, but seemingly inaccessible. I sought the opinion of my now board member John Lyman from Google Ventures on whether I should attend (secretly hoping for permission to decline so I might continue my introverted grind). To my surprise, he strongly encouraged my participation. So I booked my flight, reserved a room, and, six months later, found myself surrounded by CEOs who led billion-dollar businesses and had raised hundreds of millions of dollars, seated along with their angel investors and infamous already-exited founders. Wearing a simple skirt and T-shirt, I headed to the welcome reception.

The atmosphere was lively, with music playing, hors d'oeuvres being passed around, and approximately two hundred people mingling as if they were attending a family reunion. The only person I knew at the event was Peter Pham, the man who had nominated me for an invitation, but I couldn't find him. Overwhelmed, I grabbed some bites, wrapped them in a napkin, and retreated to my hotel room, leaving the reception behind.

I spent most of my time during the conference either in my hotel room or at the pool restaurant, only venturing out to join the morning activities and bonfire dinner on the second day. I rationalized my isolation by attributing it to my introverted nature and a never-ending flood of emails, granting myself mental permission not to seize opportunities to connect with and learn from my fellow executives. I was plagued by countless "what-if" scenarios: What if potential collaborators incorrectly believed Blavity was merely a shell company? What if an angel investor wanted to explore further opportunities post-retreat, only to lengthen my to-do list? What if, after introducing myself to someone new, they lost interest upon learning I led a media company focused on Black consumers, instead of a business-to-business, Software as a Service (SaaS) firm catering to automating mechanics' invoices? Terrified of exposing myself to increased risk and judgment, I opted to isolate myself within certain circles rather than participate in the community I had worked tirelessly to join. Oh, the irony!

Crushing our fears means we've got to hug vulnerability, flex our resilience muscles, and hold firm to our growth-driven mindset. By recognizing the value of setbacks and overcoming our fear of rejection, we can unlock our true potential and chart a course toward personal and professional fulfillment. Once I saw the sheer number of opportunities I was passing up, I revamped my conference game plan with some severe prep action.

Now when I hit up conferences, I take control! I have my assistant dive deep into research mode ahead of time. We scope out faces and information from the social profiles of other attendees as soon as that list drops. I show up to every meal and make sure I'm on time, so I can schmooze with new peeps at the table. I preblock my calendar for the week after to manage follow-ups and reduce my anxiety. This is my strategy—a calculated approach to address my apprehensions and fears. Embracing what I can control and giving myself permission to strategize. Tackling your fears changes the entire game.

So, what about you? How can you face your fears and get a better handle on what you can control? The key lies in understanding what exactly you're afraid of. Is it a fear of the unknown? Of not being good enough? Or is it the dread of rejection or failure? To understand your fears, you need to turn inward. Get in touch with yourself. Recall instances when you felt afraid and analyze them. What were the circumstances? How did you react? The answers to these questions will give you insights into how to control your fears. It's what I did.

Ask yourself: Where does my manifestation of fear as the

leader of my life lie? How do I transform it into an area I can control better rather than have it remain a stumbling block? Overcoming my own fear of failure and of success is an ongoing process. It doesn't happen overnight. Every success story is punctuated with episodes of failure. And failure, in its essence, is just an opportunity to learn, grow, and make better-informed decisions moving forward.

Fear is normal, and suppressing it will only cause it to control you. Embrace that it's okay to have fears at all. Then, armed with the knowledge and tools from the previous chapters, create a plan. A leader, when faced with fear, doesn't cower or freeze. They acknowledge the fear, analyze it, and formulate a strategy to address it.

Fear, in its essence, is a reaction to perceived threat or risk. And where there's risk, there's also the potential for growth, success, and progress. Risk can be managed. So move toward fear, not away from it, and actually manage it. Understand your fears, plan for them, and maybe even use your fear to your advantage. Remember, you're the boss of your life.

Once you start adopting a mindset that values adaptability and resilience, you can thrive amid uncertainty and harness the potential that lies within change.

UNCOVERING FEAR AND GOING ON THE OFFENSIVE

Use the following prompts to help uncover the fears that may be holding you back.

- Reflect on a past experience of rejection. Consider how it shaped you and what you learned from it. How can you apply that wisdom to future situations?
- Identify a situation where you've held back due to fear. Visualize yourself taking action and facing the potential fear head-on. What steps can you take to confront this fear in reality?
- Set a small, achievable goal that involves the risk of rejection, such as making a new connection on LinkedIn or writing out your idea for a business process change to your team lead. Take note of how you feel before, during, and after the experience.
- Practice self-compassion by writing a letter to yourself, acknowledging your fears and offering encouragement. Remind yourself that rejection is a natural part of life and it does not define you.
- Identify areas in your life where you can deliberately expose yourself to potential rejection. Create a plan to regularly engage in these activities to build emotional resilience and decrease your fear of rejection over time.

10

In 2020, in the aftermath of the first bout of COVID-19, I found myself running on fumes. I was at odds with my co-founders, drained by the impossible toll of decisions that had to be made to keep the company afloat, and frankly tired of feeling like the weight of our company was on my shoulders. I mourned the year that could've been, the balanced life I had painstakingly crafted, and a horizon that seemed to recede further into the distance with each passing day.

Despite the tumult, our company had seen its most successful quarter yet, with several subsequent profitable quarters in our wake. I had operated the heck out of the company and scaled every mountain in my path with a tenacity that deserved recognition and, quite frankly, a breather. I went to the internet and googled top countries that were safest for women to travel to solo and went online to look for houses in Costa Rica. I called up two of my friends, Melissa Butler (The Lip Bar founder) and Simone Tyler (a fellow executive at

Blavity who ran our sales team). A few months later, Simone, Melissa, and I found ourselves nestled in a car, weaving through lush landscapes on our way to a serene yoga retreat in Nosara, a gem on Costa Rica's resplendent Pacific coast. It was Thanksgiving week, but we were about to celebrate freedom.

We made a pact right then and there—the next thirty days were ours and ours alone. A vacation from the rest of the world, dictated solely by our whims and fancies. We'd been toeing the line of responsibility for far too long, treading the delicate tightrope of perfection. Now it was time to shed the shackles and unapologetically embrace our own idiosyncrasies. Who needs a bra when you can breathe free? Only juice for lunch and dinner? Why not? Deep-sea fishing despite my knack for turning green at the mere sway of a boat? Bring it on! The calendar no longer ruled my day, my desires did.

Armed with a journal and my watercolor paints, I embarked on a journey of self-rediscovery. Feasting on organic fruits from the fruit-cart man, I spent my days redesigning the blueprint of my life. Because, good Lord, my life's pillars were akin to a Jenga tower teetering on the brink of collapse. COVID destroyed the balance and original vision I'd worked to create. I needed a hard reset, and Costa Rica was just the Ctrl+Alt+Delete I needed.

Every moment of liberation, every unconventional decision, every step taken purely for the sake of joy, helped me redefine my goals and expectations. It was as though I were dismantling the intricate puzzle of my life, only to put the pieces back together in a configuration that felt more balanced, more attuned to my authentic self.

As a part of my hard reset I journaled about what I loved about my life, dreamed about what the next five years would look like, and took time to take inventory of my pillars. At the age of thirty, I was successful in my career but was at a moment when I wanted to rebalance how I was spending my time. I wrote down the following things.

MY INITIAL GOALS FOR 2021:

- Grow Blavity.org, our nonprofit, to redistribute money to Black entrepreneurs and generate more economic impact.
- Create a podcast to connect with more people who people love and listen to.
- Create a successful AfroTech business model that can scale beyond me.
- Develop mutual relationships of love and growth.
- Get a therapist to hold me accountable.
- Get better at sending gifts and create more moments of appreciation for employees and friends.
- Travel more to visit old friends in their cities now that everyone has moved.
- Train thirty CEOs per year with WorkSmart.
- Create a free version of WorkSmart content.
- And the biggest decision: Sell Blavity to a larger media company.

As I reveled in the vibrancy of Costa Rica, steeped in my own thoughts and plans, unexpected news shot through my tranquil bubble—my grandmother had fallen ill with pneumonia after having COVID. She was thousands of miles away, engaged in a slow dance with death alone in an assisted-living home in St. Louis. It felt like an iron hand had clamped around my heart, draining away the warmth of the tropical sun. Grief struck me, hard and sudden. Nothing can really prepare you for the sucker punch that grief delivers. She passed a few days after I returned from my trip. Preparing for her life transition served as a stark reminder of the ephemeral nature of life, and that time waits for no one.

But here's the funny thing about grief: It's a remarkable wake-up call. It's the universe's giant slap that wakes you up and makes you face your mortality and the mortality of the people who matter most to you. And facing your mortality is the most sobering cup of reality I wasn't entirely ready to drink.

My pillars, until then firmly rooted in the hustle of Los Angeles and an all-consuming dedication to Blavity, quickly began to sway. They seemed suddenly misaligned with the vision of a future that had crystallized amid my Costa Rican reset. I yearned for deeper connections, for family dinners that weren't stretched thin across miles and time zones. I wanted to be a presence in my yet-to-be-born nephew's life, to carve out a space for my own family someday, and to be less distracted by the material things that are so intoxicating in L.A. I wanted the freedom to lead Blavity without the financial responsibility of managing cash flow or the pressure of board meetings every ninety days.

So, I moved to Nashville, where my parents had relocated and had been living for the past ten years. Nashville presented a more balanced, wholesome new vision in which work was still important, but not so important as to become my entire being. It was a fast-growing city that was based in the South, where family values and slow living are more normalized while still being a one- to two-hour flight to major cities I needed to frequent for work: Washington, D.C., Atlanta, Chicago, and New York. I could be a kickass leader at Blavity without my personal life going down the drain. COVID gave me an opportunity to transition the company to be fully remote, which forced us to reorganize. I also learned quickly how much more productive my team and I could be working remotely without the in-and-out distractions of the office.

While still in Costa Rica, I took a few actions to put my vision into motion. I wrote an email to my Hermosa Beach landlord and broke my lease, gave most of my furniture to friends, and moved into my parents' house. So there I was, in a moment of absolute clarity, deciding to uproot my life, swap the L.A. skyline for Nashville's more subdued country music scene, and move back in with my folks. A closet became my new office and I was about to become a thirtysomething CEO bunking it with Mom and Dad. Picture that.

Under normal circumstances, the judging eyes of society on Instagram and the whispers of doubt from my inner critic would've held me back. They'd have had me believe it's ludicrous for such a public CEO of a profitable company to be living with her parents. They'd say it's a step back, not forward. They'd say it's not what successful people do.

The next step I took was putting together my request for board approval to hire a mergers and acquisition (M&A) adviser to formalize my intention to sell the company. Earlier in 2020, my co-founders and I had talked about how drained we were running Blavity, but I had held out on taking action toward officially responding to the inquiries from external companies, hiring a senior executive to join the team and help run the process internally, and shifting our financial goals to give us the best negotiating power for a sale.

But this hard reset was one of the best decisions I made in my life and completely changed the trajectory of my future happiness. It wasn't a defeat or a compromise. It was a victory. A triumph of choosing love, balance, and togetherness over prestige and societal expectations. Yes, if I moved to Nashville and sold the company, I would likely say no to sexy listening parties with celebrities, rarely walk the red carpet for movie openings, and most certainly get fewer invitations to events with the who's who of Black-owned American companies.

Yet, I chose to value the warmth of family dinners, the soft wrinkles on my parents' aging faces, and the comfort of my nephew lighting up every time he sees my face, and not to have my life's impact dictated by my title of CEO and founder of Blavity Inc. It wasn't lame, it was brave. It was a deliberate choice to prioritize these reshuffled pillars that now mattered most to me.

IS IT TIME FOR YOU TO REDIRECT YOUR LIFE?

Have you ever let yourself fully indulge without judgment from yourself and others? Who would you be if you let your guard down? Recognizing the need for a hard reset is like discerning the faint whisper of intuition over the cacophony of obligations and expectations. It's that deep-seated nudge that tells you, despite your most dogged determination, that continuing to push forward on the same path isn't the answer.

Instead, it signals that it's time to strip it all back to the bare bones, return to the drawing board, and start anew. It's the realization that your current path isn't a detour but a dead end, and the true path to your destination requires you to blaze a new trail. I've had a few hard resets in my life: when I quit my job at Intuit or when I broke up with my seemingly lovely NYC boyfriend.

Typically, hard resets don't come with flashing neon signs or manuals; they're about raw, honest self-reflection. They come when gut perseverance turns into stubbornness, when determination morphs into a mindset of lack, and when the drive to execute blinds us from seeing the broader vision.

I know how hard you work. You may be working the hardest you ever have in your life and hitting new milestones. Opportunities you used to dream of are right in front of you and the resistance and habits of your former self are also right around the corner. When you stand at a pivot point, facing a fateful choice, this is the exact moment you should slow down. Don't go where the tide of momentum pushes you. Center yourself in stillness. Choose yourself and be clear on what's next.

Whether it's thirty days or a weekend staycation, it's like taking a deep breath after a long, punishing sprint. You stop counting the miles, the milestones, and the missteps, and instead, you give yourself permission to simply be. Reduce the noise.

Now, a hard reset isn't about recklessness or neglecting your responsibilities. Yes, I realize we've spent quite a bit of time talking about discipline, work ethic, and prioritizing balance, but sometimes you need a hard reset and the only way to do that is to go all in, 100 percent. A hard reset is about giving yourself permission to explore, to indulge, to learn and grow outside the confines of judgment.

What I've found is that if you peel off the layers of societal expectations and self-imposed limitations, what's left is the unvarnished version of you, free from the confines of shoulds and musts. Suddenly, the arena of possibilities becomes huge! You begin to ask yourself, "What if I simply trusted my instincts?" "What if I indulged my whims without the fear of judgment?" "What if I followed my desires instead of my daily agenda?"

These insights can help you redirect yourself and your vision as you build from scratch.

HOW DO YOU IMPLEMENT THIS?

How do you translate this radical idea into everyday life? Here are a few tangible steps.

Set a time limit: I recommend thirty days, but take as much time as you can spare consecutively. Just like a vacation, it takes a few days to unwind and let your brain relax.

Create a safe space: This can be a physical place or a mental sanctuary, where you allow yourself to be, do, and feel anything without fear of judgment or critique for an extended period of time. A space where you feel free and secure to indulge yourself. Maybe it's a cabin near a lake, or your own home once you negotiate your parents taking your kids for a long weekend.

Question the "shoulds": During this time, every time you find yourself thinking, "I should . . ." stop and ask why. Is this something you genuinely want or need to do, or is it an obligation imposed by others or by your own expectations? During these periods, let your impulses guide you, not your to-do list.

Practice nonjudgmental observation: Pay attention to your thoughts and actions like an outsider, without labeling them as "good" or "bad." Instead of jumping to judge or justify, simply notice and acknowledge them. Keep a daily journal during this time so that you can document your thoughts. Be fully present in your experiences and gently acknowledge what arises without the need for justification or correction.

DETACHING FROM YOUR HOW

One thing the hard reset taught me very clearly was detachment. I no longer attached myself to how I thought a CEO's life must look. You've got dreams, ambitions, and, from our time together, a solid outline of steps you need to take to get you there. But what if I told you that there are times when being too attached to that plan could actually limit your potential? Yup, it's time to talk about the power of detaching from the "how," and embracing the possibility that lies beyond when you open your mind.

Why detachment? Sometimes when we become obsessed with the how, we put ourselves in a tiny little box. We become so fixated on following a rigid plan that we have put in place that we miss out on the unexpected twists and turns that could lead us to even greater joy and success. It's like wearing blinders and refusing to see the breathtaking landscape that surrounds us. We limit ourselves because the world as we envisioned it along the way doesn't quite look how we expected. In this book, we've reviewed various methods to help build a road map to the life that you want. But in our quest to manifest our visions, we often become attached to the how, rigidly clinging to plans and timelines. Look, I want you to put into practice everything you've learned here (it has worked time and time again), but I also want you to move with spaciousness for the unexpected to occur as well. When we obsess over strategy it can impair our ability to enjoy each step along the winding road. The journey itself offers invaluable lessons, growth, and fulfillment. Maybe you're on a two-week sprint and the kids just got the flu and are home from school. Okay, now it was a three-day sprint and you'll adjust. Don't beat yourself up. Or maybe you realize your Step-change Growth goals have changed, so, change! Had I stayed in L.A. because the optics told me that was the place to be for a tech founder, I would not have found the beauty and richness of intangible pleasures that I have now. If you take a reset and realize you need to adjust the vision, get to adjusting! As they say, the only constant is change.

We are all obsessed with getting A's. We're taught to measure our successes against the all-powerful grading scale as early as first grade, and if we don't stack up, we're considered unfit or unqualified for the next level. The educational system is not solely to blame; mentors, guardians, and households are also teaching from the same "results-first" mindset.

When talking to young people, there is far too much emphasis on "What outcome did you get?" and far too little on "What did you learn?"

Unfortunately, we carry this mentality into adulthood, our careers and businesses, and even our romantic relationships and friendships. We're still looking for those damn A's! We still want to be able to make our parents, teachers, and selves proud after each test. So we keep taking a test when life has asked us time and time again to put our pencils down! To go color or something, you get what I'm saying. Don't stay on a path to say you completed it if your soul's destination is shifting. Too often, we're still seeking acceptance into life's gifted program. Our preoccupation with daily outcomes, approval, and testing perfection brings on a great hesitancy to have something not go our way, hesitancy to reroute the course, preventing too many of us from making progress if the process we're driving toward isn't working out.

Refreshingly enough for me, I believe my parents did their best to break the mold. "Work as hard as you can and let the chips fall where they may," my father would repeat religiously. It was his way of saying that while I couldn't control the outcome, I could control how much quality effort I put into something. If I did my best work, the process would be more valuable than any disappointing results. If I studied hard, was engaged in the subject, and practiced after school with worksheets or with a computer program, then I should be proud of myself. If I didn't do my best work, I would easily admit it and return to identifying what held me back from reaching my personal best potential. Affirmations and approval from my parents weren't tied to grades, standardized test scores, or even how smart the teacher thought I was (or wasn't), but how *I felt I performed.* As a child, I was taught by my parents to move freely through the erroneous zone. In other words, I could jump into something new, give my best effort, and not waste time being overwhelmed with thoughts of what might not happen.

Having a family that wasn't fixated on perfect scores gave me room to be the girl who had interests, concerns, and life outside of scholastic achievement. Although I was pretty good at school, my parents intentionally did not let schoolwork consume my life or be the only place where I learned valuable lessons as I grew up. They challenged me to develop hobbies that fed my soul and my mind outside of textbooks. They helped open doors to my creative side by enrolling me in glass-blowing classes, built my self-confidence through tae kwon do, and groomed my ability to think strategically as a competitive youth chess player.

DO YOUR BEST AND LET THE CHIPS FALL WHERE THEY MAY

Embrace the mindset my Professor Dad instilled: Do your best and let the chips fall where they may. Letting go of attachment to perfect outcomes builds resilience, lessens stress, and creates space to nurture other life pillars—Relationships, Passions, Wellness—without paralysis over results.

How can you practically apply this outlook amid real-world responsibilities?

Start by identifying unreasonable attachments. Which projects, goals, or timelines cause disproportionate anxiety due to unrealistic standards? Perfectionism often takes root in our deepest motivations and strangles joy. Locate these roots.

Next, redefine your reasonable best effort given your specific constraints. Clarify available time, mental bandwidth, and competing obligations. Detach from the invented expectations exceeding your current reality. Commit to progress that sustains rather than burns out your engines.

With attachments released and effort redefined, reexamine your first steps forward. Part the clouds of imagined futures obscuring today's simple path. What actions align to your priorities and will move the needle? Revisit our basic principles in this book and prime your motivation by connecting tasks directly to your core motives and CEO Tasks that drive you forward.

I've advised other entrepreneurs to focus on progress over perfection when it comes to mastering their growth. You can't waste time being afraid to try new things. Look at your data, decide how you want to approach something and where you want to grow, and then jump into the mix. No hesitation. Screw the perfectionist voice in your head. It's not about getting an A. It's about taking steps forward. Lead with "Let's see what we can do," and "I wonder how well we can make this happen." Sometimes it's as simple as "I worked on this and did a good job; I learned something about myself." Whether it turns out to be a huge accomplishment or it doesn't work at all, at least you've learned to master the process of maximizing your personal effort and made progress toward your goal.

Lean into uncertainty as you act. Stand ever ready to flow in new directions, perceiving setbacks as feedback and iteration as advancement. Through consistency, courage, and course corrections, we master growth itself.

ARE YOU GIVING MAXIMUM EFFORT?

Imagine Sarah, a passionate journalist who dreams of becoming a renowned television commentator. She spent years honing her writing skills, getting an MBA at Columbia, and cultivating her knowledge in various fields. Sarah envisions herself delivering impactful and insightful commentary on current events and social issues to a wide audience.

She dedicates countless hours to perfecting her craft, studying the art of effective communication, and taking internships in engaging storytelling. Sarah prepares herself for the opportunity to appear on television, imagining the impact she could make through her words and analysis. She pitches her concepts to media companies and television networks, hoping to secure a spot as an on-air commentator.

However, as Sarah submits her pitches and goes through numerous auditions, she faces disappointment after disappointment. The networks do not choose her for their programs, her agent stops calling, and Sarah starts to doubt her abilities and questions if she will ever achieve her dream.

But instead of allowing herself to be consumed by the outcome, Sarah takes a step back and reminds herself of the importance of detaching from a specific "how." She shifts her focus from the end result of appearing on television to the effort she puts into her journalistic work every day and telling important stories.

On a whim, Sarah decides to explore TikTok to share her

expertise and commentary. What does she have to lose? She creates her own newsletter, where she publishes thought-provoking articles on pressing issues and shares her unique perspective. She leverages social media to engage with a growing audience and builds a loyal community around her journalistic insights.

As Sarah continues to give the world her maximum effort and engages with her audience, she starts to gain recognition for her thought leadership and personality. She receives invitations to contribute to reputable major publications, moderate panel discussions, and be a paid influencer with purpose-driven brands. Sarah realizes that by detaching from the specific outcome of appearing on television and embracing the journey, she has opened herself up to new opportunities and a wider range of platforms from which to share her voice and impact others.

Through her dedication and commitment to living the design but being open to how the process might shift, Sarah cultivates a distinct journalistic style. Her unique perspective and now huge online audience attracted the attention of television networks, and she finally received an opportunity to appear as a guest commentator on a major news channel.

Another example is James, an aspiring medical entrepreneur who dreams of launching a successful tech start-up. He has a clear vision of his product, spends countless hours developing his business plan, and seeks out med tech investors to fund his venture. However, despite his meticulous preparation and hard work (not to mention his medical degree from Harvard), James faces rejection after rejection. Each investor meeting ends without securing the funding he needs to bring his vision to life, and it's pretty clear he won't get funded in the current market conditions.

Instead of becoming disheartened, James chooses to release himself from the specific outcome of securing investors and shifts his focus to the effort he puts into building his start-up. He realizes that success is not solely dependent on external validation or financial backing but is a result of his product impact, resilience, and continuous learning.

James starts to embrace each setback as an opportunity to learn and improve. He seeks out mentors and advisers through an accelerator in Atlanta who can provide guidance and support along his entrepreneurial journey. He focuses on building a strong team, refining his product, and finding creative ways to bootstrap his start-up. By detaching from the outcome and living the design, James cultivates an unwavering belief in his vision and becomes a tenacious problem-solver.

As time goes on, James's relentless effort and unwavering commitment to his purpose start to pay off. He attracts the attention of a top professor at Georgia Tech who is connected to a venture capitalist. The seed funding he had initially sought suddenly becomes available, and his dream begins to materialize.

These narratives illustrate the power of letting go of specific outcomes and being comfortable with plot twists. Letting go doesn't mean giving up. It means shifting your focus from obsessing over the end result to giving your maximum effort in the present moment. Ambition is anything but inflexible. It's all about agile momentum. How can you keep moving quickly but still be nimble enough to swerve when needed? By placing importance on the effort we put in—rather than a fixed benchmark—we open ourselves up to new possibilities, unexpected opportunities, and a greater sense of fulfillment.

The road to living a life that's successful in all areas demands that we understand true success lies in the process, the growth, and the joy we experience along the way, regardless of what we initially envisioned. Here are a few questions to help you in this.

1. Are you giving max effort to your priority pillars?
2. What are five different ways you can live your wealthy life and vision?
3. If the outcome is slightly different from what you expected, how can you still choose to be happy?

Let your imagination run wild. Aim for out-of-the-box concepts beyond the obvious. Barriers often arise from narrow definitions of success rather than capability limitations. As you ideate adventurously, your criteria expand from "what is" to "what could be." While my heart was set on moving to Nashville, I'd also considered what a wealthy life might look like moving to Costa Rica permanently or to New York. I needed to make sure I had other options that still felt good in case life called for it.

Contentment remains a choice, determined by perspective alone. Life has a way of surprising you, despite best-laid plans. Did you enjoy the journey, learn lessons, develop new dimensions of self regardless of specific manifestations? If so, you're advancing toward your ambitions. Even if things don't go exactly as planned, you have the power to choose how you respond. Embrace the mindset that contentment is not solely dependent on the end product, but rather on your ability to find joy in the journey itself. Adjust your perspective, focus on the lessons learned, and celebrate the progress you've made.

When all else fails, you can always hit reboot and start all over again.

EVALUATING A NEW PATH

Once I got settled in Nashville, I started on the path of selling the company and went back through the framework outlined in this book. I revised my schedule and meetings, I hired a new COO who had experience at a big media company and would be a signal to potential acquirers that the business had stable senior leaders, and I revisited my Stepchange Growth goals both personally and professionally. I found a therapist and began the emotional work and journey to detach my identity and value from Blavity and to hold myself accountable through this change.

I started to give a road show of management presentations about my company to some of the biggest CEOs and investment bankers in the media industry. Management presentations are huge PowerPoint presentations including all of the financial data, the client contracts, and the behind-the-scenes of how the company works. It's an incredibly time-consuming confidential undertaking involving managing an external team of eight lawyers and three investment bankers, and keeping our board closely updated on how things are going.

As I was going through the virtual road show, I spent hours poring over my vision for Blavity in the future and how, with a larger company partnership, we could scale our audience to the next level. While everyone understood the value that a Black audience could add to their portfolio, it became apparent that none of the executives really had a clear plan for how to create value for Black consumers or advertisers who were looking to reach the new majority of America. Further, none of them had a plan for our AfroTech business and severely misunderstood the incredible impact we could have if we invested more in the events and built out products to serve talent-acquisition organizations at some of the largest companies in the world. The acquisition of Blavity was purely looked at this way: If they buy us, they get to add our revenue to their own, which increases their valuation in the marketplace, so they themselves could sell to someone else (or the stock market) at a higher price.

And this, my friend, is what didn't sit right with me. I didn't feel confident that the company would be able to remotely maintain or give us the working capital and freedom to grow our impact. And yes, while I'd be personally quite wealthy, throughout the negotiations that level of wealth and financial windfall decreased and required a variety of "if this, then that" scenarios that were dependent on market conditions, not Blavity's relative contribution to the bottom or top line of the bigger corporation. Most important, I didn't feel like I was putting the company and my employees in a position to be more likely to grow closer to our mission. To put it simply—the acquisition had evolved into a world that did not align with my Purpose Principle. Not enough security for my investors, no clear plan for our employees or for *at least maintaining* our business, and certainly not enough financial payout. So, after one year of negotiation, two letters of intent, one sixty-four-page, deeply redlined purchase agreement, and $800K in lawyer fees, I realized that the best possible outcome for my company was to keep building this thing myself and continue leading Blavity Inc. as CEO and chairperson.

I'll be honest, it wasn't easy. It required a lot of emotional labor to maintain my composure and keep my head high after spending twelve months on a process. Countless late nights, tears on the couch after calls with our legal team, and humbling conversations with my co-founders. Not to mention having to keep this entire brutal process confidential. But I did it. And the power of knowing when to walk away, when to stick it out, and when to change your mind is one of the greatest gifts you can give yourself. I met with the board, told them I was finished, and we mutually agreed to end the acquisition talks. I renegotiated my salary and responsibilities as CEO with the board and myself. If I was going to stay on as CEO then I was only going to do it while maintaining the Work-Life Integration I had worked so hard for. No more prolonged self-sacrifice at this stage, no more misaligned incentives. I know it might sound odd, but during the M&A process our leaders and I had doubled the size of our revenue and had reached new levels of free operating cash flow. I rewrote my rules, went through my pillars *another* time, and came out stronger, with a more profitable company and a new vision for what my life and business would look like in this new phase. Our current COO, Gautam Ranji (whom I had hired to get the company sale ready and lead the integration), moved to our board of directors, and I opened up job descriptions for a chief revenue officer and new chief financial officer so that we could continue operating at a senior level and maintain a lack of dependency on me.

Ultimately, my hard reset took me on quite a journey. In some ways, I ended up right back where I had started—as the CEO of Blavity. It wasn't my initial ideal outcome, but again, ambition can sometimes require openness to detours, backtracking, and multiple circles around the block. However, my destination revealed itself to be so much different and even better than I could have imagined. Why? Well, this time around, I prioritized myself, my pillars, and a ton of tiny joys that would make my pace at work more sustainable.

IN PURSUIT OF TINY JOYS

I'm here to tell you that in this pursuit we call life, it's not happiness that should be our ultimate goal. No, no, no. Happiness is often fleeting, elusive, and dependent on external circumstances.

Contentment, on the other hand, is a steady companion. It's the inner peace and satisfaction that comes from embracing the present moment, regardless of the external circumstances. It's finding joy in the simple pleasures of life, even when the world around you seems chaotic and uncertain. Contentment is a state of being that can be cultivated each and every day, regardless of what's happening in your life.

After I did a hard reset and made the move to Nashville, I

realized that true contentment lies in the little things I do for myself. So I set out on a mission to create a tapestry of tiny joys—habits and routines that would bring me fulfillment and unadulterated contentment along the way. I promised myself that I would no longer rely on external circumstances or the actions of others to determine my joy. It was time to take control of my own true happiness, one delightful moment at a time.

First on my agenda was moving out of my parents' house and buying a home I could call my own to be the epitome of my personal peace, my office, and my art studio. I scoured real estate listings, visiting potential homes in Nashville with a discerning eye. Finally, I found it—a newly built house with hardwood floors and a surround sound system that beckoned me to twirl and spin with glee. It became my sanctuary where I could wake up each morning and feel an irresistible urge to play music and get to work.

But it didn't stop there. I needed to infuse my days with more bursts of joy and fulfillment. I turned my attention to gardening. I discovered the immense satisfaction of nurturing living things, coaxing tiny seeds to sprout and flourish. My backyard transformed into a small but semiproductive space of flowers, herbs, and veggies. Full disclosure—with so much travel, I wasn't the best at keeping everything alive, but the simple act of tending to my garden every morning brought me closer to nature, grounding me and filling me with a sense of purpose and accomplishment outside of my job as CEO.

Weekend spontaneity became my middle name as I embarked on impromptu bike rides to my parents' house for Sunday lunches. The wind in my hair, the sun on my face, and the feeling of freedom as I pedaled along the familiar streets brought a rush of pure delight to my soul. Taking home delicious food only my mom could make and relishing the fact that my conversations with my parents in person could be semiweekly instead of only a few times a year as they aged.

And then there was my morning obsession with the perfect iced matcha latte. I took it upon myself to master the art of crafting this exquisite beverage in the comfort of my own home. Experimenting with different tea house–grade matcha powders, milk ratios, and sweeteners, I honed my skills until I had created a concoction that was simply divine. The act of preparing and savoring this elixir of bliss became a daily ritual, a small but powerful reminder that life's little pleasures can bring immense happiness.

These are my Tiny Joys, the building blocks of my contentment. They serve as a reminder that life is not solely defined by monumental achievements or external circumstances, but by the moments of joy we create for ourselves. They became my anchor, releasing me from the grip of attachment to outcomes beyond my control.

No longer did I experience extreme emotional highs and lows. Instead, I found solace in the steady rhythm of doing the work, giving my best, and surrendering to the flow of life. By letting go of expectations and entitlement to specific results, I opened myself up to the beauty of the present moment. And in that space, where I cultivated my Tiny Joys, I discovered a profound and unshakeable peace.

WHAT ARE YOUR TINY JOYS?

I want you to become attuned to the simple pleasures that surround you each day, whether it's savoring a delicious cup of coffee, taking a leisurely midafternoon stroll in nature, or sharing a warm snuggle in the morning with your toddler. Here are some ways you can discover the Tiny Joys to incorporate into your life:

Journaling journey: Take a trip down memory lane and recall moments in your life when you felt true joy. What activities, experiences, or interactions brought a smile to your face and warmth to your heart? Write about these moments in detail, allowing yourself to relive the emotions and sensations associated with them.

Recapturing childhood delights: Think back to your childhood and the simple joys that made your heart sing. What made you smile? Was it roller-skating at the rink, building with LEGO, or indulging in baking cookies? Revisit these nostalgic pleasures and consider how you can inject elements of them back into your adult life. Maybe you already have with our hobby challenge earlier; if so, keep it going!

Gratitude ritual: Establish a daily practice of gratitude, where you reflect on and express appreciation for the blessings in your life. For a week, write down three things you're grateful for each day, whether it's a podcaster you enjoy following, a beautiful sunset, or a delicious meal at a local restaurant. This ritual shifts your focus to the positive aspects of life and cultivates a sense of joy.

Social joy-seeking: Surround yourself with positive and
uplifting people who inspire you and give you perspective.
Seek out social activities that bring you energy, such as
game nights, volunteering at your mosque, joining
outdoor pickup games, or bringing your neighbor a gift
basket. Foster connections that bring you energy and have
no material outcome.

By doing your best and living for the journey instead of
the destination, you liberate yourself from the burdens of ex-
cessive expectations and free yourself to fully experience the
richness of each day. By embracing the prompts and exercises
shared in this chapter, you have taken a step toward nurtur-
ing a mindset that prioritizes the present and celebrates the
small joys that add meaning to your life.

These simple pleasures have the power to lift your spirits,
infuse your life with pleasure, and enhance your overall well-
being. Listen, I need you to let go of the urge to control
everything. And if I did it, the girl who began investing at
thirteen because I wanted "freedom and security," I know
you can too. Trust in your abilities to handle what comes,
with support from your pillars and a new mindset. As you
pursue your wealthy vision, sow multiple seeds of joy and
success, so that regardless of what the world has for you,
you'll be at ease.

As you move forward, remember that the pursuit of inner
joy and outer success is not only about chasing after grand
achievements or external validations. It's about embracing
the here and now, finding joy in the everyday, and savoring
the beauty that surrounds you. I want you to reach that vi-

sion you charted earlier, hit those Step-change Growth goals, bask in your Wealth Code and do it from a place of real peace, excited about your next step but just as content with the here and now. After all, it's all we have.

WHAT'S NEXT FOR YOU?

All right, you've made it to the end of this wild ride. Congratulations, you've officially rewritten your rules and started to care less about what's been holding you back. But guess what? This isn't the end of the road. It's just the beginning of a crazy, messy, beautiful journey of growth and self-discovery.

As I've said, this journey isn't some straight line from point A to point B. It's a cycle, a loop that you'll keep coming back to again and again. Just when you think you've got it all figured out, life will come along and smack you in the face with a new challenge, a new lesson, a new opportunity to grow.

And that's okay. In fact, it's more than okay. It's necessary. Every three months, or after some big life event, I want you to take a step back and reevaluate your stuff. Look at your pillars, your goals, your strategies, and ask yourself: Is this still working for me? Is this still aligned with who I am and what I want? If the answer is no, then it's time to make some changes. Tear down those old rules and rewrite them. Embrace the discomfort, the uncertainty, the messiness of growth.

And when things get tough, when you feel like throwing in the towel, just remember: You're a force to be reckoned with. You've already rewritten your rules once and you can do it again. So keep pushing forward, keep growing, keep focusing on the things that truly matter. Harness your power, embrace the journey, and stride confidently into the next phase of your incredible, unique CEO-led life. Now that you've started rewriting the rules, keep the momentum going! Visit MorganDeBaun.com for the tools and community to make your boldest moves yet.

Thank you for taking this journey with me. Thank you for being courageous enough to renegotiate your terms, to face your fears, to change the rules you're living by. I'm proud of you, and I can't wait to see the incredible things you'll achieve next.

Acknowledgments

A heartfelt thank-you to my partner, Josh, for your constant love and support, and to my son, Langston, for being my inspiration. To my parents, Sandra and Michael, thank you for the foundation you've given me.

To my co-founders, Jeff, Aaron, and Jonathan, and to board members John Lyman, Marlon Nichols, and Gautam Ranji, your belief in this journey has been everything.

Special thanks to my research editor, Heather Sundell, and to Luvvie for your advice and leading the way for Black authors of this generation. Thank you to my agent, Eve Atterman, for guiding me through this process.

Finally, thank you to my incredible chief of staff, Kate McDonald: Your exceptional leadership, attention to detail, and ability to keep everything running smoothly have been a game-changer. I couldn't have done this without you by my side.

Notes

Chapter 1: The Purposeful Life

12 **Viktor Frankl:** Viktor E. Frankl, *Man's Search for Meaning* (Boston: Beacon Press, 1962).

13 **Psychology research backs this up:** Richard M. Ryan and Edward L. Deci, "Self-Determination Theory and the Facilitation of Intrinsic Motivation, Social Development, and Well-Being," *Canadian Psychology* 49, no. 3 (2008): 182–85, doi.org/10.1037/a0012801.

13 **Researchers have also found:** American Psychological Association, "Trends in Meaning and Stability in Workplaces," *Monitor on Psychology,* January 2024, https://www.apa.org/monitor/2024/01/trends-meaning-stability-workplaces.

14 **"Providing our customers":** Trader Joe's, "About Us," https://www.traderjoes.com/home/about-us.

Chapter 2: Be a Visionary

30 **Research shows:** Patrick E. McKnight and Todd B. Kashdan, "Purpose in Life as a System That Creates and Sustains Health and Well-Being: An Integrative, Testable Theory," *Review of General Psychology* 13, no. 3 (2009): 242–51, doi.org/10.1037/a0017152.

Chapter 3: Design Your Wealth Code

56 **Consider a 2010 Princeton study:** Angus Deaton and Daniel Kahneman, "High Income Improves Evaluation of Life but Not Emotional Well-being," Princeton University, August 2010, https://www.princeton.edu/~deaton/downloads/deaton_kahneman_high_income_improves_evaluation_August2010.pdf.

Chapter 4: Dare to Be Data-Driven

83 **One international survey:** Btihaj Ajana, "Personal Metrics: Users' Experiences and Perceptions of Self-Tracking Practices and Data," *Social Science Information* 59, no. 4 (December 2020): 654–78, doi.org/10.1177/0539018420959522.

96 **"perseverance and passion"**: Angela L. Duckworth et al., "Grit: Perseverance and Passion for Long-Term Goals," *Journal of Personality and Social Psychology* 92, no. 6 (2007): 1087–1101, doi.org/10.1037/0022 -3514.92.6.1087.

Chapter 5: Build Your Team Like a CEO

113 **In experiments published in 2001**: Joshua S. Rubinstein, David E. Meyer, and Jeffrey E. Evans, "Executive Control of Cognitive Processes in Task Switching," *Journal of Experimental Psychology: Human Perception and Performance* 27, no. 4 (2001): 763–97, doi.org/10.1037/ 0096-1523.27.4.763.

Chapter 6: Hit Your Goals Like a Start-up

150 **This was first shown**: Alexa K. Stuifbergen et al., "The Use of Individualized Goal Setting to Facilitate Behavior Change in Women with Multiple Sclerosis," *Journal of Neuroscience Nursing* 35, no. 2 (April 2003): 94–99, 106, doi.org/10.1097/01376517-200304000-00005.

151 **Another study found**: Lawrence J. Becker, "Joint Effect of Feedback and Goal Setting on Performance: A Field Study of Residential Energy Conservation," *Journal of Applied Psychology* 63, no. 4 (1978): 428–33, doi.org/10.1037/0021-9010.63.4.428.

161 **Psychological research reveals:** Charlotte Lieberman, "Why You Procrastinate (It Has Nothing to Do with Self-Control)," *The New York Times,* March 25, 2019, nytimes.com/2019/03/25/smarter -living/why-you-procrastinate-it-has-nothing-to-do-with-self-control .html.

161 **In a 2013 study:** Fuschia Sirois and Tim Pychyl, "Procrastination and the Priority of Short-Term Mood Regulation: Consequences for Future Self," *Social and Personality Psychology Compass* 7, no. 2 (2013): 115–27, doi:10.1111/spc3.12011.

Chapter 7: How to Pace Your Life

180 **In 2023, Pew Research Center:** Shradha Dinesh and Kim Parker, "More than 4 in 10 U.S. Workers Don't Take All Their Paid Time Off," Pew Research Center, August 10, 2023, pewresearch.org/short-reads/ 2023/08/10/more-than-4-in-10-u-s-workers-dont-take-all-their-paid -time-off/.

191 **"Flow":** Mihaly Csikszentmihalyi, *Flow and the Foundations of Positive*

Psychology: The Collected Works of Mihaly Csikszentmihalyi (Dordrecht: Springer Netherlands, 2014), doi.org/10.1007/978-94-017-9088-8.

Chapter 8: The Power of Decisiveness

221 **action-oriented versus state-oriented:** Nathan DeWall and Brad J. Bushman, "Social Acceptance and Rejection: The Sweet and the Bitter," *Current Directions in Psychological Science* 20, no. 4 (August 2011): 256–60, doi.org/10.1177/0963721411417545.

230 **Daniel Kahneman's acclaimed 2011 book:** Daniel Kahneman, *Thinking, Fast and Slow* (New York: Farrar, Straus and Giroux, 2011), 80–81, 324, 333.

231 **Anchoring bias was first identified:** Amos Tversky and Daniel Kahneman, "Judgment Under Uncertainty: Heuristics and Biases," *Science* 185 (1974): 1124–131, doi.org/10.21236/ad0767426.

241 **In an interview with *Vanity Fair*:** Michael Lewis, "Obama's Way," *Vanity Fair,* October 2012, https://www.vanityfair.com/news/2012/10/michael-lewis-profile-barack-obama.

Chapter 9: Be the Rough Draft

264 **Social psychology proposes:** Lisa M. Williams and Kipling D. Williams, "Social Rejection, Ostracism, and Bullying: Models of Empathy and Revenge," *Current Directions in Psychological Science* 20, no. 2 (2011): 71–75, doi:10.1177/0963721411417545.

268 **six dimensions of psychological well-being:** Carol D. Ryff, "Psychological Well-Being in Adult Life," *Current Directions in Psychological Science* 4, no. 4 (August 1995): 99–104, journals.sagepub.com/doi/epdf/10.1111/1467-8721.ep10772395.

About the Author

MORGAN DEBAUN is the founder and CEO of Blavity Inc., a revolutionary media and tech company serving multicultural consumers. A serial entrepreneur, small business advocate, and corporate board adviser, DeBaun has become one of the most prominent figures in both the modern equity and inclusive tech landscape and consumer marketing world. DeBaun is an icon for a generation of entrepreneurs and ambitious professionals looking to find sustainable success and balance in a world that values the hustle and grind over everything. Visit her website for more guides and resources at MorganDeBaun.com.